Praise for
Sipping from the Cup of Wisdom

Crenshaw's two-volume work is a compelling testimony to the generative fervor of wisdom study today. It is a must-read for all students of wisdom, one that invites both appreciative and critical engagement.

—*William P. Brown*
William Marcellus McPheeters Professor of Old Testament
Columbia Theological Seminary

James Crenshaw, without a doubt, has been the leading scholar of his generation concerning the wisdom traditions of Israel. These volumes present a summation of his lifetime of good work. Crenshaw shows that the biblical tradition is open to a broad cultural reading, truth claims given in a compelling manner. This is a most welcome volume.

—*Walter Brueggemann*
William Marcellus McPheeters Emeritus Professor of Old Testament
Columbia Theological Seminary

James Crenshaw has been a leading voice in the study of wisdom literature for several decades. His knowledge of the texts and the scholarly literature about them is unparalleled. The present study comprises a culmination of his lifelong scholarly engagement with sapiential literature. *Sipping from the Cup of Wisdom* is a "house of instruction" (Sir 51:23) that all who seek wisdom and understanding should visit, to learn from a master sage.

—*Matt Goff*
Professor of Religion
Florida State University

Smyth & Helwys Publishing, Inc.
6316 Peake Road
Macon, Georgia 31210-3960
1-800-747-3016
©2017 by James L. Crenshaw
All rights reserved.

Library of Congress Cataloging-in-Publication Data

Names: Crenshaw, James L., author.
Title: Sipping from the cup of wisdom : faith lingering on the edges / by
James L. Crenshaw.
Description: Macon : Smyth & Helwys, 2017. | Includes bibliographical
references.
Identifiers: LCCN 2017025205 | ISBN 9781573129572 (pbk. : alk. paper)
Subjects: LCSH: Wisdom literature--Criticism, interpretation, etc.
Classification: LCC BS1455 .C657 2017 | DDC 223/.06--dc23
LC record available at https://lccn.loc.gov/2017025205

SIPPING FROM THE CUP OF WISDOM

volume 2

FAITH LINGERING ON THE EDGES

JAMES L. CRENSHAW

Also by James L. Crenshaw

Prophetic Conflict (de Gruyter, 1971)
Hymnic Affirmation of Divine Justice (SBL, 1975)
Samson (John Knox, 1978)
Gerhard von Rad (Word, 1978)
A Whirlpool of Torment (Fortress, 1984)
Story and Faith (Macmillan, 1986)
Ecclesiastes (Westminster, 1987)
Trembling at the Threshold of a Biblical Text (Eerdmans, 1994)
Joel (Doubleday, 1995)
Urgent Advice and Probing Questions (Mercer University, 1995)
Education in Ancient Israel (Doubleday, 1998)
Psalms (Eerdmans, 2001)
Defending God (Oxford University, 2005)
Prophets, Sages & Poets (Chalice, 2006)
Old Testament Wisdom, 3rd ed. (Westminster John Knox, 2010)
Dust and Ashes (Cascade, 2010)
Reading Job: A Literary and Theological Commentary
(Smyth & Helwys, 2011)
Qoheleth: The Ironic Wink (University of South Carolina, 2013)

To Linda Adams Crenshaw

Acknowledgments

Seven of the eight articles in this volume have previously appeared in various publications. I wish to thank the publishers for permitting me to bring them together in a single volume. I am also grateful to Keith Gammons, who generously agreed to make the essays available to a larger audience. The occasional inconsistency in transliteration of the Hebrew is a result of the different venues in which the articles appeared.

Thanks also go to Ron Mimnaugh of Duke Divinity School for technical assistance and to the expert staff of Smyth & Helwys, especially Leslie Andres. Finally, as has been true for sixty-one years, Nita has encouraged me to "search the Scriptures" even at considerable sacrifice. To her I say once again, "Thank you for everything."

CONTENTS

INTRODUCTION

Like the ancient Greeks, who crafted stories about extraordinary acts of valor and selfless devotion to country, Israelites, too, praised heroes who served as examples for the young, both salutary and unsavory. They celebrated the exploits of strong men (Samson), men who combined cunning and strength (David), women who defied convention (Jael), normally peaceful individuals who were moved to violence by marauding bands (Abraham), fearless prophets facing rulers' ire (Nathan, Jeremiah), warriors who treasured honor more than personal safety (Uriah the Hittite).

Over time, such deeds largely of heart and hand were supplemented by epochal achievements of the mind. Just as Homeric legends gave way to philosophical treatises by Plato, Aristotle, and others, biblical tales of valor receded due to changed historical circumstances. In this void created by empires from the East, daring poets such as the authors of Job and Ecclesiastes began to ponder the enigma of unjust suffering and to question the meaning of life.

Surprisingly, the adversary in the prologue to the book of Job is credited with articulating the ethical dilemma that lingers to this day. In short, will anyone serve God for naught? For this antagonist, true religion did not take into account the carrot or the stick, reward or punishment. This rejection of calculating morality that had inserted itself into the heart of Yahwism encountered sharp resistance, as the speeches of Job and his friends reveal.

It was left to the teacher who called himself Qoheleth to question the meaning of life. For him, everything was the refuse of breathing. Existence, he argued, was ephemeral, absurd, futile, transient—like chasing wind. His language moves beyond thinking the absurd to reflecting on the process of thinking itself. The poet who was capable of exquisite imagery (1:4-11; 3:2-8; 11:7–12:7) makes tiny inroads into the higher realm of philosophy. Chapter 1, the essay from which the title of these two volumes is taken, examines the contribution of sages to the Judaism that informed Jesus of Nazareth. Among other things, it develops the arguments surrounding *ḥinnām* thinking and the idea that everything is *hebel.*

Chapter 2 looks at the historical context of Qoheleth, an era that has been called a moneyed economy. On the basis of a thorough examination of the language of Qoheleth and extra-biblical sources from the fifth and fourth centuries BCE, Choon-Leong Seow has argued for a fourth-century date, for which he provides a valuable description. His analysis of the word *šalîṭ* is crucial to the argument that places Qoheleth somewhat earlier than the time most critics have considered likely.

I use a different approach to support a date of 260–250 BCE. It resembles the method applied to Sirach by Oda Wischmeyer, one focusing on culture. I inquire about the intellectual community, the religious context, economic realities, the political situation, and the institution of the family. In doing so, I am aware that authors are capable of creating "fantasy worlds" with no basis in real events. Qoheleth, I admit, has shown a propensity to do just that by adopting the persona of King Solomon.

My conclusions substantiate the claim that Qoheleth harbored skeptical realism and a certain reserve toward religious practice, even prayer. He describes a volatile, high risk economy, a highly developed "Big Brother" bureaucracy, and he is ambiguous toward the family because of a heightened sense of the ego. Even his empiricism stands in tension with traditional assertions about God that cannot be verified, making him a dubious empiricist. For him, God determines all things, throwing merit out the window.

Some things are surprising about his cultural observations: an emerging hermeneutic with special vocabulary (*pesher*); the absence of urban life and its clashes, as well as polemic against idolatry; silence about priests. Above all, the failure to mention personified Wisdom stands out. Less surprising is Qoheleth's familiarity with ideas from Mesopotamia ranging from proverbs to philosophical observations about complementary pairs and the four elements of the universe.

Chapter 3 grew out of my participation in an international conference of philosophers that met at the University of Notre Dame. The topic, the character of the God of the Hebrew Bible, has come under close scrutiny and much criticism lately and elicited strong statements from theists and atheists. For me, many of the claims made by several philosophers and the other two biblical scholars stretched credulity. Perhaps that feeling is a result of my upbringing as a Baptist and my lifelong struggle to promote a reasoned approach to the Bible in its historical context.

In my view, the Bible is a human product, just as God is a literary construct. That much can be substantiated. Everything beyond that calls for faith, which by its very nature cannot be verified. Moreover, the behavior of God should measure up to the ethical standard of humans, at the very least. One other principle is essential to my understanding of the Bible. No biblical assertion is self-validating. Quoting the Bible to back up one's theological claims only proves familiarity with Scripture.

It follows that I do not think interpreters should read Christian views into the Hebrew Bible. Early Christians and church fathers who did so and developed typologies pointing to Jesus were adapting to the needs of their age. Post-Enlightenment thinkers can hardly be content with such a practice. Precisely because I treasure the Bible so much I also insist on trying to understand it in context. I attribute that love to my Baptist past; my skepticism stems from years of observing the injustices of the world, which in part explain the intensity of my reaction to fundamentalism.

Perhaps the most startling statement by Qoheleth is that he hated life. Chapter 4 treats this idea and asks whether hatred of life was an enduring sentiment and thus not negated by the seven admonitions, the last of which takes the form of an imperative, to enjoy life. In short, does his mind change as the book progresses as some interpreters think? If so, what can one make of the inclusions that sum up his teachings in 1:2 and 12:8? Did he always think that life was utterly meaningless, totally absurd?

Qoheleth's characterization of the human condition as *hebel* echoes that of the author of the primeval story about Adam and Eve. Life, that is, can be defined as *ʿāmāl*, toilsome labor. This is one of Qoheleth's favorite words, occurring ten times in 2:18-23 alone. At root, it connotes exhaustion, and companion words in parallelism outside Qoheleth imply the odious features of being tired. He does not use these words, probably because of the scarcity of parallelism in his teachings.

Job's use of *ʿāmāl* is informative. Here the word means "misery," as in Gen 1 and Psalms. Qoheleth, however, never uses this word to indicate "misery." Instead, he chooses the exceptional senses "toil" and "wealth" that occur in the book of Job. For Qoheleth, the human condition is *hebel* (transience, insubstantial, futile, absurd, foul, vapor).

The unit with ten uses of *ʿāmāl* leads up to the conclusion of the royal experiment, moving from loathing to devaluing of everything. The language is entirely self-centered, with "for me" occupying center stage. Elsewhere Qoheleth attributes life's burden to God, with death being the hidden culprit. Injustices abound, adding to the misery brought on by the brevity of life and its lack of meaning. I can find little joy in this book, certainly no reason to call him a preacher of joy.

Chapter 5 suggests that Qoheleth's realism was shared by at least one psalmist. The author of Ps 39 also felt the weight of existence, which he, or she, calls *hebel.* In the ancient world, loose speech and its consequences were frequent topics of discussion. Knowing this, the psalmist hopes to monitor speech lest offense follow. Nonetheless, life for this poet was burdensome. Two reasons are given: the brevity of life and the heavy hand of Yahweh.

This psalm moves from voluntary silence to enforced mutism. It takes the form of three prayers. Unable to remain silent, the psalmist inquires about the length of his life, an unusual request. He thinks of life as a mere breath, totally empty. His silence also included hidden anger, which bursts forth almost unexpectedly as an accusation ("For you did it"). The translator of the text into Greek, the Septuagint, recoils from such audacity and renders it as follows ("For you created me").

The psalm continues with the charge that Yahweh consumes treasures like a moth, adding "Surely everyone is a breath." The haunting ending resembles one of Job's moods: look away from me so that I can find relief in death. Psalm 39 is joined by three other psalms that have echoes of Qoheleth's teachings. These are Pss 62, 90, and 144. Such texts allow for an interesting exercise in intertextuality, a method that is gaining status in the guild.

According to Jer 17:9, the human heart is desperately corrupt, and that seems to be a universal opinion in the Bible. We are all flawed; that is the nature of finite creatures. The story of the fall implies that things could have been different; perhaps, but the impulse to set one's own norms is overwhelming. Without a doubt, Qoheleth was flawed, but was he a genius? Chapter 6 seeks to answer this question.

Yes, and no. If by genius, we mean someone who saw clearly the nature of human existence as *hebel,* then he qualifies. He was bold enough to challenge comforting views of reality as a safe haven under the divine panoply. In addition, he recognized the futile, indeed absurd, nature of all things. He saw that in the end human effort, however heroic and well-intentioned, amounts to a huge zero.

What, then, should people do if their entire future lay outside their control, apparently in the hands of an indifferent and distant Puppeteer? Qoheleth opted for a popular choice throughout the ancient world. Make hay while the sun shines; enjoy life while (and if) able to do so. This advice hardly qualifies as the insight of a genius. Or does it?

To be sure, sparks of genius appear in his teachings: linguistic poetry about cyclic nature, the times for every matter under the sun, and the onset of old age and death. Remarkable, too, is his choice of vocabulary to communicate philosophy to students. And yet society seldom understands genius. The two epilogues represent attempts to situate him as a sage and to combat his dangerous ideas. Subsequent Jewish literature highlights the unknown and hidden dimensions of intellectual pursuits, sometimes restricting thought. Just what God placed in the mind (3:11) remains a mystery.

An eternal decree governed all humanity: you must die. A little comfort was found in the hope of being remembered, which the ancients reinforced in various ways. Qoheleth considered such effort fruitless. Everyone, he said, is subjected to a single fate, death and oblivion. To be forgotten forever awaits us all. Chapter 7 discusses remembering and forgetting in wisdom literature.

Not everyone agreed with Qoheleth about being forgotten. Ben Sira remembers heroes from sacred narrative and parades them before readers as examples for others. For him as for others in the ancient world, memory played a huge role. Society, it must be remembered, was largely oral, perhaps even in Ben Sira's day. Hence the warning in parental teachings not to forget what is said.

The power of wine and strong drink to blot out memory is a recurrent theme, even when attributed to a foreign sage such as the mother of Prince Lemuel. Most notably, this connection between wine and forgetting is explored in the speech by the court page in 1 Esd 3:20-23. Although Prov 23:29-35 does not mention the loss of memory, it shows how excessive drinking severs one from reality.

Forgetfulness can be a good thing, especially for the miserable. That is why Job is urged to forget his misery and anticipate a return to normalcy. Remembering, however, is a source of angst for Job, who calls on God to remember that he made him out of clay. Moreover, Job hopes that God will remember him for a fleeting moment and hide him in Sheol.

Qoheleth insisted that everyone is soon forgotten. The dead know nothing, and all their previous emotions are erased (love, hate, and envy). To emphasize the importance of memory and the tragedy when it is missing, he tells a story about a tiny village that could have been saved (or was saved) by a poor but wise man. Unfortunately, no one remembered that wise man.

The final chapter represents my third attempt to fathom the depths of the most scandalous story in the Bible. Both Kierkegaard and Rembrandt also were drawn again and again to this account of the offering of Isaac by the patriarch Abraham. I include this study of Gen 22:1-19 because the harrowing tale rivals Job and Qoheleth in theological profundity. I do not consider it wisdom literature although its linguistic affinities to Job and its view of God are remarkably similar.

For me, the story raises numerous questions about the character of God and Abraham. Its literary beauty, often singled out for admiration, conceals dangerous features, especially the psychological effect on children. Even if one takes the story as fiction, as I do, its harmful effects linger. Not only are Abraham and Isaac vulnerable in quite different ways; God, too, is vulnerable.

I concentrate on the literary artistry of the story which holds in abeyance everything but bare essentials, as Erich Auerbach noted in his famous study comparing the Homeric account of Odysseus's scar and the biblical story. I discuss the rich reflections on this narrative by later Jewish interpreters, some of which suggest unease over the depiction of the ancestor of their religion. The highpoint of this unease is found in 2 Macc 7, the story about a mother of seven martyrs who chides Abraham for trials whereas hers are the performances.

Can such a story as this one about the offering of the beloved son be justified? I discuss the unflattering picture of God and suggest that postenlightenment thought has rendered the biblical deity vulnerable. Asking the question, Can theism survive in this new environment?, I arrive at the notion of divine vulnerability.

chapter one

JESUS AND ANCIENT JEWISH WISDOM TRADITIONS*

Biblical sages never asked the question that is arguably the most divisive of all intellectual queries: "Does Being exist?" With one possible exception, the sayings of a non-Israelite named Agur in Prov 30:1-14, they joined their ancient Near Eastern counterparts in taking the existence of a supreme power as a given.[1] Indeed, the intelligentsia in Egypt and Mesopotamia assumed that a host of lesser gods made up a pantheon that modern scholars identify as a Divine Council. Biblical wise men appear to have found this understanding of reality acceptable, for the prologue to the book of Job describes such an assembly of gods. In this regard, the sages merely adopted the prevailing views of the day, like the unknown author of Gen 6:1-4, who mentions lustful sons of God who descended to earth and cohabited with women.

The belief in heavenly beings who functioned as a royal court occurs in several biblical texts and often reinforces ethical ideals, as in Deut 32:8 and Ps 82, which allude to patron gods of the nations and their abdication of responsibility to maintain justice on earth. Other references to the Divine Council involve a semi-Platonic notion of events in heaven that are

---

* The original appeared in Paul K. Moser, ed. *Jesus and Philosophy: New Essays* (Cambridge University Press, 2009) 41–62. Copyright Cambridge University Press, 2009. Reprinted with permission.

subsequently enacted on earth (1 Kgs 22:19), add drama to a prophetic vision involving a chilling vocation (Isa 6:1-13), or convey a sense of grandeur to the description of Yahweh as creator and savior (Isa 40–55). The few dissidents who are mentioned in the book of Psalms become objects of ridicule for their lack of faith and are burdened with the label "Fool" (Pss 14:1 and 53:1) even when divine silence encourages such radical thoughts (Ps 10:4, 11).

Now if the authors of canonical wisdom—Proverbs, Ecclesiastes, Job, Sirach (Ecclesiasticus), and Wisdom of Solomon—failed to ponder whether or not God exists, they did, however, raise the most penetrating question of all: "Am I accountable to a power higher than earthly monarchs?" "Given the existence of a transcendent being," they asked, "what difference does that make in daily experience?" Stated differently, "Does the divine countenance present a smile or a frown when humans come to mind?"

Not knowing the answer, they devoted their efforts to discovering how to gain the favor of the Supreme Being whom they identified as creator of the universe.

I. MADE IN THE IMAGE OF GOD

They began by postulating a principle of similarity between humans and deity, by no means an obvious assumption at the time.[2] The long history of veneration of deities in nonhuman form, beautifully analyzed by Thorkild Jacobsen in *The Treasures of Darkness: A History of Mesopotamian Religion*,[3] could not easily be erased from memory, especially when in popular imagination nature's potency was witnessed season after season. The secret to harnessing this energy was gradually unveiled as a consequence of the rise of city-states and the surging of political ambition; as the sovereign domain of a nation expanded, so did the god's territorial claim. Thus the benevolent deeds that had been ascribed to patron deities were credited to the god of the dominant earthly power. That process also explains the ascendancy of the biblical Yahweh, who slowly took on the features of deities whose city-states fell to a stronger Israel and Judah during the brief period of a monarchy (roughly the tenth through the first decade of the sixth century BCE). This personalization of the gods brought with it the possibility of imagining a relationship between them and humans that was ultimately akin to the way women and men relate to one another. In sociopolitical language, these bonds were called treaties. Religious associations of like-minded people were said to have been linked by covenants.

Nowhere does the idea of similarity between gods and humans occur more clearly than in Gen 1:26-27, which describes Elohim's intentions to create a being "in our image," here articulated within the Divine Council, and reports the implementation of the plan that results in "male and female" who are nevertheless said to bear the imprint of their creator. It is not necessary to resolve the issue of the exact meaning of this language about the image of God, which must certainly imply in the narrative context a physical likeness but much more, including any one, or all, of the following possibilities: self-transcendence, a verbal capacity, and dominance over other creatures. It is noteworthy that this priestly author, who was probably active during the early postexilic period (after 539 BCE), avoids hubris by having this notion of a similarity between humans and God originate with deity rather than with mortals. The only other clear reference to this idea within canonical literature (Sir 17:3) completely divests it of the slightest hint of pride, for Ben Sira states it within the context of human mortality and divine majesty, where the benefits of likeness to the divine, spelled out as dominance over creatures and intellectual capacity, pale before life's brevity and the reminder that dust is the substance from which mortals were formed and will be their sure future as well.

This dual aspect, likeness to deity and kinship with dust, rendered humans the object of intellectual ambivalence, occasionally eliciting wonder, as in Ps 8, but also satire when vulnerability encompassed miserable victims of flesh and blood, as in Job 7:17-21. Belief in such elevation to a status approaching divinity partially explains the several myths that recount the heroic efforts on the part of exceptional individuals to achieve full divinity.

The best-known example of this failed endeavor from Mesopotamia involves a certain Adapa, the most perfect of mortals, whose ascent to the assembly of the gods did not achieve the desired end because Ea, the god of wisdom, tricked him into refusing an offer of food that would have made him immortal.[4] Although the biblical story of the first couple lacks an ascent to the heavens, it nevertheless describes their frustrated attempt to attain equality with Elohim, which the narrative glosses as knowing good and evil. The two words, "good and evil," appear to function as a merism connoting "everything."[5] The presence of a second tree in the midst of the garden of Eden suggests that the myth did not only limit equality with Elohim to the cognitive realm but also embraced the temporal, or rather its transcendence. Access to the tree of life meant the possibility of sloughing off mortal robes for eternal apparel. The operative word here is "possibility," for just as the hero Gilgamesh was robbed of a branch from the tree of life by a serpent, so Adam and Eve, having succumbed to the seductive rhetoric of a clever serpent, incurred divine wrath that resulted in their expulsion from the garden and loss of access to the tree of life.

The author does not question the couple's choice of fruit from the tree of knowledge, when sampling the produce from the tree of life nearby would have given them immortality. After all, myths must ring true; humans possess knowledge, not immortality.[6]

Not surprisingly, the gods were believed to be protective of their unique status. Thus we hear about Ea's willingness to deceive even favored individuals like Adapa, who had every reason to trust the god of wisdom. The biblical Elohim is not entirely above blame either, for the serpent owes its presence in the garden to the creator.[7] For some inexplicable reason, the acquisition of knowledge, presumably the salutary result of asserting personal freedom, poses a threat that must be immediately suppressed. The outcome, at least in the eyes of the narrator, is the permanent closing of the door to full equality with God.

That closed door, however, did not prevent levitical teachers from admonishing Israelites to pattern their lives after the Lord whom they worshiped as a partner in a covenantal relationship, as Erich Fromm's *You Shall Be as Gods* recognizes.[8] The later theological term for the object of this appeal, *imitatio Dei*, acknowledges both the extraordinary potential within humans to scale ethical heights and the wide gulf separating God and mortals. Ironically, the promise placed in the mouth of the serpent in Eden became the desired destination of individuals who aspired to holiness.

For at least two reasons, this compulsion to imitate the deity approaches the ironic. First, because the gods themselves were thought to have been subject to death, a belief that found expression in myths about gods who died and rose from the dead as perfect symbols for seasonal changes that brought new vegetation, only to see it replaced in due time by barren earth.[9] Ps 82 offers another explanation for the death of the gods, specifically their failure to protect widows, orphans, the weak, and the needy from compassionless citizens with "strong elbows." Second, because the very possibility of rising above self-absorption was denied by learned teachers, this low opinion of human beings seems to have been widespread, at least among the intelligentsia, judging from such texts as The Babylonian Theodicy and an apparent proverbial saying attributed to the prophet Jeremiah. The former text has the Job-like sufferer lay full responsibility for mortals' lying ways on the gods. In Benjamin Foster's felicitous translation, the text reads,

Enlil, king of the gods, who created teeming mankind, Majestic Ea,
who pinched off their clay,
The queen who fashioned them, Mistress Mami, Gave twisted words to
the human race.
They endowed them in perpetuity with lies and falsehood.[10]

By way of contrast, the aphorism from the Bible is silent with respect to blame, simply stating that the mind is most perverse and twisted. It then inquires, "Who can grasp it?" (Jer 17:9).[11] The anticipated response is, "No one." Like the proverb about transgenerational sin and retribution ("The parents have eaten sour grapes and the children's teeth have become sensitive," Jer 31:29 and Ezek 18:2), this assertion of intellectual malady bore a bountiful harvest, for the idea took many forms, sometimes resembling the well-known Greek example of Diogenes, lantern in hand, searching for a single righteous individual. In the case of Jer 5:1, the aim was to locate someone who could ransom a sin-laden Jerusalem, but in Jeremiah's view neither the lowly nor the nobility possessed sufficient goodness to spare Zion. At other times, the idea shaped Israel's historiography in a manner that became a self-fulfilling prophecy while providing a rationale for the destruction of Jerusalem at the hands of Babylonian soldiers.

Despite these attenuations to the principle of similarity, it eventually shaped theological discourse and undergirded the concept of reward and retribution. Human standards of conduct were extended to the divine realm through an argument from the least to the greatest. If humans were expected to follow a strict code of ethics, surely, it was deduced, the gods should at a minimum live up to these standards of conduct. This kind of reasoning also meant that the gods expressed both pleasure and anger, which became a source of either joy or dismay. It therefore became incumbent on every individual to search for ways to please the deities or, in a monotheistic context, the sole deity. Alternatively, it was imperative to devise various means of dealing with divine anger, the cause of which was often shrouded in mystery.

The most poignant biblical application of the principle that God is subject to the same ethical code as humans involves Abraham. When informed of the deity's intention to destroy the cities of the plain, Sodom and Gomorrah, he is said to have uttered this bold response, "Shall not the Judge of all the earth do what is right?" (Gen 18:25).[12] The story, which belongs to the category of theodicy, illustrates the narrator's unease over attributing a possible miscarriage of justice to Yahweh. A similar refrain can be heard in the Gilgamesh Epic, where Enkidu pays the price for both his and Gilgamesh's offenses and evokes Gilgamesh's plea amounting to "On the guilty impose the punishment."

These ancient thinkers refused to travel the road later taken by Soren Kierkegaard who posited a teleological suspension of the ethical that allowed him to make sense of God's demand that Abraham sacrifice his beloved son.[13] To them, right was right, whether involving gods or humans. Much later, Immanuel Kant used the same logic to deny that the command to sacrifice Isaac issued from God.

To some degree, the mechanisms for rewarding virtue and punishing evil complicated the principle of similarity, for there is some evidence that the ancients believed that a natural law governed reward and retribution.[14] Woven into the fabric of the universe, this operative principle, they thought, was completely independent of further influence from the gods, except that they may have acted as a kind of midwife to assist the birth of weal or woe. The controversy occasioned by Klaus Koch's application of this hypothesis to the Bible under the formula *Tun-Ergehen Zusammenhang*[15] shows how difficult it is to reconcile the nexus of cause and effect with belief in an interactive deity who knows the very thoughts of every person, according to Ps 139.

Without a doubt, however, the largest challenge to comparing God to humans was ignorance. An element of mystery surrounded deity, for every revelation was believed to be simultaneously a veiling.[16] The prophet who is known as Deutero-Isaiah minces no words when expressing this idea: "Truly you are a God who hides, God of Israel, Savior!" (Isa 45:15). Even moments of exceptional disclosure such as Yahweh's revelation of the divine name as "I am that I am" (Exod 3:14) and the concession to Moses' persistent request to see the deity convey a sense of undisclosed mystery (Exod 33:1-7).[17] Foreigners also recognized divine mystery, according to the author of the book of Job, which gives a spine-curdling account of a theophany to Eliphaz that left him terrified and unable to recognize the mysterious visitor, who, one may infer, bristled at the thought that Job was more righteous than God (Job 4:12-17). Gilgamesh, too, had three dreams that left him distraught as he pondered both their originating cause and its effect.

Extra-biblical literature from the ancient Near East attests wide awareness of mystery surrounding the gods, despite their anthropomorphism. Egyptian iconography[18] best conveys this sense of the unknown, for the deities are frequently depicted in quasi-human form, with animal parts and features of winged creatures. In Mesopotamian art, the lion, symbolic of royalty, indicates both earthly and heavenly rulers. The solar disc that played such a prominent role in the ancient world nicely illustrates the combination of visibility and invisibility, for although accessible to all, the sun burns with such intensity that onlookers dare not risk more than a quick glance. Shamash's mystery is thereby protected, and humans are reminded that all knowledge is partial, particularly that concerning Being itself. The appropriation of mythic ideas pertaining to the sun god by the author of Ps 19 shows how concepts from a different religious context can enrich another one. In this instance, the sun's penetration of everything below is matched by the illuminating power of the Torah, which reaches as far as the human conscience.

To overcome partial knowledge about the heavenly realm, religious thinkers applied analogical reasoning, which by necessity assumed real continuity between what was seen and what could not be seen. In reality, analogies worked only if God thought and acted like humans. In the final analysis, metaphors conveyed truths that could not be stated otherwise: God was father, shepherd, warrior, healer, king, teacher, rock, and so on.[19] Each of these metaphors captured an essential characteristic of deity; taken literally, they were woefully inadequate.

Limited knowledge did not, however, prevent ancient artisans from crafting images of the gods. According to the second-century author of Wisdom of Solomon, the practice originated in one of three ways: (1) a bereaving father carved a likeness of his deceased son; (2) a subject of a distant ruler made an image as a token of loyalty; and (3) a gifted artist created a work of beauty that became an object of supreme devotion. Regardless of its origin, the making of visible images to represent an invisible deity served royal liturgy and personal piety well. The Babylonian *Mis Pi* ritual that symbolized the opening of the god's mouth and regular feeding is particularly illuminating.[20] The daily exercises to which the gods' statues were subjected testify to their importance in sustaining a positive relationship with the ones to whom the visible objects pointed.

Admittedly, the role of the god's statue in prophecy from Neo-Assyrian times may strike moderns as bizarre, but ancient worshipers viewed it as apt.[21] Standing in front of a statue of a god, a prophet functioned as the mouthpiece of the deity while pronouncing a divine oracle, which would subsequently be conveyed to kings Esarhaddon or Aššurbanipal, the two Assyrian kings from whose reigns prophetic texts have survived.[22] Although biblical orthodoxy forbade the worship of idols, the fervor with which this practice was denounced suggests that ordinary people were favorably impressed by idols, so much so that religious leaders found various substitutes, not the least of which was verbal. The tablets containing the Decalogue and the written Torah of Moses are the two most notable examples. Nevertheless, biblical tradents insisted that nothing in heaven or on earth adequately resembled God. Accordingly, an empty throne in the temple symbolized the presence of an invisible Yahweh. Worship at the northern sanctuaries of Bethel and Dan, however, indicates a different view of representations for deity. In these two cult centers, images of bulls, overlaid with gold, signaled continuity with the cultic ritual associated with the period of wandering in the wilderness.[23] Traditions from the southern kingdom of Judah took exception to such aids to worship, as the episode about the "golden calf" in Exod 32 illustrates.

Because communication with the gods was considered essential to the well-being of the nation and individuals alike, an elaborate system of detecting the future was devised. In Mesopotamia, specialists in reading the signs were highly trained in the art of extispicy, and careful records were kept in archives for future consultation. Diviners studied the configuration of animals' livers, the flight of birds, the trajectory of arrows, the fall of lots, and so forth, searching for clues about the intentions of the gods. Visionaries were widely believed to have seen things concealed from ordinary people, and this extrasensory gift was understood to have been bestowed on them by deity. Biblical prophecy was apparently reluctant to stress the auditory over the visual, as the superscription to the book of Amos indicates: "The words of Amos which he saw . . ." (Amos 1:1).[24] An inscription discovered at Deir 'Alla that mentions the diviner Balaam, otherwise known from Num 22–24, shows the popularity of this visual mode of receiving communications from God.[25]

The Mesopotamian world also developed a "science" of omens covering a seemingly endless array of anomalies that were thought to lend insight into the future. Perhaps the most lasting of these endeavors is astronomy, for observation of heavenly bodies was indispensable to ritual accuracy.[26] The many debates within Judaism over the correct calendar demonstrate similar interest in performing the ritual at exactly the right time.

II. QUESTIONING THE PRINCIPLE OF SIMILARITY

Such specialized research and clairvoyance notwithstanding, individuals sometimes experienced an alien God who seemed to lack even rudimentary human goodness. Personal suffering befell them for no apparent reason, and their prayers for relief went unanswered. Perplexed and bewildered, they began to question their knowledge of deity. The distraught sufferer in "I Will Praise the Lord of Wisdom" put the matter this way:

> I wish I knew that these things were pleasing to a god!
> What seems good to one's self could be an offense to a god,
> What in one's own heart seems abominable could be good to one's god!
> Who could learn the reasoning of the gods in heaven? Who could grasp
> the intentions of the gods of the depths?
> Where might human beings have learned the way of a god?[27]

Ignorance, that is, prevails among humans where the gods are concerned, and the premise that they are essentially like people flies out the window.

The author of the fictive masterpiece, the book of Job, has his hero undergo a similar collapse of a previous understanding of God when his erstwhile friend becomes an inveterate foe. Extreme loss and personal misery force Job to view God as a wild beast intent on devouring prey. Then when God finally shows up, Job can no longer recognize the face in the tempest. He has gone from the center of Yahweh's attention, his pride and joy, to the outer edges of thought where humans are no longer the measure of all things, indeed where Leviathan and Behemoth have replaced Job as objects of Yahweh's boasting.[28]

It is unclear whether the root cause of this loss of confidence in the basic affinities between humans and deity is personal or national. Instances of individual dismay over the contradiction between ancestral belief and actual experience probably lie behind narratives like the one focusing on Gideon's sharp retort to an angel who seemed blissfully unaware that assurance of Yahweh's presence rang hollow after foreign raiders had destroyed Israel's grain fields (Judg 6:12-13). When such personal questioning of divine governance was fueled by more than empty stomachs, specifically a failed cult, the angst intensified to near-breaking point. That is what happened in the wake of Jerusalem's destruction as depicted in the agonizing cry preserved in the book of Lamentations, one that ends in utter confusion: ". . . unless you have completely rejected us; [you] have raged against us mightily" (Lam 5:22).

A witness to the vanishing hope associated with the royal sanctuary in Zion has left an even more penetrating analysis of that dark period. If not the actual composer of the "confessions," then at least their primary subject, Jeremiah struggled valiantly with what he perceived to be a scandalous transformation of Yahweh. The one whom the prophet had known previously as a fountain of living water had become in his mind a deceitful rake bent on destroying a loyal spokesman (Jer 20:7). The lonely journey into disenchantment, presented here as deeply personal, is universalized in the book of Job. In general, despite Job's foreign ancestry according to the biblical text, Jewish interpreters have viewed him as a cipher for the nation Israel, whereas Christians often have seen him as a single individual. Both groups of interpreters have been troubled by some aspects of his character, which they have managed to explain away by adopting an allegorical approach. Many modern readers admire Job's rebellious spirit rather than viewing it as a flaw in his character.

Among religious leaders, the initial shock occasioned by cognitive dissonance eventually brought adjustments to the basic understanding of God. The most notable change concerned the way Yahweh was thought to interact with humans. The idea of the deity's intimate involvement by appointing leaders and by controlling the course of history to benefit a chosen people was replaced by the concept of a distant, silent creator. Revelation, once believed to have been immediate and episodic, became looked upon as derivative, with written texts identified as the font of knowledge. In some circles, however, divine pedagogy that included hunger and thirst was not understood as signaling Yahweh's absence but rather an intimacy involving whispered guidance about where to walk on dangerous paths (Isa 30:20-21). Rare individuals have always managed to interpret adversity as confirmation of profound trust, or as in the case of the author of Ps 73 to look beyond calamity or injustice to buttress traditional belief.

In this confusing spiritual environment, even prophets who stood in a long tradition of boldly announcing Yahweh's words abandoned that confident mien and began to interpret the fuller ramifications of what others had said rather than deliver a new oracle from God.[29] In such fallow ground apocalyptic easily took root,[30] pushing divine activity into the foreseeable future and introducing angels with names like Gabriel and Uriel who assisted God in disclosing the secrets of the hidden realm to special individuals like Enoch and Ezra. More important, this sea change brought mainstream intellectualism into line with sapiential thought, until now something of a maverick because of its emphasis on human achievement rather than on God's control of history.[31]

These adjustments to religious thinking were necessitated by a combination of other factors as well. First, it became apparent that the claim to speak in the name of Yahweh was in essence *testimony* to a perceived encounter with transcendence. Moreover, that *testimony* was by its very nature broken, for it involved fallible humans—intellectually, ethically, and culturally. As conflict among prophets demonstrated, the audacious claim to be a mouthpiece for Yahweh did not assure authenticity.[32] Second, every attempt to speak theologically brought one face to face with personal limitations, ultimately issuing in little more than stammering. The indescribable and unutterable did not lend itself to articulate speech, as religious mystics have long recognized. Third, visual acuity was severely hampered when gazing into eternity. The best one could hope to do was catch a glimpse of holiness, as if through stained-glass windows, hardly more reliable than observing shadows on the wall of a cave.

The effect of the religious crisis on the point at which faith and daily experience came together was enormous. The central assumption that reward and retribution corresponded exactly with one's deeds gave way to belief in random distribution of both the benefits of virtue and punishment for evil deeds without regard to either merit or blame. Admittedly, that association of deed and consequence had no thorough grounding to start with, for exceptions like Abel and Josiah were well known. Still, hardened dogma alone explains comments like that expressed in Ps 37:25 denying want on the part of righteous people, the jaundiced reasoning by Job's three friends, and the near-certitude in the book of Proverbs that virtue was rewarded and vice punished. Against such a dogmatic background, the radical dismissal of orthodoxy with a rhetorical flick of the wrist ("Who knows?") by Qoheleth, the speaker in Ecclesiastes, makes sense. For him, the firm belief that one could control destiny by rational means had become fatally flawed, for time and chance governed all things. Subjection to fate's cruel mockery of both good and evil was a far cry from shaping one's own future by applying ancestral knowledge to daily experience.

The removal of Yahweh from ordinary affairs created a void that was soon filled by a mediating figure. At emotionally charged moments, Job gave voice to the possibility that someone would bridge the chasm between him and God. Variously referred to as a conciliator (Job 9:33), a heavenly witness (16:19), and a vindicator (19:25), this figment of Job's imagination who, Job hoped, would bring about a change in Yahweh's treatment of him never materialized. A mediating figure did come to play a significant role in the sapiential pedagogy of the unknown author of Prov 1–9 and in Ben Sira's instruction of aspiring scribes of second-century Judaism. This female persona, *ḥokmāh*, developed from metaphorical beginnings (cf. the four metaphors for divine attributes that are mentioned in Ps 85:10) into a hypostasis, an earthly manifestation of the invisible God.[33]

To strengthen her mediating function, she was given an extraordinary pedigree, one originating in heaven and antedating the created world (Prov 8:22-31). In addition, she was linked with primordial sages of Mesopotamian lore (Prov 9:1) and later identified as the visible expression of the divine Torah revealed to Moses. In short, she was God's universal will that reached all the way back to the garden of Eden and also the covenantal presence at Zion (Sir 24:1-23). Above all, however, she was thought to possess divine attributes and to be an extension of God similar to the relationship between the sun and its rays (Wis 7:22-26). As such, she took on herself a soteriological role that had previously belonged to the spirit, thereby rewriting religious history.

III. A CLOUD OF UNKNOWING

Much has been made in scholarly literature of a crisis among biblical sages brought on by a collapse of belief in divine order regulating the universe. The basic thesis, presented cogently by Hartmut Gese and Hans Heinrich Schmid,[34] seems to correspond to what transpired in the ancient Near East, first in Egypt and later in Mesopotamia and Israel. Dogma tends to harden over time, bending with each perceived counter-argument until finally breaking under the weight of reality. The books of Job and Ecclesiastes, together with comparable literature from Egypt and Mesopotamia, attest to a temporary breakdown of a worldview.

At the same time, however, this testimony to the inadequacy of religious consensus reveals the extraordinary resilience of the human mind, its creative capacity when old views are shown to be bankrupt. Crisis therefore becomes an occasion for a religious breakthrough.[35] That is precisely what happens when the author of the book of Job replaces retributive justice with the concept of gratuitous love. The centrality of the Hebrew word *ḥinnām* in the prologue signals this remarkable change in perspective. The fact that it is placed in the mouths of both the Adversary and Yahweh indicates agreement on the issue underlying all that follows (Job 1:9; 2:3). As the ensuing poetic dialogue demonstrates with increasing exactitude, dogma is seldom surrendered without a fight. For what seems an eternity, the argument moves within the realm of discourse established by the old belief in reward and retribution. Remarkably, Job is caught in this treacherous web even when challenging it, for apart from the principle of retributive justice he has no basis for complaint. Only the divine speeches fall outside this restrictive box; in the end, ambiguous syntax and grammar make it impossible to determine whether or not Job finally embraced the radical understanding of relating to Yahweh without cause (Job 42:6).[36] The ironic epilogue dramatically underscores the unpredictable nature of *ḥinnām*, while also demonstrating divine freedom.[37]

Now if the book of Job explored a radically new principle that destroyed every vestige of a calculating morality, Ecclesiastes began to flirt with philosophical issues beyond the question, "What is true virtue?" For Qoheleth, the only topic worthy of serious consideration was that of meaning. His approach was unabashedly anthropocentric: "What is good for mortals?" Moreover, he set himself up as supreme judge about everything under the sun, giving pride of place to experience but also accepting much conventional wisdom, especially concerning creation.

Qoheleth's view of all things as *hebel* closely resembles that of the Greek philosopher Monimus, for whom mist was the best term to indicate everything. Appropriately, *hebel* was nearly as elusive as vapor, for it had various nuances: breath, transience, idol, stench.[38] Qoheleth took advantage of this richness, although the majority of his uses convey something like absurdity or futility. His assessment of things as *hebel* was all encompassing, so much so that it elicited hatred of life. For him, religion brought no comfort, for a distant and silent Elohim dispensed favors and calamities gratuitously, without rhyme or reason. Death was certain; anything beyond that moment was a mystery. Nothing therefore carried enduring worth: not work, not fame, not life itself. There was simply no profit, nothing in excess, despite all human striving.

The macrostructure of Ecclesiastes emphasizes Qoheleth's disenchantment with human existence. After initial superscription, motto, and thematic statement, the book has an exquisite poem about nature's ceaseless rhythm (Eccl 1:4-11). It closes with a poignant description of human aging and demise in a context of nature's extraordinary rejuvenation (Eccl 11:8–12:7). The prominence of earth, air, fire, and water in the first poem is hardly accidental, for Qoheleth was attempting to juxtapose what he took to be the essential substances of the universe with transient mortals.[39] The closing poem sets death in an ambiguous context suggesting an apocalyptic cataclysm and perdurance, as if Qoheleth could not choose between competing philosophical views about the future of the universe.

This fascination with philosophy extends beyond the two poems mentioned above. Qoheleth reflected on his own intellectual process in a way that resembles second-order thinking. Peter Machinist has pointed to Qoheleth's choice of vocabulary, specifically *ḥešbōn*, *maʿăśeh*, *miqreh*, and *ʿōlām*, as proof that he had made a rudimentary breakthrough with respect to thinking about thought itself.[40] Qoheleth was fully aware that he had to connect vital pieces of cognition in additive fashion in order to arrive at the larger picture (Eccl 7:27).[41]

The case for viewing Qoheleth as a pioneer in the attempt to think philosophically in a language that hardly encouraged such an enterprise can be strengthened further by recognizing the manner in which he used the particle *kōl* ("everything"). Qoheleth's use of the word "everything" coincided with universalist tendencies in some late biblical literature.[42] The similarities with Greek philosophical explorations of concepts for totality need not indicate dependence, although Qoheleth may well have been familiar with popular philosophy of his day. In Ben Sira's case, the use of the expression "He is the all" (Sir 43:27) must surely imply acquaintance with the Stoic notion, *tó ón*.

Joseph Blenkinsopp has advanced the hypothesis of a Stoic source for the well-known poem about a time for everything in Eccl 3:1-8.[43] The philosophical presupposition of these fourteen opposites is, in his view, the Stoic concept of the principle governing the universe itself. Whether in the end Blenkinsopp's view will ring true remains to be seen, but his readiness to interpret Ecclesiastes in the light of Greek philosophy is not off the mark. In my view, the fairly mundane nature of the opposites in Qoheleth's list, except for the first and last (birth/death; war/peace) makes this text less akin to Stoic teaching than Ben Sira's use of comprehensive concepts such as good and evil in the service of theodicy (Sir 39:17–40:11).

The cumulative weight of thinking about God's relationship with humans as gratuitous and denying both meaning and permanence to anything under the sun pushed toward acceptance of epistemological agnosticism. The result was increasing emphasis on mystery, for the authors of both Job and Ecclesiastes agreed that the true nature of God was veiled. By necessity revelation implied divine inscrutability, as well as esotericism. The latter idea became full-blown in apocalyptic literature and in sectarian Judaism.

The covenanters from Qumran pondered the *raz nihyeh*, mystery that is to be,[44] while considering themselves and their righteous teacher to be keepers of heavenly secrets. That sense of chosenness flourished in various apocalyptic accounts of special people who were escorted into heaven, given divine mysteries of creation, and allowed to return to earth with secret knowledge. This speculation occurred, it should be noted, simultaneously with flourishing mystery religions in the Greco-Roman world. Precisely when knowledge of deity was strongly questioned in favor of *theos agnostos*, teachers sought to fill the void with gnostic responses: knowledge comes via special revelation and conveys elite status on those "in the know." In 2 Cor 12:2-4 the apostle Paul debunked such elitist attitudes that grew out of special revelation, suggesting instead that personal weakness made strong by God was the only cause for boasting. In this context, he managed to report on his own mystical experience while also allowing the experience to retain its basic secrecy.

In Jewish circles, the expression *'ēn mispār* arose to express the vast gulf between what could be known about deity and what remained hidden. Ben Sira conveyed the same idea differently: "although we speak much, we cannot reach the end . . ." (Sir 43:27a). In a word, beginnings and endings stand outside human purview—like divinity. Religious breakthroughs like *ḥinnām* and *hebel* do not take place without resistance, even when traditional views have become obsolete because of changing times. The astonishing thing is that the two canonical works of wisdom literature after Job and Ecclesiastes resumed older thinking as if the radical insights, *ḥinnām* and *hebel*, never existed. There is a difference, however, for both Ben Sira and the unknown author of the strongly hellenized Wisdom of Solomon[45] consciously sought to provide rational theodicies grounded in psychology and philosophy.[46] So much for *ḥinnām* thinking about the relationship between God and humans or for *hebel* as the descriptor of all existence. Reaching back into sacred history, Ben Sira identified the Mosaic legislation as Israel's wisdom before the court of international inquiry. By introducing the idea of proportional punishment at the hands of an infinitely patient deity, Wisdom of Solomon tried to exonerate Yahweh from the charge of cruelly exterminating Egyptians and Canaanites.[47] Traditional theology flourished once more: God could be known and was just, according to Ben Sira and Wisdom of Solomon. Furthermore, the prospect of death, so troubling to Qoheleth, seems not to have disturbed Ben Sira unduly, and the neoplatonic idea of an immortal soul eased its burden for the author of Wisdom of Solomon.[48]

IV. SIMILARITY RESTORED?

The penultimate chapter in Wisdom of Solomon introduces a parallel notion to *ḥokmāh*. It states that the divine word leapt from the royal throne in heaven and stood on earth, touching heaven at the same time, and brought death to inhospitable Egyptians who worshiped created things instead of their maker (Wis Sol 18:14-19). Such fearsome figures of gigantic proportions were familiar lore in the ancient world, perhaps the most memorable being Sheol, whose insatiable appetite was symbolized by lips that touched both heaven and earth. The personification of the divine word is anticipated in poetic lyrical texts in Deutero-Isaiah (Isa 55:10-11), but this type of rhetoric was widespread.

The author of Wisdom of Solomon could never have imagined the future role of this particular personification. Incarnational theology was clearly aided by the equation of the Hebrew concept of *ḥokmāh* with two Greek words, *sophia* and *logos*. The natural translation of *ḥokmāh* to *sophia* in the Septuagint was the first step toward such theology, and Stoic teaching about a universal rational substance that resided to a lesser degree in the human intellect was the second. Notwithstanding the discrepancy in gender, the identification of *sophia* with *logos* made it possible to think of a single individual as both *ḥokmāh/sophia* and *logos*. When Christians began to view Jesus as God's eternal wisdom, it was but a small step to see him as the incarnation of the divine word. The result was the restoration of the principle of similarity, now applied absolutely with reference to Jesus. Here in the person of Jesus was a second Adam, truly God and truly man, according to later Christian orthodoxy.

What, then, did the theologians responsible for the Synoptics and the Gospel of John think he believed about *ḥinnām* and *hebel* as the most accurate descriptions of the human dilemma? They have preserved just enough information to indicate an awareness of gratuitous love, specifically the allusion to innocent Galileans who were killed by Pilate or eighteen unfortunate persons on whom a tower fell (Luke 13:2-5) and Jesus' refusal to attach blame either to a blind man or to his parents (John 9:1-3). The recognition that the sun shines on individuals irrespective of their conduct (Matt 5:45) and the emphasis on the heavenly Father's readiness to forgive fit within *ḥinnām* thinking just like the stories about victims of special circumstances.

This limited acceptance of *ḥinnām* theology is only half the story, for it is dwarfed by another theme, the retributional, that clashes with belief that God freely dispenses good things to all without regard to worth. Even the observation about sun and rain falling on one and all is set within a context of reward and retribution. The many exhortations to earn divine favor by means of exceptional virtue within the Gospels give a wholly different impression from the reminder of God's providential care. So do the frequent threats of hell fire awaiting all who fail to respond obediently to Jesus' teachings. The tradents who transmitted the Gospels depict a Jesus who leaned more heavily in the direction of a dogmatic position that had been found wanting by at least two representatives of the sapiential enterprise than toward disinterested righteousness.

How did *hebel* thinking fare in the representatives' recollection of the tradition associated with Jesus? Less well than *ḥinnām* theology. Qoheleth's sense of the grand absurdity left no place for manipulative behavior by humans, however selfless the act. In his view, Elohim did not respond in a predictable manner, regardless of how virtuous an individual became. Such a dark assessment of reality would seem to have been attractive to Jesus' followers, who were trying to make sense of his death on the cross, the supreme scandal facing any theodicy. The marvel is that the Gospel writers refused to cast their eyes "under the sun" but appealed to apocalyptic hopes that, in the language of Jonathan Z. Smith,[49] abandoned locative spirituality for the utopian.

For all they knew, Jesus was caught up in the same web that had entangled the sages who preceded him. Like them, he tried to unite justice and mercy in his understanding of God. Like them, too, he found the task impossible. However sublime the concept of gratuitous love may have been, it had an unwelcome corollary: the total loss of a bargaining chip when finally ushered into divine presence. And however true *hebel* thinking rang in the shadow of death, it left individuals without hope. Because the Gospel writers believed that the God who had raised Jesus from the grave could be trusted to make all things new, they grounded this conviction in a worldview burdened by retributive morality and a utopian escape from reality itself. In doing so, they cast their vote for the principle of similarity and remained oblivious to the epistemological revolution ushered in by the unknown authors of the books of Job and Ecclesiastes.

Notes

1. The initial remark by Agur, *le'îtî'ēl le'îtî'ēl we'ukāl*, has been understood as an expression of exhaustion spoken to an individual whose name was Ithiel and as a denial of theism that robbed the speaker of ability. Scholars disagree about the language, whether Hebrew or Aramaic, and tend to view the extent of the literary unit as either minimal (vv. 1-4) or maximal (vv. 1-14). They also question the integrity of the unit, sometimes recognizing an internal debate between a skeptic and a dogmatist. The possibilities are examined in James L. Crenshaw, "Clanging Symbols," 51–64 in *Justice and the Holy*, ed. Douglas A. Knight and Peter J. Paris

(Philadelphia: Fortress Press, 1989), reprinted in James L. Crenshaw, *Urgent Advice and Probing Questions: Collected Writings on Old Testament Wisdom* (Macon GA: Mercer University Press, 1995) 371–82.

2. Karel van der Toorn, "Sources in Heaven: Revelation as a Scholarly Construct in Second Temple Judaism," 265–77 in *Kein Land für sich allein: Studien zum Kulturkontakt in Kanaan, Israel/Palästina und Ebirnâri für Manfred Weippert zum 65. Geburtstag,* ed. Ulrich Hübner und Ernst Axel Knauf (Freiburg: Universitätsverlag Freiburg and Göttingen: Vandenhoeck & Ruprecht, 2002) has argued that the collapse of a worldview based on the principle that the gods resembled humans led to the idea of revelation and to elitism. If gods and humans were inherently different, all knowledge of deity must have come from revelation, which lifted its recipients above everyone else. When written texts were involved, elitism increased, for very few people could read. (James L. Crenshaw, *Education in Ancient Israel: Across the Deadening Silence* [New York: Doubleday, 1998] and David M. Carr, *Writing on the Tablet of the Heart: Origins of Scripture and Literature* [Oxford/New York: Oxford University Press, 2005]).

3. New Haven: Yale University Press, 1976. Jacobsen applies three adjectives— natural, royal, and familial—to successive millennia of religious development in Mesopotamia. With the emergence of city-states and strong rulers, the tendency to view gods as embodiments of nature itself gave way to terminology involving kings. This practice declined when families gained influence amid growing concern for gods with parental attributes.

4. "The gods may lie, cheat, steal, and deceive each other, the very actions that humans may be punished for. These possibilities make for a certain drama in the universe, if at the same time for a certain moral bleakness" (Benjamin R. Foster, *From Distant Days: Myths, Tales, and Poetry of Ancient Mesopotamia* (Bethesda MD: CDL Press, 1995) 2. Although given a moral rationale, the biblical account of the flood implicitly indicts Yahweh for perpetuating violence and authorizes Sovereignty as if the deity were above challenge for what would clearly be a moral outrage if done by humans.

5. A striking similarity occurs in the Gilgamesh Epic, where a harlot who has introduced Enkidu to the wonders of sex informs him as follows: "Thou art wise, Enkidu, art become like a god!" (James B. Pritchard, ed., *Ancient Near Eastern Texts Relating to the Old Testament* [Princeton NJ: Princeton University Press, 1969] 75, hereafter *ANET*)

6. James Barr, *Biblical Faith and Natural Theology: The Gifford Lectures for 1991* (Oxford: Clarendon Press, 1993) makes a persuasive argument for viewing the biblical story as implying that Adam and Eve were mortal prior to their disobedience. The Ugaritic "Tale of Aqhatu" has its hero reject an offer of immortality by Anatu with these words:

"Fib not to me, O Maiden;
For to a Youth thy fibbing is loathsome. Further life—how can mortal attain it? How can mortal attain life enduring? Glaze will be poured [on] my head, Plaster upon my pate;
And I'll die as everyone dies,
I too shall assuredly die." (*ANET*, 151)

7. Biblical literature reveals varying degrees of willingness to attribute respon-sibility for evil to Yahweh, even when forced to do so by an emerging sense of monotheism (James L. Crenshaw, *Defending God: Biblical Responses to the Problem of Evil* [Oxford & New York: Oxford University Press, 2005]). Hence the emergence of the figure who eventually was given a personal name, Satan. At first an official in divine service, the satan eventually was removed from the role of certifying authentic loyalty and became an antagonist. Nevertheless, Satan was always thought to be subject to God's authority.

8. Greenwich CT: Fawcett Publishing Inc., 1966.

9. Jonathan Z. Smith has challenged the very notion of dying/rising gods as inaccurate ("Dying and Rising Gods," in *The Encyclopedia of Religion*, ed. Mircea Eliade [New York: Collier Macmillan Publishers, 1987] and *Drudgery Divine: On the Comparison of Early Christianities and the Religions of Late Antiquity* [Chicago: University of Chicago Press, 1990]).

10. *From Distant Days*, 323. Utnapishtism, the hero of the flood in Mesopotamia, had a similar view of human nature when instructing his wife to devise a scheme to prevent Gilgamesh from lying about falling asleep. "Since to deceive is human," Utnapishtim said, "he will seek to deceive thee" (*ANET*, 95). Receptive to her hus-band's advice, she baked bread each day Gilgamesh slept, and upon awaking he saw the irrefutable evidence that he had succumbed to sleep, the tell-tale sign that he was a mortal.

11. The irony of theological claims by humans, who are by nature perverse, is sel-dom acknowledged (James L. Crenshaw, "Deceitful Minds and Theological Dogma: Jeremiah 17:5-11," 105–21 in *Utopia and Dystopia in Prophetic Literature*, ed. Ehud Ben Zvi [Helsinki: The Finnish Exegetical Society and Göttingen: Vandenhoeck & Ruprecht, 2006], reprinted in Crenshaw, *Prophets, Sages & Poets* [St. Louis: Chalice Press, 2006] 73–82, 222–24). Ignorance, one result of a perverse mind, was widely ceded, as in the following proverb from Mesopotamia.

> . . . The will of god cannot be understood,
> The way of god cannot be known:
> Anything divine is [impossible] to find out. (*From Distant Days*, 387)

A prayer to Marduk with an agnostic sentiment strikes a strong note of dismay: "Men, by whatever name, what can they understand of their own sin? Who has not been negligent, which one has committed no sin? Who can understand a god's behavior?" (*From Distant Days*, 247). Similarly, a prayer "To Any God" states that "Men are slow-witted and know nothing, no matter how many names they go by, what do they know? They do not know at all if they are doing good or evil!" (*From Distant Days*, 271).

12. James L. Crenshaw, "The Sojourner Has Come to Play the Judge: Theodicy on Trial," 83–92 in *God in the Fray: A Tribute to Walter Brueggemann*, ed. Tod Linafelt and Timothy K. Beal (Minneapolis: Fortress Press, 1998). Abraham's ques-tion to God in this story provides the title for an examination of theodicy by various scholars: *Shall Not the Judge of All the Earth Do What Is Right? Studies on the Nature of God in Tribute to James L. Crenshaw*, ed. David Penchansky and Paul L. Redditt (Winona Lake IN: Eisenbrauns, 2000). Whereas this volume is thematic, another recent treatment of theodicy combines theme with canon (*Theodicy in the World*

of the Bible, ed. Antti Laato and Johannes C. de Moor [Leiden and Boston: Brill, 2003]).

13. *Fear and Trembling* (Garden City NY: Doubleday, 1941). R. W. L. Moberly gives a theological defense of the divine test in Genesis 22, but he fails to reckon seriously with the theological consequences of mandating such a monstrous test for a faithful servant (*The Bible, Theology, and Faith: A Study of Abraham and Jesus* [Cambridge: Cambridge University Press, 2000]).

14. John J. Collins, *Encounters with Biblical Theology* (Minneapolis: Fortress, 2005) 126, links natural theology with upwardly mobile Jews of Alexandria. He also recognizes a flaw in Wisdom of Solomon, namely tension between particularism, fueled by ethnic survival, and universalism. Collins finds a precedent for natural theology within wisdom literature, the linking of act and consequence, and in the idea of personified Wisdom (101).

15. "Is There a Doctrine of Retribution in the Old Testament?" 57–87 in *Theodicy in the Old Testament*, ed. James L. Crenshaw (IRT 4; Philadelphia: Fortress Press; London: SPCK, 1983). Koch's article first appeared as "Gibt es ein Vergeltungsdogma im Alten Testament?" *ZThK* 52 (1955): 1–42. The English translation is an abridged version.

16. Samuel E. Balentine, *The Hidden God: The Hiding of the Face of God in the Old Testament* (Oxford: Oxford University Press, 1983); Kornelis H. Miskotte, *When the Gods Are Silent* (New York and Evanston: Harper & Row, Publishers 1967); and Karl Rahner, *Encounters with Silence* (Westminster MD: Newman Press, 1965), provide different readings of the same religious experience.

17. The linguistic possibilities of this disclosure retain its mystery. It can be read to imply divine causation, philosophical being, or a meteorological phenomenon.

18. Othmar Keel, *The Symbolism of the Biblical World: Ancient Near Eastern Iconography and the Book of Psalms* (Winona Lake IN: Eisenbrauns, 1997).

19. William P. Brown, *Seeing the Psalms: A Theology of Metaphor* (Louisville KY: Westminster John Knox, 2002) introduces an innovative way of viewing the book of Psalms from the perspective of its rich use of metaphors.

20. John F. Kutsko, *Between Heaven and Earth: Divine Presence and Absence in the Book of Ezekiel*, Biblical and Judaic Studies 7 (Winona Lake IN: Eisenbrauns, 2000) 57, n 109 refers to convenient discussions of the ritual referred to as washing/opening the mouth.

21. Karel van der Toorn, "From the Oral to the Written: The Case of Old Babylonian Prophecy," 219–34, and Martti Missinen, "Spoken, Written, Quoted and Invented: Orality and Writtenness in Ancient Near Eastern Prophecy," 235–72 in *Writings and Speech in Israelite and Ancient Near Eastern Prophecy*, ed. Ehud Ben Zvi and Michael H. Floyd, Symposium 10 (Atlanta: Society of Biblical Literature, 2000).

22. Simo Parpola, *Assyrian Prophecies*, State Archives of Assyria 9 (Helsinki: Helsinki University Press, 1997) reproduces the texts in translation and ventures a controversial synthesis of the religious worldview they presuppose, one greatly resembling early Christianity.

23. Patrick D. Miller, *The Religion of Ancient Israel* (London: SPCK; Louisville, Kentucky: Westminster John Knox Press, 2000) and Mark S. Smith, *The Early History of God: Yahweh and the Other Deities in Ancient Israel* (New York: Harper & Row, 1990) trace both the evolution of religious thought and its diversity. For Smith, Canaanite influence on Israelite religion was far reaching.

24. The unusual syntax of this verse has been treated by Francis I. Andersen and David Noel Freedman in *Amos*, AB 24A (New York: Doubleday, 1989) 188–90. The problem arises from the twofold use of the relative *'aser* with no clear antecedent for the second occurrence.

25. Baruch A. Levine has provided a translation with introduction and notes in volume 2 of *The Context of Scripture: Monumental Inscriptions from the Biblical World*, ed. William W. Hallo (Leiden and Boston: Brill, 2003) 140–45.

26. J. Edward Wright, *The Early History of Heaven* (Oxford/New York: Oxford University Press, 2000) gives an informative analysis of the origin of astronomy in the biblical world.

27. Foster, *From Distant Days*, 305.

28. No individual can adequately describe the vast literature on the book of Job, although James L. Crenshaw, "Job, Book of," 858–68 in *ABD*, vol. 3, ed. David Noel Freedman (New York: Doubleday, 1992); Samuel E. Balentine, *Job* (Macon GA: Smyth & Helwys, 2006); and Carol Newsom, "The Book of Job," *NIB*, vol. 4 (Nashville: Abingdon Press, 1996) indicate its general character.

29. John Barton, *Oracles of God: Perceptions of Ancient Prophecy in Israel after the Exile* (New York: Oxford University Press, 1986).

30. A perceptive introduction to apocalyptic thinking can be found in the various publications of John J. Collins, particularly *The Apocalyptic Imagination: An Introduction to the Jewish Matrix of Christianity* (New York: Crossroad, 1984); "Early Jewish Apocalypticism," 282–88 in *ABD*, vol. 1 (New York: Doubleday, 1992); and "The Reinterpretation of Apocalyptic Traditions in The Wisdom of Solomon," 143–55, *The Book of Wisdom in Modern Research: Studies on Tradition, Redaction, and Theology*, ed. Angelo Passaro and Geirceppe Bellia, Deuterocanonical and Cognate Literature Yearbook 2005 (Berlin/New York: Walter de Gruyter, 2005).

31. James L. Crenshaw, *Old Testament Wisdom: An Introduction* (Louisville: Westminster John Knox, 1998) and Gerhard von Rad, *Wisdom in Israel* (Nashville: Abingdon Press, 1972).

32. James L. Crenshaw, *Prophetic Conflict: Its Effect Upon Israelite Religion*, BZAW 124 (Berlin and New York: Walter de Gruyter, 1971) discusses the futile effort to formulate adequate criteria by which people could determine which prophets to heed and whom to ignore.

33. Alice M. Sinnott, *The Personification of Wisdom*, SOTS MS (Aldershot: Ashgate, 2005); Judith E. McKinlay, *Gendering Wisdom the Host: Biblical Invitations to Eat and Drink*, JSOT SS 216 (Sheffield: Sheffield Academic Press, 1996); Gerlinde Baumann, *Die Weisheitsgestalt in Proverbien 1-9*, FAT 16 (Tübingen: J. C. B. Mohr [Paul Siebeck], 1996); and Silvia Schroer, *Wisdom Has Built Her House: Studies on the Figure of Sophia in the Bible* (Collegeville MN: The Liturgical Press, 2000).

34. "Die Krisis der Weisheit bei Kohelet," 139–52 in *Les Sagesses du proche-Orient ancient: Colloque de Strasbourg 17-19 Mai 1962* (Paris: Presses Universitaires de France, 1963) and *Wesen und Geschichte der Weisheit*, BZAW 101 (Berlin: Töpelmann, 1966) respectively. Martin Rose, "De la <<Crise de la Sagesse >> à la << Sagesse de la Crise >>," *Revue de théologie et de philosophie* 131 (1999): 115–34 stresses the creative potential in a crisis of belief. One may compare the positive correlation between evil and the creative in literature and art.

35. Eric Weil, "What Is a Breakthrough in History?" *Daedalus* (Spring 1975): 21–36 (*Wisdom, Revelation and Doubt: Perspectives on the First Millennium B.C.*). In my view, two remarkable intellectual revolutions occurred in ancient Israel. The first was the transition from polytheism to monotheism recorded in Ps 82. The sentence of death, imposed by Elohim on the gods for failing to maintain justice, signals this radical shift in worldview. The second revolution was the belief that humans might transcend death through faithful service of God as indicated in Ps 73 (James L. Crenshaw, "Love Is Stronger Than Death: Intimations of Life beyond the Grave," 53–78 in *Resurrection: The Origin and Future of a Biblical Doctrine*, ed. James H. Charlesworth [New York and London: T & T Clark, 2006]).

36. Newsom, "The Book of Job," 629, discusses five possible translations of Job 42:6. They are as follows:

> 1. "Therefore I despise myself and repent upon dust and ashes" (i.e., in humiliation);
> 2. "Therefore I retract my words and repent of dust and ashes" (i.e., the symbols of mourning);
> 3. "Therefore I reject and forswear dust and ashes" (i.e., the symbols of mourning);
> 4. "Therefore I retract my words and have changed my mind concerning dust and ashes" (i.e., the human condition);
> 5. "Therefore I retract my words, and I am comforted concerning dust and ashes" (i.e., the human condition).

37. Aversion to unresolved endings is widespread. It dictates the practice in synagogues of ending the Scripture reading on a positive note. Similarly, it has produced wholly unanticipated endings in literature and film, for example, Goethe's *Faust* and the movie *Fatal Attraction*. The epilogue to the book of Job overlooks Job's ten children and his servants, whose deaths seem to matter little more than those of extras in a movie. This feature of the biblical book presents a serious challenge to the method that governs the stimulating analysis of the epilogue by Kenneth Numfor Ngwa (*The Hermeneutics of the "Happy" Ending in Job 42:7-17*, BZAW 354 [New York and Berlin: Walter de Gruyter, 2005]). He uses a threefold dynamic: inward toward the center in search of unity, outward toward other experiences in search of diversity, and forward toward the transcendent search of meaning. In Ngwa's view, the epilogue transcends any strict concept of retribution, but as I read the text an ironic wink lingers despite every attempt to resolve the tension between the prose and poetry. God's action is still outrageous, even if construed as outside the norms of a human concept of reward and retribution. The epilogue sabotages the message of the poetic dialogue.

38. Ethan Dor-Shav, "Ecclesiastes, Fleeting and Timeless," *Azure* 18 (5765/2004): 67–87 reflects continuing interest in a topic that was widely researched in the last half of the twentieth century. Witness two recent commentaries by Thomas Krüger and Ludger Schwienhorst-Schönberger, namely *Kohelet* (*Prediger*), Biblischer

Kommentar Altes Testament 19 (Neukirchen Vluyn: Neukirchener Verlag, 2000) and *Kohelet,* Herders theologischers Kommentar zum Alten Testament (Freiburg: Herder, 2004).

39. Norbert Lohfink, "Die Wiederkehr des immer Gleichen. Eine frühe Synthese zwischen griechischen und jüdischen Weltgefuhl in Kohelet 1, 4-11," 95–124 in *Studien zu Kohelet,* Stuttgarter biblische Aufsatzbande 26 (Stuttgart: Verlag Katholisches Bibelwerk GmbH, 1998).

40. "Fate, *miqreh,* and Reason: Some Reflections on Qohelet and Biblical Thought," 159–75 in *Solving Riddles and Untying Knots: Biblical, Epigraphic and Semitic Studies in Honor of Jonas G. Greenfield,* ed. Ziony Zevit et al. (Winona Lake IN: Eisenbrauns, 1995).

41. James L. Crenshaw, "Qoheleth's Quantitative Language," 83–94, 224–30 in *Prophets, Sages & Poets,* also appearing in *The Language of Qohelet in Context: Essays in Honour of Prof. A. Schoors* (Leuven: Peeters, 2007). This article discusses incipient philosophy in the heavy use of quantitative terminology by Qoheleth and offers a rationale for such language among sages in the second century.

42. Norbert Lohfink, "Koh 1, 2 <<Alles ist Windhauch>>—universale oder anthropologische Aussage," 125–42 in *Studien zu Kohelet.*

43. "Ecclesiastes 3.1-15: Another Interpretation," *JSOT* 66 (1995): 55–64.

44. Daniel J. Harrington, *Wisdom Texts from Qumran* (London and New York: Routledge, 1996).

45. John J. Collins, *Jewish Wisdom in the Hellenistic Age,* OTL (Louisville KY: Westminster John Knox, 1997).

46. James L. Crenshaw, "The Problem of Theodicy in Sirach: On Human Bondage," *JBL* 94 (1975): 47–64, reprinted in *Urgent Advice and Probing Questions,* 155–74.

47. Moyna McGlynn, *Divine Judgment and Divine Benevolence in the Book of Wisdom,* WUNT 139 (Tübingen: Mohr Siebeck, 2001) 25–53 and Giuseppe Bellia-Angelo Passare, "Infinite Passion for Justice," 307–28 in *The Book of Wisdom in Modern Research.* The articles from a Conference of Biblical Studies organized by the Theological Faculty of Sicily, "St. John the Evangelist," and held March 22–23 in 2002 reveal the extraordinary vitality of current Italian scholarship on the Book of Wisdom, along with notable contributions by David Winston, John J. Collins, Émile Puech, and Maurice Gilbert.

48. Michael Kolarcik, *The Ambiguity of Death in Wisdom Chapters 1–6: A Study of Literary Structure and Interpretation* (Rome: Editrice Pontificio Istituto Biblico, 1991).

49. *Map Is Not Territory: Studies in the History of Religions* (Leiden: Brill, 1978).

chapter two

QOHELETH IN HISTORICAL CONTEXT*

In the initial stages of searching for the historical context of Qoheleth, scholars concentrated above all on geography. For them almond trees, cisterns, the technological innovation of the pulley for drawing water from deep wells, meteorological factors, and peculiarities of language indicated an Israelite location rather than Alexandria or Phoenicia. Proximity to sacred space permitted them to narrow the search to Jerusalem or its immediate environs.

Recent efforts range more widely as interpreters take another look at the Hellenistic impact on Qoheleth, particularly symposiastic philosophy and the Zenon archives.[1] Defying the near-consensus that the book of Ecclesiastes is to be dated in the middle of the third century BCE, C. L. Seow has adapted the linguistic approach D. Winston applied to Wisdom of Solomon and concluded that the fourth century alone saw the use of *šalît* as Qoheleth employs it.[2] Because I do not wish to duplicate what others have done, I have chosen to turn the spotlight on the culture reflected in Qoheleth's own words, somewhat in the manner of O. Wischmeyer's analysis of Sirach. I shall ask what Qoheleth says about the intellectual community, the religious context, the economic realities, the political situation, and the institution of the family. Then I shall reflect

* The original appeared in *Biblica* 88 (2007): 285–99. Reprinted with permission.

on some surprising omissions, especially personified *ḥokmāh*, as well as the tenuous claim that Qoheleth was an epistemological empiricist. In a bow to a current trend, I shall illustrate the principle of intertextuality with regard to Ps 39. My closing observations will examine Qoheleth's modernity.

Through it all, I ask you to keep in mind that even Qoheleth's assessment of historical reality was not entirely accurate, for new things really do happen. Even if his experiential approach to learning[3] is not entirely without precedent among earlier biblical sages, his self-conscious reflection on the process of thinking itself marks a new stage in the epistemology of ancient Semites.[4] Now if his own assessment of the historical context[5] was not entirely accurate, how much more my own views will undoubtedly be riddled with half-truths. Perhaps even partial truths are better than nothing if they stimulate fuller revelation from you, my esteemed listeners and soon-to-be partners in dialogue.

I. KNOWLEDGE

I begin by looking at the intellectual scene, since Qoheleth was above all a *ḥākām*, wise man, at least in the view of the first epilogist.[6] Incidental references to a flourishing intellectual life highlight the tedium that often results from persistent study and compositional activity aimed at preserving insights from the past. Technical vocabulary such as *pešer* attests early attempts to develop a suitable hermeneutic, one that later flourishes at Qumran but has not yet attained the sophistication of rabbinic *pešat* and *derash*.[7] "In your face" polemic represents epistemological agnosticism and indicates competing views about absolutist claims, but not the stifling of intellectual curiosity that Ben Sira adopts to counter hubris. Such conflict suggests rival intellectual camps, a sure sign of an open society confronting alternative value systems, one with high appreciation for refined rhetoric and literary craft.[8] The extension of instruction to ordinary citizens (*hā'ām*) reflects confident professional leadership.

The sources of different understandings of reality are not entirely clear. Reflective thinking about the cognitive process has its counterpart in the Hellenistic environment, although Qoheleth's move in the direction of second-order thought may be an indigenous development associated with the attempt to transform Hebrew into a medium for conveying philosophy.[9] The use of *miqreh* to indicate human destiny, the technical nuance of *ḥešbôn* as the bottom line in an economic balance sheet, and the temporal extension of *'ōlām* resemble Greek thinking sufficiently to raise the issue of influence,[10] as does Qoheleth's choice of *hebel* to characterize everything in the visible world in the same way the philosopher Monimus spoke of smoke or mist as the defining term.[11] The faint resemblance between Qoheleth's well-known poem about a time for everything and the Stoic division of the universe into balanced opposites may indicate the influence of Greek popular philosophy.[12]

Two additional features of Qoheleth's language allow for the possibility of cross-cultural exchange with the Hellenistic world: first, the reference to four basic elements of the universe (earth, air, fire, and water), and second, the totalizing sense attributed to the particle *kōl*.[13] From these humble beginnings, a later Ben Sira will ponder life's necessities and pay lip service, at the very least, to the Stoic formulation of cosmic unity

"He is the all, τό ον."[14] His two different lists of essentials for living apply to contrasting circumstances. When confronted with people in need, one can eke out a meager living with little. Hence the Spartan four items of bread, water, clothes, and house appear in a context of generosity toward the needy. The longer list of water, fire, iron, salt, flour, milk, honey, wine, oil, and clothing occurs in a section dealing with divine largesse, where bounty abounds. The two texts illustrate an important interpretive principle: apparent contradictions in a literary document sometimes may stem from diverse social contexts and literary purposes. Qoheleth's essentials, closer to Ben Sira's short list, include bread, wine, clothes, oil, and a lover.[15]

The similarities between Qoheleth's advice about how to enjoy life and Siduri's counsel to Gilgamesh point farther east to Mesopotamia. While two authors could have reached similar conclusions independently, the striking affinities between Qoheleth's advice and that given to Gilgamesh to dissuade him from a futile search for immortality may not be fully explained by the notion of polygenesis,[16] especially in light of the mention of the proverb about a threefold cord in both Qoheleth and the Gilgamesh Epic.

The centrality of personal observation to Qoheleth's epistemology is a factor of his frequent use of expressions like "I saw," "I knew," "I thought," "I said," "I concluded." Such language tends to obscure tell-tale signs of a wholly different understanding of knowledge alongside the experimental: the acceptance of ancestral tradition, particularly about the noumenal world.[17] This extraordinary combination of empirical conclusions and unverifiable assertions about a distant Elohim give his teachings a modern stamp, for we today readily endorse a scientific worldview while maintaining teachings grounded in faith. Qoheleth's ambivalence toward traditional ideas about the creator and judge places him in the camp with skeptics who possess a vision of a better universe but doubt that it will ever materialize. Consequently, the refrain, "Everything is utterly futile—and shepherding the wind," echoes throughout the book.

II. RELIGION

Just as Qoheleth's teachings reveal a robust intellectual society, they also point to a religious community that is struggling to grasp the implications of a loss of certainty. In some circles, nostalgia for the certainties experienced in the past invests the present moment with a tinge of disappointment. Death, the pervasive issue, has become an acute problem because of an emerging consciousness of the ego.[18] The age-old question about survival beyond the grave is suddenly profoundly existential.[19] Qoheleth's response is to throw his hands up and exclaim, *mî yôdēaʿ*.[20] The general tenor of his teachings suggests that he rejected the belief in either a form of immortality like that envisioned in Ps 73:23-26 or a resurrection of the body.[21] The resulting loss of meaning pervades virtually everything Qoheleth says and provides the catalyst for the seven exhortations to enjoy life before death inaugurates eternal darkness devoid of memory. The striking non sequitur of his logic is that hatred of life does not issue in suicide but rather generates classic literature.

To be sure, remnants of official religion persist. Funerals retain their significance despite their inherent susceptibility to crass commercialism and self-glorification. Professional mourners fill the streets as they have done from time immemorial when death enters a house, and they are matched by professional singers with a merrier tune. Caution reigns in the sacred precinct, presumably because of fear that what is promised in difficult circumstances may be quickly forgotten in better times, thus invoking divine anger. Prayer in the house of God is thought to be wasted effort because of the distance separating the speaker from the one addressed. This neutrality, perhaps hostility, toward the cult is theological rather than the result of priestly malfeasance. Fear of God as piety plays a minimal role for Qoheleth;[22] dread like that before a human despot has replaced it.

The remote creator may have withdrawn from providential interaction with humans, but they are nonetheless said to be recipients of random gifts from God.[23] Unfortunately, at least from the perspective of justice, these tokens of divine generosity are dispensed without regard to merit.[24] Everything that happens is determined by the deity, rendering useless all human effort to shape the future and negating the sapiential enterprise.

Even potentially helpful gifts such as a sense of eternity or the hidden are emptied of positive value, resulting in epistemological agnosticism (3:11). In this instance, as in the similar reference to a gift of joy (5:17-20), linguistic ambiguity prevents modern interpreters from a clear grasp of what is being said.

III. ECONOMY

A perceptive sage once observed that socioeconomic circumstances affect religious views (Prov 30:7-9). Too many worldly goods produce practical atheism; too few produce desperate acts that dishonor God. Qoheleth's era was characterized by unprecedented economic volatility. Fortunes were made and lost; the risk was high, the potential for wealth enormous. In this bustling economy, social standing was often fleeting. Talented individuals accumulated vast wealth at the expense of enjoyment, working incessantly and spending restless nights worrying about losing it to thieves and seeing it squandered by costly employees. Investments in mercantile enterprises on the high seas provided a risky alternative to pastoral and agricultural endeavors, themselves subject to the whim of nature. Obsession with capturing the optimal moment to venture forth in either of these tasks threatened the whole activity, as did the attempt to bolster human labor by magic, whether spells or a divining rod.[25]

In such a moneyed economy, a crucial issue was how to sustain prosperity, in a word, to register a profit at the end of the day as well as over the long haul. Who will inherit my vast wealth, and will the person who benefits from my labor use it wisely?

That seems to have been a perennial question raised by the well-to-do. Earlier unwritten laws that guaranteed the family's land to the firstborn or to a legitimate successor are circumvented because much of the land has been appropriated for bureaucracy or lost through enforced debt. Even the privileged elite, however, have no assurance that society will be stable. Kings have been known to fall, and prisoners have risen to the throne. Consequently, princes may be forced to walk while former slaves ride on horses. This reversal of fortune may have been sufficiently common in Israel and Egypt to generate a literary convention.

Like most societies, this one has pockets of wealth and pockets of poverty. We hear of gold and silver vessels, costly perfumes, expensive clothes, oils, and wine, in addition to royal opulence. We also hear about slaves, concubines, and wretched victims of oppression who have no defender.

Laborers toil at catching fish and fowl, repair walls, wield axes, patch leaking roofs, grind grain, guard estates, sow seed, harvest crops, and engage in countless other daily activities.

IV. POLITICS

Watching over this volatile situation is a many-tiered bureaucracy. At the very top is a foreign sovereign, and beneath him are powerful appointees with two goals: to increase revenues for the king and secretly to direct as much money as possible into their personal treasuries.

Absolute power not only corrupts; it also instills fear in the people who are subject to it. Caution therefore commends itself in all interactions with a sovereign, as well as when conversing with others about anything that might be interpreted as critical of one whose might is construed as right. In Qoheleth's world, an Orwellian "Big Brother" is an ever-present threat, making gossip doubly dangerous. Even tiny villages are not safe from a ruler's expansionist policy, particularly when the local leadership lacks intelligence. The long arm of the king reaches out to seize taxable income and to claim young men for military duty, from which Qoheleth admits no exclusion,[26] unlike Deuteronomy and Persian sources.

Despite all this negative perspective on royalty and real politics, Qoheleth's initial self-presentation is that of king. He boasts of unprecedented accomplishments reminiscent of the Solomonic anecdote in 1 Kgs 3:4-15; 5:9-14; 10:23. The picture of a king using his wealth to build houses and gardens for pleasure, all too familiar from the ancient world, functions as a royal travesty. The use of the indirect object *lî* ("for myself") nine times in 2:4-9 highlights the self-absorption of a kingship emptied of royal ideology. In a proper world, and in ideal fantasy, rulers apply their wealth and power to correct injustice, specifically grievances of widows, orphans, the poor, and strangers.[27]

They also maximize the yield of cultivated land.

If Qoheleth has heard of philosopher-kings, he surely has serious reservations about the utility of such a concept. When one contrasts his treatment of regality with that of Pseudo-Solomon, it becomes clear that Qoheleth considers kingship something less than an ideal toward which the wise ought to strive. For the first-century author of Wisdom of Solomon, however, regality achieves its true manifestation in the sage, whose union with *ḥokmāh* actually fulfills the philosopher's dream for a perfect society. Whereas Qoheleth unmasked royal ideology, Wisdom of Solomon recovered it.[28] The *arché* of Prov 1:7 becomes *telos*, *ḥokmāh* functioning like *rûaḥ* in Israel's sacred narrative.

V. FAMILY

In Qoheleth's world, how does the family fare? We are told that conception occurs as mysteriously as the wind's movement, and that God is at work in both. Young people, present as addressee but never vocal, are encouraged to enjoy life while youthful vigor lasts, a sure indication that such advice reflects the thoughts of an older person. They are also warned against a femme fatale, which is a traditional motif in ancient wisdom, so permeated by androcentrism. Nevertheless, they are exhorted, "Enjoy life with the woman you love." This unusual expression[29] instead of the usual word for "your wife" forges a link with the eroticism celebrated in Song of Songs.

Disappointments are known in the intimacy of the family. The joy associated with anticipated birth gives way to sorrow when an infant is stillborn. Miserliness creates bitterness, sickness prevents enjoyment of accumulated goods, and advanced years bring days in which one can find no pleasure. Flies spoil costly perfume, brigands attack travelers, snakes bite their charmers and day laborers; the less agile or careless fall into pits or ravines.

In this society, individualism thrives unchecked. Qoheleth's heightened ego goes beyond the usual scribe's striving for immortality by leaving a literary legacy, at least of his name as copier of documents. Although Qoheleth hides his identity, when he does momentarily expand the horizon of thought to entertain a principle of solidarity, he continues to think about personal advantages that come from an associate. When attacked by robbers, he observes, a companion can come to the rescue; if one falls (into a pit), a friend can help him up, and a person can stave off the cold of night by lying close to someone.

SOME STRIKING OMISSIONS

Several things stand out in this account by their near-absence. There are few indications of urban life despite the fourfold reference to Jerusalem, no references to ethnic groups, no cultural clashes. Priests do not seem to have filled the void left by the collapse of the Davidic monarchy and a decisive decline in prophetic status. Apocalyptic thinking, if present at all, is greatly subdued, lacking its identifying features that become prominent during the first century.[30] The evils of idolatry are not mentioned, although this theme that developed into lively ridicule of rival religions is widely attested in late canonical and intertestamental literature.[31] Perhaps most perplexing of all is Qoheleth's total silence about the descent of heavenly Wisdom in feminine form.

Personified Wisdom. This last omission requires further scrutiny in light of the role of an extraordinary female in Prov 8:22-31, Ben Sira, and Wisdom of Solomon. The hiatus in the book of Job after the promising beginning in Proverbs may partially explain Qoheleth's reluctance to venture in a direction that the poet who composed Job 28 backed away from after partially opening a door.[32] If the best one can hope for is a confession from the dual powers of Sheol and death that even they have only heard a secondhand report of her, the better part of prudence may be to concede failure in locating Wisdom and to leave her dwelling place to God. In adopting this position, however, Qoheleth misses out on at least four contributions of such speculation about personified Wisdom.

First, this intriguing figure brings the deity into everyday life in a way that responds effectively to a perceived absence as a consequence of a defunct cult. The theological impact of the Babylonian victory in Jerusalem, YHWH's residence, must surely have contributed to an overwhelming sense of disquietude, either from the suspicion that the gods of Babylon were superior to Judah's[33] or from the heavy burden of guilt that shifted the responsibility for the defeat to human shoulders. The nostalgia for a lost past that surfaced in connection with the restored temple in the late sixth century indicates that the newly constituted community in Jerusalem sensed an aching void.

It was left to Ben Sira to figure out how to use the concept of personified Wisdom to link cult and written Torah. In his view, heavenly Wisdom chose the holy city as a dwelling place and ministered to God in the temple. Most important, she was present to all in the teachings transmitted from God through Moses. The torah was thus given universal application, an important transcending of nationalism. The author of Wisdom of Solomon moved in a different direction: Wisdom guided the people of God in the same way the Spirit did. Indeed, Wisdom is said to be the external manifestation of God, a pure hypostasis of divine attributes. By these means, guilt was assuaged and divine presence assured.[34]

Second, warfare's destabilization of the family structure[35] in Judah found a harsh sequel in the Persian satrapy, which administered a policy of taxation that threatened the fabric of society. Debt incurred during drought or from diseases of crops led to the enslaving of children, and foreign political appointees under Ptolemaic rule exercised irrepressible control over the lives of adults. In this situation women assumed a greater role in holding families together, and for that task personified Wisdom served as model. The eroticism associated with this mysterious figure strengthened that important function.

Third, the return of priestly hierocracy under Ezra's leadership contributed to a growing sense of transcendence. The distancing of the deity[36] entailed a rich repertoire of divine names, at least two of which accentuated the gulf separating humans from their creator. For Qoheleth the epithet of choice, *ha'elōhîm*, was the general name for God preceded by the definite article, best translated by "the deity." Although it is difficult to say for certain, given the textual status of Sirach, Ben Sira seems to have preferred the Hebrew equivalent of *'upsistos*, probably *'elyôn*.[37] Wisdom's mediation of the heavenly deity softened the consequences of a priestly desire to protect divine prerogatives and majesty.

Fourth, the growing attraction of Hellenism to Jewish youth who dared to compare what they knew of Greek philosophy with the Hebraic tradition must have weighed heavily on parents and teachers. Qoheleth appears to have been spared the open confrontation with Greek ideas and customs that Ben Sira experienced, particularly those associated with symposia, medicine, and philosophical debate about divine justice. The equation of wisdom with the universal logos as envisioned in Wisdom of Solomon placed Jewish thinking on a trajectory similar to that of Hellenism.[38]

The prevalence of female deities in the ancient Near East and their likely attraction in Israel's popular religion may suggest a fifth function of personified Wisdom: the elevation of the feminine into the heavenly court. Both Prov 8:22-31 and Sir 24:1-23 ascribe a heavenly origin to this extraordinary figure.[39]

EPISTEMOLOGICAL AMBIGUITY

Qoheleth's silence about personified Wisdom is more than compensated for by his vocal position on the deity's activity. The language of giving prevails here, along with that of divine work (*ma'aśeh*). This fascination with things concealed from the naked eye by one who otherwise lays claim to an empirical approach to knowledge calls for additional investigation. What access did Qoheleth have to the deity's interaction with the world and humans?

To answer that question, we must turn to a famous crux, the claim that Elohim has placed something in the mind (*lēb*) but at the same time prohibited humans from finding its full sense or possibly from discovering it at all (3:11). The promising beginning that the creator made everything beautiful or appropriate in its time gives way to a syntactical anomaly, *mibbelî 'ăšer lō'* plus a verb, transforming promise into sober lament. What secret has been planted in the intellect, according to Qoheleth?

The temporal emphasis in the preceding poem, 3:2-8, and the vocalization in the Masoretic Text have led many interpreters to something like "a sense of eternity," *ha'ōlām* having not yet taken on the meaning it has in rabbinic literature, "the age to come." In my view, this temporal rendering is less satisfactory than revocalizing to *ha'elem* and translating it "the unknown," a meaning of the root *'lm* that is attested in Eccl 12:14, at Ugarit, and in Job.[40] The first translation implies that no one can discover the future, while the second denies access to the mystery lying at the very heart of human existence.

On either reading of this difficult verse, Qoheleth states that human beings are recipients of a revelation that guards its precise content. The closed door contributes a sense of finitude, either from inability to master time or from ignorance about meaning itself. The negative spin on revelation matches that of the Joban author in the other two direct references to divine disclosure within wisdom literature. The nocturnal specter who disturbed Eliphaz's deep sleep (*tardēmâ*) and left him trembling in awe conveyed a single thought: "Can a mortal be more just than Elohim; can a man be purer than his maker?" (Job 4:17).[41] Similarly, the divine speeches in Job 38–41 leave Job's agonizing questions unanswered while undermining his anthropocentrism. Knowledge, they seem to say, must be discovered on one's own rather than hazarding direct revelation. While Qoheleth's brush with divine disclosure lacks *mysterium tremendum et fascinosum*, its lingering effect is unmatched by what has preceded in the poem about times.

One other text in Ecclesiastes has been said to involve direct communication from the deity. In it, Qoheleth comments on what *ha'elōhîm* does to or for persons to whom much has been given (5:19).[42] The verse refers to an abbreviated recollection during one's life "because the deity does something (*ma'aneh*) with joy of the heart." The verb *'ānâ*, here in the hiphil participial form, has three distinct meanings: (1) to answer; (2) to afflict; and (3) to occupy oneself with. For me, the overwhelming mood of the book supports a reading that emphasizes the downside of pleasure. For this reason, I prefer the translation "For the deity afflicts him with joy in the mind." In other words, humans experience pain in the very pondering of pleasure, either because it fails to appear or is ephemeral.

These two (?) references to a one-way communication between deity and humans provide no adequate basis for mediated revelation via personified *ḥokmāh* or for Qoheleth's many assertions about God. For all his insistence on empirical epistemology, Qoheleth recognizes the fragmented nature of learning based on sight and sound. Although his sweeping epistemological claims give the impression that he personally evaluates all his observations, the content often comes from tradition. The tensions within his thought derive partly from his failure to reconcile what his eyes observed and what his ancestors transmitted to him. His rhetorical style therefore matches his powerful assertion that everything is illusory (*hebel*). Axioms lie alongside tautology, constituting what has been called a rhetoric of erasure[43] or a relativizing of all absolutes.

INTERTEXTUALITY (PS 39)

This conclusion about Qoheleth's religious legacy raises a question about intertextuality,[44] particularly that involving affinities with certain psalms. For our purposes, the most significant psalm is the thirty-ninth, which, like Qoheleth, universalizes *hebel* as the essence of humankind. The crucial verses read as follows:

> Tell me, YHWH, my end (*qiṣṣî*),
> and what is the length of my life; Let me know how fleeting (*ḥādēl*) [it
> is]. You made my life handbreadths,
> its span as nothing before you (*negdekā*);
> surely every human is (*hebel*) breath.[45]
> Surely man walks as an image (*beṣelem*);
> surely his fortune (*yehemāyûn*) is but a breath;
> he amasses but does not know who will gather it. (Ps 39:5-7)

The psalmist's dim view of existence is matched by a grim assessment of YHWH's indifference, represented in the image of a moth devouring a treasure and punctuated by a summary judgment, "Surely every person is a breath" (39:12).

The psalmist's exercise in ambiguity corresponds to his concept of human existence. Troubled by life's brevity, he asks for a clue as to when nonexistence will begin for him. Like Qoheleth, the psalmist uses a form of the verb *hālak* as a euphemism for dying,[46] together with the particle of nonexistence, *ʾēnennî* (39:14).[47] Like him, too, the psalmist compares daily life to walking in darkness, as in a shadow (cf. Qoh 6:4), unless the sense is that of likeness to an image (39:7).[48]

The unusual *ʾāmartî* that opens the psalm recalls Qoheleth's repeated formula for deliberation,[49] although without the accompanying *belibbî*, but the alternation between *ʾanî* and *ʾānōkî* (vv. 11 and 13) contrasts with Qoheleth's exclusive use of *ʾanî* for the personal pronoun "I." The progression from "autobiographical" reflection[50] to somber thoughts about human existence parallels Qoheleth's move from the royal experiment to hatred of life.[51] The near-blasphemous charge hurled at YHWH in v. 6 that human life is but a trifle to God uses *negdî*, the same word as that indicating the presence of the wicked in v. 2. The similar accusation in v. 10 that the afflictions experienced by the poet are YHWH's doing and the almost unprecedented lament devoid of resolution underline the psalmist's dismay, comparable to the effect of Ps 88, which begins with the comforting epithet *YHWH ʾelōhê yešûātî*, but what follows rings a more ominous bell. A troubled Qoheleth never addresses deity and avoids the personal name YHWH completely. The psalmist shares Qoheleth's anxiety generated by ignorance about who will benefit from his labor, and he also joins Qoheleth in an almost unprecedented lament devoid of resolution.

I make no claim of textual dependence in either direction, but I wish to emphasize the similarity in thought between this psalm and Qoheleth, if only to confirm that he was not alone in viewing life as *hebel*. The sentiment expressed in Ps 39 is hardly matched by that in Ps 62, which uses the notion of *hebel* and *kāzāb*[52] to downplay human threats against him when God acts as both refuge and deliverer (Ps 62:10). The picture of all of one's personal enemies on a single scale and weighing no more than a breath (*hebel*) arises from a profound trust that is absent from both Ps 39 and Qoheleth. The sixfold use of *ʾak* in Ps 62, twice as many as in Ps 39, merely punctuates the poet's certainty of special care from above. The description of human frailty in Ps 144:4 also arises as a means of conveying the insubstantiality of danger from enemies. Because mortals are like *hebel*,[53] their days like a passing shadow (v. 4), one need not fear hostile forces, except that death is itself a force with which to reckon. The plea for the eradication of the wicked in this bellicistic psalm[54] demonstrates the psalmist's awareness of vulnerability while at the same time pointing to a power before whom all mortals pale.

CONCLUDING OBSERVATIONS

In sum, even if I have reliably interpreted the clues that Qoheleth left behind about the world around him, I must consider the possibility that it is entirely the product of fantasy. Behind the text lie dramatic human events, to be sure, but are they figments of the author's imagination? It is well known that individuals and institutions often conceal some facts and expose others to the light of day for the purpose of shaping historical memory in a way that promotes their own prestige and survival. Writers have the ability to construct symbolic worlds wholly consistent with their chosen rhetorical strategy. Qoheleth's use of the royal travesty enables him to retain anonymity and proves that he was not above fiction in the service of a rhetorical plan. The task confronting every interpreter, therefore, is to link social data with mental styles present in ancient social life.

The modern anthropological turn[55] that shifted the focus away from deity to humans requires not only that interpreters be alert to the ancient social/historical environment within a text but also that they recognize their own context. This remarkable turn helped bring about a collapse of a one-sided theology that bore the catchword "salvation history."[56] The resulting turn to biblical literature emphasizing the human initiative, to which I have devoted a lifetime of research and writing, will be salutary only if it preserves the memory of transcendence. Qoheleth did so, although with brutal honesty, not unlike Czesław Miłosz, who writes,

> "For me, skeptical philosophy.
> That doesn't ascribe to men any higher qualities, Nor to the God man created.
> Then I could be in harmony with my nature.
> Yet I repeat, 'I believe in God,' and I know That my belief has no justification." "To Spite Nature."[57]

Reflecting further on the consequences of atheism, he observes,

> "If there is no God,
> Not everything is permitted to man.
> He is still his brother's keeper
> And he is not permitted to sadden his brother
> By saying that there is no God." "Second Space."[58]

Like Miłosz, many post-Enlightenment philosophers and sociologists have struggled to justify a nod toward theism. With the perceived implausibility of the ontological, cosmological, and teleological arguments for the existence of God, the focus shifted earthward to moral consciousness with Immanuel Kant, to the human mind with Sigmund Freud and Ludwig Feuerbach, to society at large and the prevailing culture with Émile Durkheim, to a collective psyche with Carl Jung, to the longing for transcendence and images driving it in Friedrich Schleiermacher and Martin Heidegger, and to nature, not humans, for Julian Huxley. As these thinkers demonstrate, it is not easy to abandon the concept of transcendence.[59]

Qoheleth, too, experienced an imperiled worldview that forced him to adopt a wary position vis-à-vis sapiential tradition. Caught in an epistemological bind, he explored new ways of interpreting reality. Whether critics choose to speak of a "crisis of wisdom" or a "wisdom of crisis"[60] matters little if they overlook his radical theological revision. Breakthroughs by necessity require breakdowns,[61] enabling the intellect to forge something new from the ashes of the familiar. Such novelty is often disturbing to those whose thoughts focus on the past rather than the open future. Qoheleth's Elohim is hardly the comforting Lord of traditional piety.[62] In this, as in so many things, Qoheleth is thoroughly modern.[63]

Notes

1. See above all C. Uehlinger, "Qohelet im Horizont mesopotamischer, levantinischer und ägyptischer Weisheitsliteratur der persischen und hellenistischen Zeit," 155–247 in *Das Buch Kohelet: Studien zur Struktur, Geschichte, Rezeption und Theologie*, ed. L. Schwienhorst-Schönberger, BZAW 254 (Berlin/ New York: de Gruyter, 1997); R. Bohlen, "Kohelet in Kontext hellenistischer Kultur," 249–73 in *Das Buch Kohelet*; and R. Harrison, "Qoheleth in Socio-Historical Perspective," Ph.D. diss., Duke University, 1991.

2. C. L. Seow, "Linguistic Evidence and the Dating of Qohelet," *JBL* 115 (1996): 643–66. In "The Social World of Qoheleth" (*Scribes, Sages, and Seers: The Sage in the Eastern Mediterranean World* [Göttingen: Vandenhoeck & Ruprecht, 2008] 189–217), he lowers the date to the fourth century. Debate about the place of composition has waned, with scholars tending to accept Jerusalem as the most likely scene of Qoheleth's activity.

3. M. V. Fox, "Qohelet's Epistemology," *HUCA* 58 (1987): 137–55 and "The Inner Structure of Qohelet's Thought," 225–38 in *Qohelet in the Context of Wisdom*, ed. A. Schoors (BETL 136; Leuven: University Press, 1998) considers Qoheleth's view of knowledge unprecedented. The novelty of the water pulley is disputed. Perhaps its use by commoners, implied in 12:6, is new even if the wealthy were familiar with the device as early as the eighth century in the Levant.

4. P. Machinist, "Fate, *miqreh*, and Reason: Some Reflections on Qohelet and Biblical Thought," 159–75 in *Solving Riddles and Untying Knots*, ed. Z. Zevit et al. (Winona Lake IN: Eisenbrauns, 1995). For this type of thinking in classical Greece,

see Y. Elkana, "The Emergence of Second-Order Thinking in Classical Greece," 40–64 in *The Origins and Diversity of Axial Age Civilizations*, ed. S. N. Eisenstadt, SUNY Series in Near Eastern Studies (Albany NY: State University of New York Press, 1986). Qoheleth's refusal to acknowledge newness contrasts with exilic and postexilic prophecy, which anticipates a new heart, spirit, covenant, exodus, even a new creation (heaven and earth).

5. The emphasis of *Qohelet in the Context of Wisdom* was the international environment for the entire sapiential enterprise

6. Most modern interpreters think the inclusion in 1:2 and 12:8 set the intervening material apart from what precedes and follows, although there is some debate about the number of epilogues (one, two, or three). The identical expression for something additional, *weyōtēr*, suggests the division as follows: 12:9-11 and 12:12-14. Alternatively, *sōp dābār* seems to introduce a concluding observation, yielding 12:9-12 and 12:13-14. Some critics therefore view 12:12 as a gloss from a third hand.

7. D. Dimant, "Pesharim, Qumran," *ABD* 5 (1992): 244–50.

8. Captured nicely in the title of a book by A. Schoors, *The Preacher Sought to Find Pleasing Words: A Study of the Language of Qoheleth*, Orientalia Lovaniensia Analecta 41 (Leuven: Peeters, 1992).

9. O. Loretz, "Anfänge jüdischer Philosophie nach Qoheleth 1, 1-11 und 3, 1-15," *Ugarit-Forschungen* 23 (1991): 223–44 and M. Rose, "Qohelet als Philosophe und Theologe. Ein biblisches Votum *für universitas*," 177–99 in M. Kreig & M. Rose, eds., *Universitas in theologia—theologia in universitate. Festschrift für Hans Heinrich Schmid zum 60. Geburtstag* (Zurich: Theologischer Verlag, 1997).

10. Machinist, "Fate, *miqreh*, and Reason." The function of *hešbôn* as an economic term for the bottom line and the uncertain reading of *h'lm* in 3:11 may weaken the case for Qoheleth's innovative epistemology.

11. The many investigations into Qoheleth's use of *hebel* acknowledge its polyvalency (vapor, breath, ephemerality, idol). No single word captures its richness, although futility/absurdity come closest when the emphasis is not on brevity. N. Lohfink, "Koh 1, 2 <<Alles ist windhauch>>—universale oder anthropologische Aussage," 126–28 in *Studien zum Kohelet*, Stuttgarter biblische Aufsatzbande 26 (Stuttgart: Kathologische Bibelwerk, 1998) and T. Krüger, *Qoheleth* (Minneapolis: Fortress Press, 2004) 43, n. 8 link Qoheleth's views with those of Monimus.

12. J. Blenkinsopp, "Ecclesiastes 3:1-15: Another Interpretation," *JSOT* 66 (1995): 55–64.

13. The proverb about a three-ply cord occurs in the Gilgamesh epic ("Two men will not die; the towed boat will not sink. A three-ply cord cannot be cut"). On *kōl*, see my "Qoheleth's Quantitative Language," in Crenshaw, *Prophets, Sages & Poets* (St. Louis: Chalice Press, 2006) 83–94, 224–30.

14. O. Kaiser, "Die Rezeption der Stoischen Providenz bei Ben Sira," *JNSL* 24 (1998): 41–54; S. L. Mattila, "Ben Sira and the Stoics: A Reexamination of the Evidence," *JBL* 119 (2000): 473–501; and U. Wicke-Reuter, *Göttliche Providenz und menschliche Verantwortung bei Ben Sira und in der Frühen Stoa*, BZAW 298 (Berlin/New York: de Gruyter, 2000).

15. J. L. Crenshaw, "Beginnings, Endings, and Life's Necessities in Biblical Wisdom," 95–103, 230–33 in *Prophets, Sages & Poets.*

16. The combination of "exact order" of the four items (feasting, fresh clothes, washing one's head, and lover) plus the inevitability of death is striking indeed.

17. J. L. Crenshaw, "Qoheleth's Understanding of Intellectual Inquiry," 205–24 in *Qohelet in the Context of Wisdom* (=29–41, 207–11 in *Prophets, Sages & Poets*).

18. P. Höffken, "Das EGO des Weisen," *Theologische Zeitschrift* 4 (1984): 121–35 and J. L. Crenshaw, "The Shadow of Death in Qoheleth," 573–85 in *Urgent Advice and Probing Questions* (Macon: Mercer University Press, 1995).

19. S. Burkes, *Death in Qoheleth and Egyptian Biographies of the Late Period,* SBL DS 170 (Atlanta: Society of Biblical Literature, 1999) documents the profound impact of an untimely demise, arguably the most problematic aspect of finitude.

20. J. L. Crenshaw, "The Expression *mî yôdēaʿ* in the Hebrew Bible," *VT* 36 (1986): 274–88 (= *Urgent Advice and Probing Questions*, 279–91).

21. J. L. Crenshaw, "Love Is Stronger than Death: Intimations of Life beyond the Grave," 53–78 in *Resurrection: The Origin and Future of a Biblical Doctrine,* ed. J. H. Charlesworth (New York/London: T & T Clark, 2006).

22. E. Pfeiffer, "Die Gottesfurcht im Buche Kohelet," 133–58 in *Gottes Wort und Gottes Land (Fs. H. W. Hertzberg),* ed H. Reventlow (Göttingen: Vandenhoeck & Ruprecht, 1965).

23. H.-P. Müller, "Wie sprach Qohälät von Gott?," *VT* 18 (1968): 507–21; A. Schoors, "God in Qohelet," 251–70 in *Schöpfungsplan und Heilsgeschichte: Fs. E. Haag.* (Rome: Paulinus, 2002); and L. Gorssen, "Le cohérence de la conception de Dieu dans l'Ecclésiaste," *Ephemerides theologicae lovanienses* 46 (1969): 282–324.

24. J. L. Crenshaw, *Defending God: Biblical Responses to the Problem of Evil* (New York: Oxford University Press, 2005) and A. Schoors, "Theodicy in Qohelet," 375–409 in *Theodicy in the World of the Bible,* A. Laato and J. C. de Moor, eds. (Leiden: Brill, 2003).

25. J. L. Crenshaw, "From the Mundane to the Sublime (Reflections on Qoh 11:1-8)," 61–72, 217–22 in *Prophets, Sages & Poets.*

26. Actually, exclusionary practices enabling people to escape military duty are familiar from Deuteronomy, and wealthy people in Persian and Greco-Roman times paid others to fulfill such obligations.

27. L. Kalugila, *The Wise King,* ConBOT 15 (Lund: Gleerup, 1980).

28. R. Vignolo, "Wisdom, Prayer and Kingly Pattern. Theology, Anthropology, Spirituality of Wis 9," 255–82 in *Deuterocanonical and Cognate Literature. Yearbook 2005: The Book of Wisdom in Modern Research,* A. Passaro and G. Bellia, eds. (Berlin/New York: de Gruyter, 2005).

29. One expects a personal pronoun on *ʾiššâ,* not the relative *ʾašer* followed by a verbal form of *ʾāhab.* Seow's textual basis for translating "your beloved spouse" is hardly persuasive (Gen 30:4, 9; 1 Sam 25:43; Deut 22:22). See Seow, *Ecclesiastes* (New York: Doubleday, 1997) 301. His additional remark that the Akkadian word in the Gilgamesh Epic is *marhitu* "wife" rather than *sinništu* woman," while interesting, carries no weight.

30. Interpreters who characterize Qoheleth's thought as apocalyptic seize upon his insistence that one cannot predict the future and his images in the final poem. At most, the latter indicate inchoate eschatology. In my view, they do not describe cosmic doom, "the end of human existence" (contra Seow, *Ecclesiastes*, 380). Qoheleth never mentions typical features of later apocalyptic (revelation during heavenly journeys, the cosmic conflict between good and evil) nor does he use bizarre images of animals.

31. M. Gilbert, *La critique des dieux dans le livre de la Sagesse*, Analecta Biblica 53 (Rome: Pontifical Biblical Institute Press, 1973).

32. See the essays by E. Greenstein, C. A. Newsom, and E. van Wolde in *Job 28: Cognition in Context*, ed. van Wolde (Leiden/Boston: Brill, 2003) 253–80, 299–305, 1–35 respectively.

33. The legend in the Apocalypse of Baruch that has YHWH's angels remove the sacred vessels from the temple for safekeeping and tear down the wall of Zion before inviting the Babylonian soldiers to enter the city because the Guard has left addresses the concern that a foreign deity could defeat the God of Israel (2 Baruch 6–7).

34. Among the several recent monographs on this remarkable figure, two deserve special attention. They are S. Schroer, *Wisdom Has Built Her House: Studies on the Figure of Sophia in the Bible* (Collegeville: The Liturgical Press, 2000) and A. M. Sinnott, *The Personification of Wisdom*, SOTS MS (Aldershot: Ashgate, 2005).

35. See the collection of essays in J. Blenkinsopp et al., eds., *Families in Ancient Israel* (Louisville: Westminster John Knox, 1997).

36. S. E. Balentine, *The Hidden God: The Hiding of the Face of God in the Old Testament* (Oxford: Oxford University Press, 1983) explores the vocabulary for divine remoteness most helpfully.

37. The problem of ascertaining the divine epithets in Ben Sira is demonstrated by J. Fichtner, *Die altorientalische Weisheit in ihrer israelitisch-jüdischen Ausprägung* (Giessen: Töpelmann, 1933).

38. The debate about the extent of antagonism toward Hellenism or accommodation involves complex decisions about the nature of literature and the ambiguity of historical reconstruction.

39. Evidence from Khirbet 'el Qom and Kuntillet 'ajrud, as well as Elephantine, indicates that a female deity held some attraction for Jewish worshipers, at least in areas remote from central religious authority in Jerusalem.

40. J. L. Crenshaw, "The Eternal Gospel (Ecclesiastes 3:11)," 23–55 in *Essays in Old Testament Ethics*, ed. Crenshaw and J. T. Willis (New York: Ktav, 1974=*Urgent Advice and Probing Questions*, 548–72). The poem in 3:2-8 with its temporal *ʿēt* hardly governs the theme in what follows, for *rā'îtî* signals a new section along the lines of 3:9, where *yitrôn* dominates. While *beʿittô* and *mērōš weʿad-sôp* extend the temporal sense of 3:2-8, the central idea is that of hiddenness.

41. One suspects that theological conservatism explains the reluctance among some translators to acknowledge the *mem* privative in this verse, rendered correctly in KJV and NIV.

42. N. Lohfink, "Qoheleth 5:17-19—Revelation by Joy," *CBQ* 52 (1990): 625–35.

43. B. L. Berger, "Qohelet and the Exigencies of the Absurd," *Bib Inter* 9 (2001): 174.

44. The seminal study by M. Fishbane, *Biblical Interpretation in Ancient Israel* (Oxford: Clarendon Press, 1985) applies to the canon a type of analysis that has been widespread in secular literary criticism. Interpreters of Qoheleth have long recognized affinities with Gen 1–11.

45. Perhaps the first *kōl* is a gloss, and one should translate "Surely every mortal is (but) a breath."

46. Eccl 1:4; 3:20; 5:14-15 [15-16]; 6:6; 9:10; 12:5. The verb *hlk* is often an ellipsis for "going to the ancestral tomb." In 12:5 this destination is identified as an eternal home.

47. A. Schoors, *The Preacher Sought to Find Pleasing Words*, 152; B. Isaksson, *Studies in the Language of Qoheleth with Special Emphasis on the Verbal System*, Acts Universitatis Uppsaliensis 10 (Uppsala: Almqvist & Wiksell International, 1987); and J. L. Crenshaw, "Qoheleth's Quantitative Language," 88–89.

48. The word *'nissāt* in v. 6 may be a musical notation like *selā*; otherwise it states as an established fact that every human is *hebel*. The peculiar *yehemāyûn* in the same verse may be explained by *hehāmôn* in 1 Chr 29:16, which seems to bear the nuance "wealth," specifically the total gift the people brought forth for constructing the Solomonic temple.

The previous verse uses the felicitous expression, "For we are sojourners before you, and residents in a shadow like all our ancestors; we lodge on earth without hope" (1 Chr 29:15).

49. A similar linguistic usage occurs in Ps 82:6 ("I once thought you were deities, all of you children of Elyon").

50. M. V. Fox, "Frame-Narrative and Composition in the Book of Qohelet," *HUCA* 48 (1977): 83–106 inaugurated a novel way of viewing Qoheleth, one that has been strengthened by T. Longman III, *Fictional Akkadian Autobiography: A Generic and Comparative Study* (Winona Lake IN: Eisenbrauns, 1991). In this reading, a narrator introduces a fictional speaker, Qoheleth, and ultimately dismisses his teaching as inadequate.

51. T. Krüger, *Qoheleth* (Minneapolis: Fortress Press, 2004); L. Schwienhorst-Schönberger, *Kohelet* (HThKAT; Freiburg: Herder, 2004); Seow, *Ecclesiastes*, interpret Qoheleth's sayings as ultimately positive, a view that strains against the overwhelming pessimism throughout the book that is accentuated by the inclusion in 1:2 and 12:8.

52. On the belief that human nature is inherently flawed, see J. L. Crenshaw, "Deceitful Minds and Theological Dogma: Jer 17:5-11," 105–21 in *Utopia and Dystopia in Prophetic Literature*, ed. E. Ben Zvi (Helsinki & Göttingen: Finnish Exegetical Society, Vandenhoeck & Ruprecht, 2006) = *Prophets, Sages & Poets*, 73–82, 222–24.

53. E. Dor-Shav, "Ecclesiastes, Fleeting and Timeless," *Azure* 18 (2004): 67–87 captures the vibrancy of Qoheleth's favorite image for what appears as reality.

54. E. Zenger, *A God of Vengeance? Understanding the Psalms of Divine Wrath* (Louisville: Westminster John Knox, 1995) gives a theological defense of this divine attribute, but J. Miles, *God: A Biography* (New York: Vintage Books, 1995) 308–28 shows how unattractive this literary portrait of the biblical deity really is.

55. On this language, see G. Bellia, "Historical and Anthropological Reading of the Book of Wisdom," *The Book of Wisdom in Modern Research*, 83–111 and J. L. Crenshaw, "Introduction: The Shift from Theodicy to Anthropodicy," 1–16 in *Theodicy in the Old Testament* (Philadelphia: Fortress Press; London: SPCK, 1983)=141–54 in *Urgent Advice and Probing Questions*.

56. B. Childs, *Biblical Theology in Crisis* (Philadelphia: Westminster, 1970).

57. C. Miłosz, *Second Space: New Poems* (New York: Harper Collins Publishers, Inc., 2004) 19–20. M. Jarman, *Questions for Ecclesiastes* (Ashland OR: Story Line Press, 1997) draws poetic inspiration from Qoheleth's questions about meaning.

58. Miłosz, *Second Space*, 5.

59. J. Mitchell Corbett, ed., *Through a Glass Darkly: Readings on the Concept of God* (Nashville: Abingdon Press, 1989).

60. M. Rose, "De la <<Crise de la Sagesse>>a la <<Sagesse de la Crise>>" *RThPh* 131 (1999): 115–34.

61. E. Weil, "What Is a Breakthrough in History?" *Daedalus* (Spring 1975): 21–36= *Wisdom, Revelation and Doubt: Perspectives on the First Millennium B.C.* and S. N. Eisenstadt, 1–25, 127–34, and 227–40 in *The Origins and Diversity of Axial Age Civilizations*.

62. Neither is the YHWH depicted in the Bible.

63. J. L. Crenshaw, *Ecclesiastes* (Philadelphia: Westminster, 1987); *Urgent Advice and Probing Questions*, 499–585; and *Prophets, Sages & Poets*, 29–41, 61–72, 83–103, 207–11, 217–22, 224–33.

chapter three

QOHELETH AND SCRIPTURAL AUTHORITY*

For many Christians, the age of scriptural authority is a relic of the past, like dinosaurs, duels, and Desotos. For others, every word of the Bible is divinely inspired, inerrant, and universally binding. Ironically, the opposing camps are united in selectively ignoring parts of sacred writ. No one, to my knowledge, obeys the specific command in Exod 22:29b, attributed to the deity, to sacrifice firstborn sons along with the first animals to leave the womb. Nor do devout Christians greet all the brothers with a holy kiss, even those who obey the ban on women speakers in congregational meetings. In short, the principle of "picking and choosing" the parts of Scripture to obey is alive and well in both the progressive and conservative camps of Christendom.

For modern Jews, who are not burdened with the belief in an inerrant Bible, oral tradition formalized in Talmud and Mishnah stands alongside Scripture and prevents a written text from becoming an idolatrous object. A theory of gradations in scriptural authority, with Torah carrying more weight than the *Prophets and Writings*, further weakens the possibility of making a fetish of the Bible. Nevertheless, Judaism, too, is marked by

* The original appeared in Isaac Kalimi et al., eds., *Scriptural Authority in Early Judaism and Ancient Christianity* (DCLS 16. Berlin/New York: Walter de Gruyter, 2013) 17–41. Reprinted with permission.

competing understandings of the degree to which contemporary conduct should be controlled by written texts.

The other Abrahamic tradition, Islam, also supplements the Bible with its own holy text. Here, too, this version of divine will, the Qur'an, carries greater authority for Muslims than the two testaments that precede it. That is also true of the Church of the Latter Day Saints, whose Book of Mormon is thought to embody divine truths that go beyond those within the Bible itself. Both religions, however, have produced groups with different degrees of adherence to the mandates of Mohammed and Joseph Smith.

A by-product of the selective process within Christianity is the creation of distinctions between priests and laity, with priests bearing the onus of more rigorous adherence to divine commands. In Judaism, a similar distinction occurs, although membership in the priesthood is by birth and not the result of a voluntary choice. Protestantism has resisted such distinctions on the basis of the principle of the priesthood of all believers, while elevating the ministry in ways approximating that of priests in Catholic and Episcopal circles. Authority has its own allure, especially when combined with the expected rewards of being holy.

I. DIMINISHING SCRIPTURAL AUTHORITY

Why has belief in scriptural authority become problematic? For one thing, globalization has exposed the localized nature of sacred texts. As a result, every claim of universality, whether found within a text or put forth by an interpreter of that particular religious tradition, becomes a case of special pleading. No text is self-validating, and claiming to be exclusively true does not make it so, however often the assertion is made.

Each "holy book" becomes the religious repository of a special group. Those who reside outside this community do not find its teachings authoritative, even if they grant the inspirational power of specific insights now and again. Christians may admire the *Bhagavad Gita* or the teachings of Confucius, but this appreciative response does not include obeisance. Similarly, the Buddhist who finds certain features of the Bible to be commendable is still free to reject all its mandates. In a word, only adherents of a special religious tradition are in any way obligated to regulate their lives according to its teachings.

This point can be broadened to include the nonreligious. Vast numbers of people lack a sacred text. Regardless of the political or religious context in which they find themselves, atheists do not consider the Bible authoritative.

To them, all talk about the authority of the Bible is meaningless. The same can be said of modern secularists, some of whom may prefer the agnostic label because of the atheist's necessity to make a leap of faith. Honesty compels agnostics to recognize that disproving a deity's existence is just as impossible as demonstrating that one exists.[1]

These three things—globalization, secularism, and diminishing scriptural authority—weigh heavily on Christians. Changes in the culture have rendered much of the Bible offensive to the intellect. All too frequently, the "narrated story" of God[2] depicts a warrior and like-minded followers. The Bible treats slavery as an acceptable social practice, women as by nature subject to men, and anything other than heterosexuality as an offense to society and to the deity. In some places it sanctions genocide, adopts an ideology of a chosen people, and reports miracles that are scientifically implausible (e.g., the sun standing still or going backwards). It mandates customs with no rational basis such as restrictions in diet, mode of dress, the mixing of different kinds of cloth, and the like. In a word, some sections of the Bible belong in a museum that houses outmoded artifacts.

This same Bible depicts a loving God who is deeply involved in the lives of human beings, an involvement of pathos[3] and extreme suffering because of human sin. This God champions the cause of the defenseless—the widow, the orphan, the poor, the stranger; works with human agents to establish social justice; teaches the principle that we ought to love our neighbors as ourselves; gives meaning to history, instilling the imagination with a vision of peace on earth; transforms all of life into little moments of holiness; eliminates the sharp distinction between thought and deed; provides useful myths of origins and symbols that structure existence, and much more.

The Bible has been influential in shaping Western culture, especially in providing hospitals to care for the sick and schools to train the mind. It has encouraged acts of charity toward the poor and philanthropy in general. Its teachings about a dependable universe have helped to provide a matrix for the rise of science, and its teleology has enriched literature from history to fiction. The Bible has shaped languages like English and German, and its rich spirituality has fed hungry souls for millennia.

In short, the embarrassing and the ennobling fill the pages of the Bible. The former arouses suspicion that the Bible is a huge lie;[4] the latter encourages those who hear a divine voice behind it. The modern controversy over the Bible began long ago. When two prophets, Jeremiah and Hananiah, proclaimed contradictory messages (surrender to the Babylonians; resist them) and each claimed to speak in YHWH's name, who was the true prophet? Not surprisingly, the resulting conflict could not be resolved.[5] Consequently, even today we are left with the naysayers and the defenders.

The extremes to which defenders of scriptural authority will go are richly illustrated in a recent publication of papers that were presented at a philosophical symposium held at the University of Notre Dame with the theme taken from Isa 55:8, "My ways are not your ways." The title of this volume—*DIVINE EVIL?*—is especially provocative.[6] The interrogative reflects the controversy between progressive and conservative authors represented in its pages. Assertions of scriptural authority stand over against rejections, and proponents of these competing views refused to budge an inch. The main arguments of the defenders follow, with my response.[7]

1. Whatever God does is right.

By definition, God is good. It follows from this conviction that God can do no wrong. Human beings are mistaken when they attribute evil to the deity, for they do not understand the divine will sufficiently to make such a judgment. Although many acts of God may give the impression of being immoral and downright cruel, God must have a reason for behaving in this way. The giver of life can take it back, whether by a universal flood, by catastrophic forays against cities like Sodom and Gomorrah, by genocidal action against a single ethnic group like the Amalekites for being inhospitable, by punishing an infant for the sins of a father, the warrior king David, and so on. Such conduct by the deity need not be disturbing to believers,[8] for they can count on the goodness of God to control divine action.

But a God whose power determines what is right is not worthy of worship. As early as Epicurus, the logical dilemma intrinsic to belief in divine goodness and power in the face of the reality of evil was recognized. Since evil is undeniable, one of the other two ideas has to be abandoned or at the very least modified. Either God is not fully good or not almighty. Often it is conceded that God freely chooses to limit divine power, but seldom is belief in divine goodness surrendered by believers. A rabbinic *midrash* makes the point emphatic by having angels advise the Creator that he cannot have both a world and justice.

To state the matter differently, surely God ought to exemplify an ethical standard equal to that of humans. Good people do not subject faithful friends to tests that involve murder, nor do they kill others and cause pain just to win a wager. Decent citizens do not engage in genocide, show irrational favoritism, and inflict suffering on those who do not reciprocate love. When God's actions in the Bible are examined against such an ethical standard, they often fail to measure up to it.

Furthermore, once a gift has been exchanged, it becomes the sole property of the recipient. We do not take back the book we have given to a friend any more than we ask for the return of a perennial we have bestowed on a fellow gardener. If life is a divine gift, it is no longer God's to take back.

2. The human concept of justice does not apply to God.

Divine transcendence means that the deity remains outside every ethical argument about goodness. Only humans are subject to norms of behavior that make society possible. God is not a member of society and does not have to abide by its rules. Abraham was completely mistaken when arguing that God act justly by sparing the condemned cities in which innocents resided.

"Shall not the judge of all the earth do what is right?"[9] rests on the premise that mortals resemble God. The principle of similitude,[10] enunciated in the priestly account of creation and reinforced by the notion of *imitatio dei*, is rendered null and void by an absolute break between creator and creature.

Even the vilest act by human standards, the testing of an obedient servant by ordering him to sacrifice his beloved son[11] or killing another servant's sons and daughters to satisfy a bet with a celestial being,[12] is acceptable because God is exempt from the standards of human decency. God has the right to find out whether Abraham loves him more than anything else and whether Job's goodness is calculated on being rewarded for service.

The numerous attempts to defend divine justice over the millennia are misguided, and theodicy[13] is a fruitless enterprise, despite huge sections of the Bible that bear witness to the human struggle to understand the unthinkable in a universe governed by a good God.

But justice is justice, whether practiced by God or by humans. The peril of adducing two different standards of justice, one for God and another for human beings, was recognized by the author of Genesis 18 and by various other biblical thinkers.[14] That is why they struggled so valiantly to understand God's interaction with them. Like Jeremiah, they endeavored to affirm divine justice as a mystery, but they were not willing to abandon the concept or to create a unique definition of justice for God alone. In short, they did not opt for a teleological suspension of the ethical in order to justify a horrific command like that issued to Abraham in Genesis 22.

3. God uses historical events to teach morality and to foster spiritual growth.

For biblical authors, history was the arena of divine activity, just as it was for the intellectuals in surrounding cultures.[15] The rise and fall of city-states occurred according to a divine plan, with sin determining the extent of decline. History was written and revised with this principle as the guiding light. A failed kingdom was deemed guilty of serious transgression, and a prosperous one was believed to have been obedient to the deity. City-states that worshiped gods other than YHWH did not deserve to survive because of the danger they posed to weaker Israelites. The threat of sin was serious, causing the downfall of both kingdoms, Ephraim and Judah.

This theory of history applied to all nations. God mandated the destruction of cities such as Jericho and larger ethnic groups like the Canaanites. In addition, God controlled the actions of the rulers of powerful kingdoms, even Assyria and Egypt. The world was a huge chessboard, and God moved the pieces around to arrive at the ultimate goal, checkmate. The nature of the game requires that some pieces fall along the way, and the end justifies the means, even if there is no logical rationale for determining winners and losers.

But a pedagogy that involves mass destruction is abominable. Theological instruction that comes at the cost of dividing ethnic groups into hate mongers or that is achieved on false pretenses comes at too great a cost. Stories about the eradication of whole peoples damage those whose memory includes gruesome accounts, whether they are based on actual history or are no more than the fruit of an active imagination. Clearly, the ancient Near Eastern context makes it probable that at least some of the atrocities in the Bible were real. Fabrications certainly occurred, but so did battles that were fought in the name of YHWH. Survival depended on defending life and property, and the lure of power was often irresistible.

4. Some historical events in the Bible are merely symbolic.

Ancient historiographers were more interested in propaganda than in reporting actual facts. They often wrote to promote the causes of their royal sponsors. Accordingly, they composed narratives that reflected favorably on the reigning monarch. In doing so, they used rhetoric that appealed to the emotions. The victory over local powers was merely spiritual, and the transformation of a cultural battle into mortal conflict was motivated by a desire to stress the importance of total allegiance to YHWH.

Modern readers are wrong in thinking that God actually mandated the total destruction of cities or peoples, that celestial beings married women, that an Assyrian army consisting of 185,000 soldiers was slain by the divine breath, that the patriarchs engaged in morally questionable behavior, and so on. Just as the Homeric stories of the gods were really about conflicts other than what seems on the surface to be the case, biblical accounts also point to something on a higher plane than the historical.

But an allegorical interpretation of Scripture does not rule out the literal. Even the church fathers Origen and Tertullian, like their Alexandrian Jewish predecessor Philo who practiced a hermeneutic involving allegory, recognized that texts are first and foremost historical.[16] That is, literature derives from a specific context, and the primary task of an interpreter is to understand that setting and its implications for reading. The subjectivity of the allegorical method leaves its practitioners free to impose their own will on a text, for they do not acknowledge even the semblance of objective control. The text means what they want it to mean, and that leaves room for *eisegesis* of all sorts.

5. Both the canonical context and its larger ancient Near Eastern counterpart correct questionable features of the Bible.
The composition of the Bible took place over centuries; during this time, many ideas changed for the better. In the process, some disturbing aspects of conduct were discarded. By this process, the Bible continually pointed to nobler instincts, at the same time interjecting a teleological hope that leads beyond the Hebrew Bible.

The distinctive nature of the Israelite people even bathed borrowed ideas in a radical negativity, changing them completely to fit into the worldview of those who worshiped YHWH. Mythic themes dealing with the flood and proverbial teachings take on a unique character once they are combined with concepts peculiar to YHWH's followers.

But uplifting features of the Bible, no matter how sublime, do not atone for its many troubling aspects. As a matter of fact, sometimes the sublime and the obscene lie side by side. The best example of this phenomenon can be found in Job's Oath of Innocence in chapter 31 of the book bearing his name. Although it soars to the heavens in one moment, it descends to the lowest depths with its reprehensible view of women, acceptance of slavery, and condescending attitude toward the poor.[17]

Furthermore, the emphasis on progress through the centuries leads naturally to a view of Christianity as superior to Judaism from which it sprang and drives a wedge between sister faiths, making a mockery of the bond that the Apostle Paul considered the divine purpose behind the two. In addition, it overlooks the disturbing views that persist to the end of the Bible. Progress, that is, occurs but not in all things.

6. Metaphorical language and stylistic features in the Bible have been confused with literal discourse.

An analogy with language involving modern athletes illustrates this point. Players frequently exaggerate the scope of their victory by saying something like "We slaughtered the opponents." Those who are familiar with the boasts of exuberant athletes easily recognize similar claims of victory in the field of battle. The story about Joshua conquering the people of Jericho and many other accounts of military exploits resulting in the death of whole populations are really boastful exaggeration. When stylistic phrases such as "Israel (or its agents) put everyone to the sword" appear several times, readers can conclude that the authors are using familiar stereotypical expressions to universalize a favorite view of the conquest. The language refers to cultural wars, not to success on the field of battle.

But even if the language of genocide were symbolic, which is doubtful, the effect of such metaphorical trumpeting of victory is harmful to the psyche. Children who are taught national history in which savagery is normal will be tempted to behave in a similar manner, especially if the historical record has nothing to indicate that the language is symbolic. The nonexistence of Jericho in the thirteenth century does not erase the fact that canonical authors had no compunctions about attributing mass destruction to Joshua and his god. No linguistic slight of hand can divest *herem* of its sinister nature, and the eradication of a people's system of values is reprehensible aside from their disappearance at the hands of YHWH.

7. Stories of atrocities in battle are retrojections from a later time that illustrate a spiritual truth.

The biblical record is governed by theological interests rather than historical facts. When much of the history was finally committed to writing, centuries had passed and the authors of stories dealing with national origins were far removed from the event themselves. By necessity, the history was fabricated out of the active imagination of writers. The highlighted experiences were only ones that contributed to the religious insights the authors hoped to convey to a receptive audience. The conquest of Canaan and the many atrocities associated with the early judges never took place. The spiritual conflict between the Israelites and neighbors did not leave a trail of mangled bodies.

The desire to put the best face on one's history is widespread, as citizens of the United States can easily appreciate. The popularity of a purist version of this nation's founding and even of the conflict between the North and the South shows how people tend to glorify their past. Ancient Israel was no different. Its historians wrote a story that justified the existence of a people fiercely eager to preserve its distinctiveness. Ideology prevailed, as usual, and the record of atrocities must be read through a lens that filters out the gory details.

But imposing one's own ideology on the recording of events from the past makes a mockery of history. The authors of the biblical stories present the narrative as factual. They may be writing imaginary stories but they do not offer a clue as to their rhetorical strategy. Throughout the entire process, they give the impression of transmitting facts. Worse still, they interject theories that have lasting repercussions, specifically the idea that Israel is a chosen nation and that the land has been set aside for them for posterity.

8. In reading the Bible, the rule of faith is primary.

No one comes to a text without bringing a counter text to bear on it. The principle of interpretation and the linguistic system in which one has been educated determine the interpretation of a given text, as any history of hermeneutics amply documents. The approaches are endless (*midrash*, patristic and medieval exegesis, historical criticism, romantic criticism, feminist criticism, Afro-American readings, structuralism, postmodernism, cognitive criticism, queer criticism, and so on). Because complete objectivity is impossible and the mind is not blank, readers impose their own world on texts. Therefore the crucial task facing readers is to choose the most appropriate lens through which to view a written document. Readers have inherited a long tradition of interpretation; they can select a hermeneutic of suspicion or one of charity. Those who think the latter approach is the right one find guidance in the past. Fortunately, both Christians and Jews possess a rich interpretive tradition. For Christians, the rule of faith (doctrines codified in creeds over the centuries) illumines texts, and the Holy Spirit protects against heresy. The rule of faith is both Christocentric and Trinitarian.

But the rule of faith fails to do justice to a sacred text that belongs to two religions. The application of a Christian principle to the Hebrew Bible yields a meaning that has nothing to do with its original sense and widens the gulf between Judaism and Christianity. Historical criticism is forced to take a back seat to patristic ways of interpreting Scripture, and doctrinal issues shape the questions brought to the text and the answers derived from it. After all, one person's heretic is another person's saint.

9. Christology ought to shape all reading of the Bible.

Just as Philip in Acts 8 explained the story of the suffering servant in Deutero-Isaiah as a proclamation about Jesus, readers look for typologies in the Hebrew Bible that are fully disclosed in the Galilean Bible. Because Jesus is believed to be God's son and the Holy Spirit is God's presence after the son's departure to heaven, all talk about deity must take into account Jesus of Nazareth. The son was present at the moment of creation, as implied by the plural in God's initial words, "Let us make humankind in our own image," and he was present when God visited Abraham and Sarah to inform them that they would become the parents of a son in their old age. Similarly, the Holy Spirit guided the Israelites out of Egyptian bondage, communicated the divine will to prophets, and manifested itself to sages as personified Wisdom.

But the earliest Christians did not agree about the Trinity, a doctrine formally introduced into a creed of the church after much controversy. To use this late doctrine when interpreting the Hebrew Bible is to impose a theological dogma from very different times on literature that arose long before such a belief was introduced. The plural in Gen 1:26 derives from the celestial court; the visitors in Gen 18:2 are called men; and the spirit in the Hebrew Bible does not reflect Trinitarian language.

10. God acts like a surgeon in removing a threat to the divine will.

It is generally agreed that surgeons operate to remove cancerous growth or diseased organs. While the operation may cause pain, the ultimate goal is to heal patients. By analogy, the great Physician surgically removes sin from society in its various guises—idolatry, pride, rebellion, venality, and the like.

But surgeons remove diseased organs; they do not intentionally kill patients. Even if Exod 15:26 calls YHWH a healer, the analogy above is flawed, for it seeks to explain how God can take human lives, which is altogether different from healing the sick. In addition, this argument depends on the identification of whole peoples as cancerous primarily because they pay allegiance to gods other than YHWH. Groups do not fall into categories like sinful and innocent, for they consist of individuals, each with a distinctive character.

11. The existence of heaven makes everything relative.

Originating in martyrdom and in an intense sense of divine presence,[18] belief in a future life with God in some heavenly abode acts as a powerful incentive to ethical conduct. It also has a negative side, legitimating poverty and social injustice by promising a better existence in the next life. Even an early departure can become less burdensome when it is explained as God's way of preventing later disobedience, or so it seemed to the unknown author of Wisdom of Solomon.

But no one really knows what happens after death; heaven therefore falls into the category of hope, one sustained by faith. The controversial idea was rejected by the authors of the books of Job, Ecclesiastes, and Sirach. And it is difficult to see how the prospect of heaven can make up for the injustices that occur on earth. Ethicists know that virtue is its own reward, and anyone who does good simply to attain heaven or to escape hell is not truly virtuous.

12. God can kill without inflicting pain.

Because nothing is impossible to deity, God can make death completely devoid of suffering. Divine anesthesia removes one of the objections to the idea that the deity takes human lives either to promote the divine plan or as punishment for sin. Plague, sickness, warfare, natural disasters, or any other cause of death do not impugn the goodness of God.

But murder is murder whether administered with or without causing suffering. The notion of divine anesthesia merely dances around the real problem. It does not remove the fact that God is still responsible for killing human beings. No matter how peaceful the final moments of the dead, the agent of their demise is still culpable.

In summary, the Bible depicts a deity who often does disturbing things, and no amount of rationalizing erases the scandal created by such action. Modern attempts to defend God's justice are no improvements on the ancient ones that I have discussed at some length elsewhere. They are (1) the atheistic response; (2) alternative gods; (3) the demonic; (4) limited power and knowledge; (5) split personality; (6) divine discipline; (7) punishment for sin; (8) suffering as atonement; (9) deferring justice until the next life; (10) mystery; and (11) questioning the problem.[19]

II. THE INTRINSIC NATURE OF LITERATURE

Those of us who are surrounded by the written word can scarcely imagine the radical change brought about by the discovery of writing. One important transition was recognized in the remark by Thamous, the patron of literature, to the putative inventor, Thoth, that writing will lead to an eventual decline in the power of memory. With a few exceptions such as blind bards, religious preservers of sacred texts, and "idiot savants," Plato's description of the transition between an oral and a written culture is accurate.

Loss of memory is not the only result of this important shift in communication, as Plato perceived. As long as the messenger was present to deliver a word to an intended audience, anyone who had trouble grasping any part of the speech could ask for clarification. That access is missing when a text is substituted for a speaker. Texts are mute, and the burden of interpretation shifts to readers.

While the burden of successful communication stays the same regardless of the mode of delivery, the clues change greatly. Gestures and tonal quality belong to oral delivery, and these aids to hearers range from the straightforward to the subtle. Written texts have their own intrinsic clues to meaning, and these, too, vary with each composition.

The secret of good reading is to uncover the signifiers left by the author. Only after that task has been carried out in minute detail can readers go on to extrapolate meanings never considered by the author, insights that have arisen because of changed circumstances and that accommodate an old message to the very different worldview of a current reader.

I have described close reading as the demand imposed on readers by a text. In short, one examines each word in the same way he or she studies the body of a lover, slowly and admiringly, always searching for that which brings pleasure and creates awe. At the same time, flaws are not overlooked but are recognized as a necessary condition of being finite. Furthermore, lovers make the best critics, for they force us to acknowledge our own shortcomings.

Like lovers, every written text is unique. Each author has a distinctive style, vocabulary, and message. Only by discovering these three can readers hope to grasp what is actually said. That is why knowledge of the language in which a text appears is required for accurate reading. That is also why familiarity with the rhetorical patterns in the time of the author is essential. It also means that interpretation of the Bible is an esoteric discipline, however much one recoils from drawing this conclusion.[20]

When we turn from texts in general to the Bible, as I have just done, the issue of authority complicates things. In my own experience, I have observed that religious zealots have used the authority of the Bible to advance their conservative social agenda. In doing so, they have seldom shown love for Christian brothers and sisters who disagreed with them. As I survey the global scene, it seems undeniable that other sacred texts generate similar rancor among those who profess allegiance to them. As a rule, belief in the authority of sacred texts has tended to divide people rather than bringing them together.

The conclusion that I draw from this situation is that the idea of the authority of sacred texts is often a convenient tool for those who are interested in power above everything else. Unscrupulous manipulators of the weak have rightly seen that the text has no intrinsic authority, that in reality people exercise the only existing authority. The philosopher Ernest Sabatier understood this fact when observing that individuals who choose to ignore the mandate of Scripture insert themselves into the position of authority. Everyone does just that. It follows logically that human beings are the final authority, and the Bible plays a subsidiary role.

Because the Bible was written in an age vastly different from the modern one, many of its ideas do not pass the test of reason. A pre-scientific worldview, a pre-Copernican universe, and theo-centrism stand over against the secular society that has shaped our sensibilities. At what point does scriptural authority begin to erode? When the sun stands still, seas divide themselves for the benefit of a wandering band of former slaves, a corpse raises another to life, an army of 185,000 soldiers is stricken and Zion spared? Or does the erosion begin the moment foreign texts such as the *Instruction of Amenemope* are incorporated into the Bible? Alternatively, does its sway over readers dwindle when a psalmist prays for the murder of the children of an enemy; when YHWH behaves worse than either you or I would ever do; when slavery, genocide, and anti-feminism surface; when God threatens destruction of the whole human race except for 144,000 men who have not lain with women; and when a basic story line contributes to anti-Semitism?

This indication of only a few objectionable features in the Bible reveals why a shift from text to reader is mandatory, despite the dangers inherent to this move. Choosing a canon within the canon occurred in the earliest days of Christendom when Jesus was asked to name the greatest commandment of all. That process of selectivity continued with Marcion and to a lesser degree survives even today. For some Christians, the choice involves something as extensive as the deuterocanonical literature in the Septuagint, while for others it comes down to individual observations about divorce, sex, military combat, and any number of commands and directives that no longer seem obligatory.

The facts demand a minimal view of scriptural authority. Because the Bible was written by humans rather than by God, it is flawed just like its authors. It is essentially their own perception of reality, one that is in many ways alien to contemporary readers. Nevertheless, it has nurtured Jews and Christians for a very long time, perhaps because of its humanity, not in spite of it. Skeptical philosophy on the edges of faith seems just about right,[21] and that is the position put forth by Qoheleth.

III. QOHELETH

What position is that? In the first place, Qoheleth speaks in his own voice, not that of God. In this regard, he stands alongside the other authors of the wisdom corpus, all of whom present their ideas as their very own.[22] Experience, not divine revelation, lies behind the observations by the various composers of the books of Proverbs, Job, Ecclesiastes, Sirach, and Wisdom of Solomon. In these books, revelation plays a minimal role, seldom occurring (e.g., in a report of a dream in Job 4:12-17; in the personification of wisdom, especially in Prov 8:22-31 and Sir 24; and in speeches attributed to YHWH in Job 38:1–40:2; 40:6–41:26).[23] Some other canonical books, especially Psalms and Song of Songs, also speak from a human perspective, in these instances either to bring human misery before the deity, along with praise,[24] or to celebrate the strong passions that accompany love between the sexes.[25] These works, however, are sufficiently different from the sapiential corpus to discourage scholars from including them in wisdom literature.

The uniqueness of the wisdom books has led to extreme views that label them an alien body and pagan[26] on the one hand and thoroughly *YHWHistic* on the other hand.[27] A more moderate view in which difference is recognized but not judged to be deficient has held sway. The emphases in other canonical works are not a valid measure to apply to wisdom literature, for it has long been known that central features of Israel's past are missing from it until the early second century: the names of the patriarchs, Mosaic and Davidic traditions, the centrality of Jerusalem and its cult,[28] and narratives in the service of the Israelites. The early sages were interested in discovering how to cope with problems that arose in daily experience. Only with Ben Sira[29] and the unknown author of Wisdom of Solomon[30] did sages incorporate Israel's sacred traditions into their teachings, perhaps as a matter of national pride in the face of an aggrandizing Hellenism.[31]

More than any other sage, Qoheleth calls attention to his own ego as the source of his teachings.[32] He goes out of his way to stress the investigative mode of discovery that lay behind everything he said. He says that he determined to explore wisdom and folly, even going so far as to examine madness too. This language is so pervasive in his observations that it has led Michael Fox to label Qoheleth the first empirical thinker in the Bible.[33]

Perhaps that judgment would be altered if the authors of Prov 7:6-27 and 24:30-34 had left more of their teachings to posterity.[34] In both instances, sages derive their insights from careful examination of behavior, which then leads to useful analogies. Experience taught them that sexual sleuths pose a threat to innocent youth and that laziness leads to want. In the absence of such additional data from these two authors, scholars are left to ponder Qoheleth's empiricism.

In doing so, they would do well to consider the numerous places in Qoheleth's teachings where an empirical approach would necessarily have left him speechless. It would never have taught him for example, that God made everything beautiful or appropriate in its time, and put something in the human mind but made it inaccessible to the recipient of this peculiar gift (3:10-11). Nor would an exclusively empirical approach have enabled Qoheleth to conclude that God mysteriously bestows life breath on a fetus (11:5). The same judgment applies to the several observations about angering the deity, indeed to everything involving transcendence.[35] Divine activity, that is, lies outside the scope of empirical investigation. Anything that Qoheleth says about God is a conclusion based on unprovable assumptions. Even his many references to divine gifts show to what extent Qoheleth combines "cultural givens" with his empirical approach to knowledge.

In short, Qoheleth observes, examines, reflects on, ponders, and explores reality as it presents itself to him, but he brings a host of assumptions to bear on what he sees. These preconceived notions about the deity are the depository of human voices over the centuries, but they cannot be subjected to the test of logical verification. In his teachings, readers come face to face with a religious quest like their very own if they take religion seriously. The operative word is quest, not divine disclosure.

The second point to be made about scriptural authority and Qoheleth is that despite his emphasis on observation, he is open to life's deep mysteries. Not only is the miracle of birth seen as the realm of divine activity,[36] but death is also plumbed for its relationship to the deity.[37] In a word, the life breath returns to its source. Life between these two episodic events is bathed in light that is sweet to look upon but laden with irksome toil (*ʿāmāl*). Nevertheless, adoration alone does not suffice, for in Qoheleth's mind God also demands awe and even fear.

Sometimes Qoheleth chooses language that reinforces a sense of mystery. That is particularly true of the unusual *bôreʾeykā* in 12:1, which has been taken to mean creator, grave, and well. Interpreters who think creator makes no sense in context understand the word to be a double reference symbolizing death and one's wife. The latter connection is based on the description in Prov 5:18 of a wife as the cistern from which a husband drinks.[38]

At other times, Qoheleth seems to bend over backwards to be ambiguous, as in 5:19 where the participle *maʿaneh* occurs with Elohim as subject.[39] Precisely what does God do with the joy of the mind? Answer? Afflict? Keep one busy? Because experience itself is capable of several interpretations, Qoheleth's language reflects actual reality. His choice of a verbal root with at least three different meanings seems to suggest indecisiveness inherent to reality.

His reading of daily events is profound, openly acknowledging the ambiguities of existence.[40] When the facts do not support a positive view of things, Qoheleth does not hide his face in the sand and pretend that things are rosy. The randomness of so much that we encounter forces him to question the reason for all human endeavor. With that simple step, the whole system of reward and retribution collapses, and with it the controlling principle that shapes the biblical record.

Third, Qoheleth's pedagogy is dialogic. He realizes that every important truth is complex, so much so that its opposite also holds some truth. Accordingly, he frequently contradicts himself, partly because his own thought has changed over the years and partly because he recognizes his own limitations as an observer of reality. Qoheleth would have agreed with the author of the Babylonian "Dialogue between a Master and a Slave," who saw positives and negatives for most choices available to humans, e.g., dining, marrying, hunting, going for a ride in the country, making war, agreeing to lend money or goods, giving one's possessions away, and committing suicide.[41]

That is why a rhetoric of erasure functions nicely for Qoheleth's thought.[42] One insight cancels another, erasing the original and substituting its opposite, at least for the moment. In his world, a "yes" is naturally followed by a "but."[43]

Fourth, under the sun, that is, on earth, all things are relative. Absolutes, if they exist at all, belong to another world. Wisdom is good, but only up to a point. The effort to arrive at knowledge brings considerable pain, and riches do not always follow success in acquiring wisdom. Poor but wise men actually exist, even if often ignored and unappreciated.[44] The profit motive is not reinforced by the actual results of any given effort, for chance inevitably enters the equation.

From these observations, it follows that Qoheleth acts as an iconoclast. He takes existing views and transforms them, in the process introducing chaos. The sequence is one of orientation, disorientation, and reorientation.[45] For those whose comfort zone requires the status quo, Qoheleth poses a huge risk. In his mind, nothing is sacrosanct, and everything is subject to questioning. Popular wisdom, the accumulation of the insights of astute observers from the past, does not escape Qoheleth's scrutiny, even when seemingly borne out in daily experience. That is how he can question the prevailing prejudice about women being morally corrupt (7:23-29).[46]

Fifth, more than any other biblical author, Qoheleth attends to time's passage. From birth to death we stand under this powerful force, but we can never bend time to make it serve us. Our moments are determined and we act like puppets in a powerful drama until death stills our voice and immobilizes us. Ironically, nature outlasts humans who have populated the earth.[47]

For Qoheleth, even in death we are not unique; animals join us in that experience. Our equality with beasts serves two purposes: to instill fear and to promote reflection. The result of his own thought processes is to underline human ignorance about our ultimate destiny, a shrugging of the shoulders and whispered question, "*mî yōdēaʿ*" (Who knows?). In the face of rising speculation about a future life beyond death, Qoheleth soberly reminds us that nobody really knows what takes place after death, if anything other than decomposition.

Time does more than seal human destiny. It makes possible the multiple opportunities to love and hate, laugh and cry, speak and be silent, plant and uproot, sew and rip apart, and much more. And although we may not be able to read the time chart so as to profit from it in the way earlier sages thought they could, we are not paralyzed by ignorance. Instead, we risk loss and defeat, knowing that life always proceeds according to time's agenda.

Sixth, Qoheleth understood the essential nature of human existence, which he called *hebel*.[48] By this word he means something approximating mist, vapor, the transitory or ephemeral, foulness, futility, and absurdity. Nothing fell outside this domain, in his view, unless it existed beyond the sun.[49] Under the sun, existence consisted of something akin to a breath, vital yet elusive like the wind. Life evokes the images of human beings either feeding on or chasing after the wind.[50]

Precisely because he viewed everything in a negative light and came to hate life, Qoheleth sought to redeem things by seizing the moment insofar as possible.[51] Hence he advises the young to savor existence while possible. The bloom of youth fades quickly, and a dark future awaits, one made no less oppressive by exquisite metaphors describing the end. These images of a shattered lamp and a broken cord magnify the truth that everything is *hebel*.

Seventh, Qoheleth looked death in the face and did not flinch. Still, he was not able to persuade the messenger to play a game of chess to forestall the inevitable.[52] He would probably have agreed with an Egyptian sage who suggests that death's real name is "Come."[53] The appointment with death may not read Samarra, as in John O'Hara's first novel, *Appointment in Samarra*,[54] but it has been inscribed in stone. Time flows into a gaping abyss in which everyone sooner or later comes to rest.

This realization may explain why death hovers over everything Qoheleth says. That single reality lends urgency to what he sought to convey to the people (*hā'ām*).[55] All instruction (1) originates in the human mind; (2) is open to transcendence but not privy to its secrets; (3) takes the form of a dialogue with opposing understandings; (4) scorns absolutes; (5) recognizes the dominance of time's passage; (6) identifies everything as *hebel*; and (7) stares death in the face even while submitting to its power.

To recapitulate, scriptural authority has diminished in modern society for understandable reasons. Even in biblical times a few authors do not make a pretense of deriving their insights from a divine source, and of these Qoheleth strikes nearly all readers as an intruder in a sacred canon. His teachings underscore the human element in Scripture. For some readers, that is a problem, as it seems to have been for his first readers (12:9-14).[56] For others, it is a testament to the integrity of a courageous and original thinker. It may be that logical persuasion is the finest authority available to mortals. Authority based on anything else is surely *hebel*, transient, and at times even foul.[57]

Notes

1. Arguments for the existence of God (e.g., the cosmological, ontological, teleological, proofs from design, morality, and consciousness) succeed, if at all, only in bringing comfort to theists.

2. Many readers of the Bible naively take the depiction of deity in its pages to be an accurate account of divine character and conduct. They would be better served to view the narrated story as a product of an active human imagination. The result would relieve them of trying to defend God's actions and force them to come to the defense of humans. Theodicy would give way to anthropodicy.

3. The name associated with the notion of divine pathos is Abraham Joshua Heschel, who turned the Aristotelian concept of the unmoved mover upside down. According to Heschel, YHWH was the most moved mover, and the prophets stood apart from others in society precisely because they participated in divine pathos. The similarity between Heschel's view of divine pathos and the Christian understanding of Jesus' death on the cross is obvious.

4. Bart Ehrman, *Forged: Writing in the Name of God—Why the Bible's Authors Are Not Who We Think They Are* (San Francisco: HarperOne, 2011).

5. The struggle to distinguish authentic prophets from inauthentic ones led to the compilation of criteria by which to test those claiming to speak on YHWH's behalf. I have examined those tests of true prophecy and found them wanting. See my *Prophetic Conflict: Its Effect upon Israelite Religion* (BZAW 124; Berlin: Walter de Gruyter, 1971; SBL, 2007).

6. Edited by Michael Bergmann, Michael J. Murray, and Michael C. Rea (Oxford and New York: Oxford University Press, 2011). The subtitle of this volume, *The Moral Character of the God of Abraham*, lacks a question mark.

7. The twelve arguments come from the defenders of the moral character of YHWH. In the elaboration, I have tried to strengthen some arguments by adding things the speakers could have said.

8. For a pastoral perspective on difficult biblical texts about YHWH, see Eric A. Seibert, *Disturbing Divine Behavior: Troubling Old Testament Images of God* (Minneapolis: Fortress Press, 2009). Neither of Seibert's solutions solves the problem, for who is equipped to say when the depiction of YHWH strays from the actual character of deity, and how can a Christocentric reading of the Hebrew Bible do anything but distort its original intent?

9. This text provided the title for a Festschrift in my honor edited by David Penchansky and Paul Redditt (Winona Lake IN: Eisenbrauns, 2000). Its contributors reveal the extent to which biblical texts trouble interpreters.

10. Karel van der Toorn, "Sources in Heaven: Revelation as a Scholarly Construct in Second Temple Judaism," in *Kein Land für sich allein: Studien zum Kulturkontakt in Kanaan, Israel/Palästina und Ebirnâri für Manfred Weippert zum 65 Geburtstag*, ed. Ulrich Hübner and Ernst Axel Knauf (Freiburg: Universitätsverlag Freiburg & Göttingen: Vandenhoeck & Ruprecht, 2002) 265–77, thinks the collapse of a worldview based on the principle that the gods resembled humans led to the idea of revelation and elitism. See also his "Why Wisdom Became a Secret: On Wisdom as a Written Genre," 21–29 in *Wisdom Literature in Mesopotamia and Israel*, ed.

Richard J. Clifford (Atlanta: Society of Biblical Literature, 2007). For a discussion of the concept of similitude in wisdom literature, see James L. Crenshaw, "Sipping from the Cup of Wisdom," 41–62 in *Jesus and Philosophy: New Essays*, ed. Paul K. Moser (Cambridge: Cambridge University Press, 2009).

11. For analysis of Genesis 22, see James L. Crenshaw, *Defending God: Biblical Responses to the Problem of Evil* (Oxford & New York: Oxford University Press, 2005) 57–65, 213–16. The story about Abraham sacrificing Isaac continues to fascinate interpreters; see the extensive bibliography on page 214, note 9, to which may be added Isaac Kalimi, "'God, I Beg You, Take Your Beloved Son and Slay Him': The Binding of Isaac in Rabbinic Literature and Thought," *Review of Rabbinic Judaism* 13 (2010): 1–29.

12. Equally intriguing is the story about Job and the dialogue that is associated with it. For my latest perspective on this book and its influence through the centuries to the present, see James L. Crenshaw, *Reading Job: A Literary and Theological Commentary* (Macon GA: Smyth & Helwys, 2011).

13. Theodicy as a problem was not limited to the biblical world. For discussion of the broader context, see Antti Laato and Johannes C. de Moor, eds., *Theodicy in the World of the Bible* (Leiden & Boston: Brill, 2003). Biblical exclusivism, however, heightened the problem where YHWH was concerned. See James L. Crenshaw, "Theodicy," 551–55 in *NIDB*, vol. 5 (Nashville: Abingdon Press, 2009) and "Theodicy in the Book of the Twelve," 175–91 in Paul L. Redditt and Aaron Schart, eds., *Thematic Threads in the Book of the Twelve*, BZAW 325 (Berlin & New York: Walter de Gruyter, 2003); repr., Crenshaw, *Prophets, Sages & Poets* (St. Louis MO: Chalice Press, 2006) 173–82, 253–57. For a look at prophetic literature generally and the problem of theodicy see Crenshaw, "Theodicy and Prophetic Literature," 236–55 in *Theodicy in the World of the Bible*, also in *Prophets, Sages & Poets*, 183–94, 257–61.

14. See James L. Crenshaw, "The Sojourner Has Come to Play the Judge: Theodicy on Trial," 83–92 in *God in the Fray: A Tribute to Walter Brueggemann*, ed. Tod Linafelt and Timothy K. Beal (Minneapolis: Fortress Press, 1998), repr., *Prophets, Sages & Poets*, 195–200, 261–64.

15. The earlier view that the biblical concept of YHWH's role in guiding history toward a favorable outcome for Israel was unique, placing Israel over against its environment, has given way to a new reading of the situation that emphasizes semblance. The groundbreaking monograph was Bertil Albrektson's *History and the Gods*, Con BOT 1 (Lund: Gleerup, 1967). Its impact is chronicled in Robert Gnuse, *Heilsgeschichte as a Model for Biblical Theology*, College Theology Society Studies in Religion 4 (Lanham, New York & London: University Press of America, 1989).

16. Church fathers like Origen and Augustine depended on allegory to explain troublesome aspects of biblical literature, but they regarded the literal sense (historical) as primary and the figurative as secondary. The allegorical and tropological meanings served more like window dressing.

17. Crenshaw, "A Good Man's Code of Ethics (Job 31)," 42–45 in *Prophets, Sages & Poets* and *Reading Job*, 131–33; Samuel E. Balentine, *Job* (Macon GA: Smyth & Helwys, 2006) 471–510; Edwin M. Good, *In Turns of Tempest: A Reading of Job with a Translation* (Stanford CA: Stanford University Press, 1990) 309–18; Carol

A. Newsom, "The Book of Job," 548–57 in *NIB*, vol. 4 (Nashville: Abingdon Press, 1996); and J. Gerald Janzen, *Job* (Atlanta: John Knox Press, 1985) 210–16.

18. I advance this thesis in "Love is Stronger than Death: Intimations of Life beyond the Grave," 53–78 in James H. Charlesworth, ed., *Resurrection: The Origin and Future of a Biblical Doctrine*, Faith and Scholarship Colloquies Series (New York & London: T & T Clark, 2006). See also Pius James D'Sousa DCD, *Stronger than Death: Intimations of Afterlife in the Book of Psalms* (Bangalore, India: Dhyanavana Publications, 2010).

19. Crenshaw, *Defending God*.

20. This statement is not to be construed as ruling out the study of Scripture by nonspecialists. In my experience, they often bring new insights into the practical application of the Bible to life. Two distinct types of study are involved. One has as its goal the accurate interpretation of the author's words in their historical setting; the other aims at deriving spiritual sustenance from what has become normative for believers.

21. The language is derived from the Nobel Prize winner Czeslaw Miłosz, who writes, "In any case, I discovered that what fits me is a skeptical philosophy. That doesn't ascribe to man any higher qualities, nor to the God man created" (*Second Space: New Poems* [New York: Harper Collins, 2004] 20).

22. James L. Crenshaw, *Old Testament Wisdom: An Introduction*, 3rd ed. (Louisville: John Knox Press, 2010); John J. Collins, *Jewish Wisdom in the Hellenistic Age* (Louisville: Westminster John Knox Press, 1997); and Leo G. Perdue, *Wisdom Literature: A Theological History* (Louisville and London: Westminster John Knox, 2007); Perdue, *The Sword and the Stylus: An Introduction to Wisdom in the Age of the Empires* (Grand Rapids MI: Eerdmans, 2008), and Perdue, ed., *Scribes, Sages, and Seers. The Sage in the Eastern Mediterranean World*, FzRLANT 219 (Göttingen: Vandenhoeck & Ruprecht, 2008). Perdue ranges more widely than either myself or Collins in that he includes scribes and seers in his study of wisdom literature.

23. In an article titled "Is the 'Wisdom Tradition' a Tradition?" *CBQ* 73 (2011): 50–71, Mark Sneed faults me for neglecting the place of revelation in biblical wisdom. Had he bothered to read the third edition of my *Old Testament Wisdom*, he would have seen the error in that assessment. Regrettably, his criticism of my views rests on the first edition from 1981 and on articles from 1969 and 1976.

24. The three-volume commentary by Amos Hakham, *The Bible Psalms with the Jerusalem Commentary* (Jerusalem: Mosad Harav Kook, 2003) reveals the rich treasures within rabbinic interpretation, while Robert Alter, *The Book of Psalms* (New York/London: W. W. Norton & Company, 2007) brings his expertise in literary criticism to bear on the biblical text. Susan Gillingham, *Psalms Through the Centuries*, vol. 1 (Oxford: Blackwell Publishing, 2008) examines the reception history of Psalms, and Laurance Wieder, *Words to God's Music. A New Book of Psalms* (Grand Rapids MI: William B. Eerdmans, 2003) lends a poet's voice to transform ancient views into modern concerns.

25. Michael V. Fox, *The Song of Songs and the Ancient Egyptian Love Songs* (Madison WI: University of Wisconsin Press, 1985) brings out the universal aspects of love songs; Ann W. Astell, *The Song of Songs in the Middle Ages* (Ithaca and London: Cornell University Press, 1990) reveals their abiding presence, and Ariel

and Chana Bloch, *The Song of Songs* (Berkeley: University of California Press, 1995) provide a fresh translation and commentary for these expressions of desire.

26. Horst-Deitrich Preuss, *Einführung in die alttestamentliche Weisheitsliteratur*, UT 383 (Stuttgart: Kohlhammer, 1987). His view is vigorously opposed by Franz-Josef Steiert, *Die Weisheit Israels—ein Fremdkörper im Alten Testament?* FThSt 143 (Freiburg: Herder, 1990).

27. Gerhard von Rad, *Wisdom in Israel* (Nashville: Abingdon, 1972) best represents the continuity between sacred narrative and poetry in the rest of the canon and wisdom literature. Of the many advocates of this perspective, Katherine Dell, *"Get Wisdom, Get Insight": An Introduction to Israel's Wisdom Literature* (Macon GA: Smyth & Helwys, 2000) and *The Book of Proverbs in Social and Theological Context* (Cambridge: Cambridge University Press, 2006) gives the clearest presentation of the facts.

28. Leo G. Perdue, *Wisdom and Cult*, SBL DS 30 (Missoula MT: Scholars Press, 1977) is the most notable exception to the view that sages were not interested in the cult.

29. Studies of Ben Sira have flourished lately; two collected works demonstrate the progress that has been made toward a fuller understanding of his teachings. They are Angelo Passaro and Giuseppe Bellia, *The Wisdom of Ben Sira: Studies on Tradition, Redaction, and Theology*, Deutero-canonical and Cognate Literature Series 1 (Berlin/New York: Walter de Gruyter, 2008) and a collection of articles by Friedrich Reiterer, ed. Renate Egger-Wenzel, *"Alle Weisheit stammt vom Herrn . . . ," Gesammelte Studien zu Ben Sira*, BZAW 375 (Berlin/New York: Walter de Gruyter, 2007).

30. John Collins's valuable introduction to Jewish wisdom in the Hellenistic age has been supplemented by Leo G. Perdue, *The Sword and the Stylus*, 292–371 and *Wisdom Literature*, 267–324.

31. Martin Hengel, *Judaism and Hellenism*, vols. 1–2 (Philadelphia: Fortress Press, 1974). Samuel L. Adams, *Wisdom in Transition: Act and Consequence in Second Temple Instructions* (Leiden/Boston: Brill, 2008) shows how a changing worldview affects a fundamental concept.

32. Peter Höffken, "Das EGO des Weisen," *TZ* 4 (1984): 121–35.

33. "Qohelet's Epistemology," *HUCA* 58 (1987): 137–55 and *A Time to Tear Down & a Time to Build Up: A Rereading of Ecclesiastes* (Grand Rapids: Wm. B. Eerdmans, 1999).

34. James L. Crenshaw, "Qoheleth's Understanding of Intellectual Inquiry," 205–24 in Antoon Schoors, ed., *Qohelet in the Context of Wisdom*, BETL 136 (Leuven: University Press, 1998) shows how much Qoheleth depends on traditional teaching.

35. Qoheleth's view of God has been widely explored; see L. Gorssen, "Le cohérence de la conception de Dieu dans l'Ecclésiaste," *Ephemerides theologicae lovanienses* 46 (1969): 282–324; Hans-Peter Müller, "Wie sprach Qohälät von Gott?" *VT* 18 (1968): 507–21; Dietrich Michel, "Gott bei Qohelet: Anmerkungen zu Kohelets Reden von Gott," *Bibel und Kirche* 45 (1990): 32–36; Stefan de Jong, "God in the Book of Qohelet: A Reappraisal of Kohelet's Place in Old Testament

Theology," *VT* 47 (1997): 154–67; A. Schoors, "God in Qoheleth," 251–70 in *Schöpfungsplan und Heilsgeschichte: FS Ernst Haag* (Rome: Paulinus, 2002); and Klaas Smelik, "God in the Book of Qoheleth," 177–81 in A. Berlejung and P. van Hecke, eds., *The Language of Qohelet in Its Context*, OLA 164 (Leuven: Uitgeverij Peeters, 2007). For me, Qoheleth's use of Elohim rather than the Tetragrammaton, Shaddai, Eloah, or such nomenclature is telling.

36. James L. Crenshaw, "From the Mundane to the Sublime (Reflection on Qoh 11:1-8)," 61–72, 217–22 in *Prophets, Sages & Poets*.

37. Shannon Burkes, *Death in Qoheleth and Egyptian Biographies of the Late Period*, SBL DS 170 (Atlanta: SBL, 1999).

38. Choon-Leong Seow, *Ecclesiastes* (New York: Doubleday, 1997) 351–52 argues persuasively that Qoheleth may have meant all three of these (Creator, well [wife], and grave [death]), which was indeed the interpretation put forth in the first century by Rabbi Akabya ben Mahallel.

39. Norbert Lohfink, "Qoheleth 5:17-19: Revelation by Joy," *CBQ* 52 (1990): 625–35 views the entire context positively.

40. Thomas Krüger, "Meaningful Ambiguities in the Book of Qoheleth," 63–74 in *The Language of Qohelet in Its Context*, and L. Wilson, "Artful Ambiguity in Ecclesiastes 1:1-11," 357–65.

41. Edward L. Greenstein, "Sages with a Sense of Humor: The Babylonian Dialogue between the Master and His Servant and the Book of Qoheleth," 55–65 in *Wisdom Literature in Mesopotamia and Israel*.

42. B. L. Berger, "Qohelet and the Exigencies of the Absurd," *Bib Inter* 9 (2001): 174 uses this felicitous language.

43. Hans Wilhelm Hertzberg, *Der Prediger*, KAT, n.s. 17, 4 (Gutersloh; Mohn, 1963) makes frequent use of the idea conveyed by Zwar/aber, listing as many as twenty-four on page 30 of his commentary.

44. James L. Crenshaw, "Poor but Wise (Qoh 9:13-16)," 153–66 in *Celebrate Her for the Fruit of Her Hands: Studies in Honor of Carol L. Meyers*, ed. Susan Ackerman (Winona Lake: Eisenbrauns, 2015).

45. The commentary by Thomas Krüger makes exemplary use of the concept of deconstruction in interpreting Qoheleth's thought (*Qoheleth* [Minneapolis: Fortress Press, 2004]).

46. No satisfactory interpretation of 7:23-29 has appeared. The current trend is to see the *misogynism* as a traditional view that Qoheleth challenges. The literature is rapidly expanding (see note 57 on pages 16–17 in my article, "Qoheleth's Quantitative Language," 1–22 in *The Language of Qohelet in Its Context*).

47. Carolyn J. Sharp, "Ironic Representation, Authorial Voice, and Meaning in Qohelet," *Bib Inter* 12 (2004): 37–68 explores the possibilities inherent to an ironic reading of Qoheleth. Ironically, she does not see the extent to which her commitment to canonical criticism shapes her positive reading of Qoheleth.

48. The most thorough analysis of *hebel* in Ecclesiastes is that by Douglas B. Miller: *Symbol and Rhetoric in Ecclesiastes: The Place of Hebel in Qohelet's Work* (Atlanta: Society of Biblical Literature, 2002). Ethan Dor-Shav, "Ecclesiastes,

Fleeting and Timeless," 67–87 roots this concept firmly in cognition about death. Franz Rosenzweing has said that all thinking about God begins with the reality of death.

49. "(1) Under the sun, the tangled knots of human carnage expose envy, greed, and bloated ego, their frayed edges masking a pained journey from trust to abuse, promise to betrayal, passion to indifference.

(2) Above the sun, a master weaver twists diverse threads in many directions to reveal a pattern of hope and pardon for abused and abuser.

(3) Beneath the heavens, victims cry out for measured justice, an eye for an eye. "A moment's satisfaction for past wrongs, finally avenged."

(4) Beyond the sun, no one assesses guilt, or even merit! Forgiveness reigns in a kingdom that knows no end." (James L. Crenshaw, *Dust and Ashes. Poems* [Eugene OR: Cascade Books, 2010] 18)

50. *Hebel* occurs thirty-nine times in Ecclesiastes, and the phrase *re'ut rûah* appears seven times. A variant, *ra'yon rûah*, makes two appearances.

51. Augustus Gianto, "Human Destiny in Emar and Qohelet," 473–79 in *Qohelet in the Context of Wisdom*, puts a positive spin on the brevity of life. See also R. Norman Whybray, "Qoheleth, Preacher of Joy," *JSOT* 23 (1982): 87–98 and Stefan Fischer, *Die Aufforderung zur Lebensfreude im Buch Kohelet und seine Rezeption der ägyptischen Harfnerleider,* Wiener Alttestamentliche Studien 2 (Frankfurt: Peter Lang, 1999).

52. This observation evokes a scene in a film by Ingmar Bergman, *Wild Strawberries*; it depicts the death angel refusing to play chess to stall the moment of death).

53. Stela of Taimhotep. See Miriam Lichtheim, *Ancient Egyptian Literature*, vol. 3 (Berkeley: University of California Press, 1980) 63.

54. New York: Harcourt Brace & Company, 1934. O'Hara got the title from Somerset Maugham's retelling of an old story in the Babylonian Talmud illustrating death's inevitability.

55. The peculiar use of *hā'ām* instead of *lemûdîm* to designate Qoheleth's audience may suggest a broadening of sapiential instruction to include everyone willing to listen.

56. The emphasis on fearing Elohim and keeping the commandments places Qoheleth at some distance, for this type of instruction is close to that of Ben Sira. On the relationship of Qoheleth and Ben Sira, see Maurice Gilbert, "Qohelet et Ben Sira," 161–79 in *Qohelet in the Context of Wisdom*. Gilbert argues against positing an influence of Qoheleth on Ben Sira.

57. Studies on scriptural authority reach diverse conclusions because of the assumptions lying behind them. See Telford Work, "Authority of Scripture," *NIDB*, vol. 1 (Nashville: Abingdon Press, 2006) 352–53. Work writes that the collapse of belief in the unity of Scripture and tradition in the Enlightenment produced "camps of historicists, spiritualists, experientialists, fundamentalists, pragmatists, liberationists, and outright skeptics" (353). He thinks the apostolic and patristic consensus is making a comeback. If so, it corresponds to the current movement

toward the right in Christendom. Scriptural authority is treated extensively in *ABD*, vol. 5 (New York: Doubleday, 1992) 1017–56. The entries cover Judaism, Eastern Orthodoxy, Roman Catholicism, the early church, the medieval church, the Protestant Reformation, the wake of the Enlightenment, and the Post-Critical period. In the last of these entries, Walter Brueggemann emphasizes the authorizing feature of the Bible, its summons to establish justice, and its classic nature that extends beyond faith communities and the academy into the public arena. He thinks these two categories overcome the tyranny of the church and the academy where authority is concerned, bringing newness of life. James Barr's remarks in "Scripture, Authority of," 794–97 in *IDB, Supplementary Volume* (Nashville: Abingdon Press, 1976) are still some of the most astute in print.

chapter four

QOHELETH'S HATRED OF LIFE: A PASSING PHASE OR AN ENDURING SENTIMENT?*

For the author who had YHWH pronounce a curse on the first couple and the agent of their nemesis, life was filled with hardship. In biblical times, the obstacles to a rosy view of reality originated in nature or were the result of human malfeasance. Whatever optimism an individual managed to conjure up was quickly erased by natural disasters and man-made carnage. Hunger and thirst, disease and warfare, back-breaking labor and mental anguish tempered the faintest glimmer of optimism. Worse still, injustice in a world believed to be ruled by a benevolent deity cast a pall over divine faithfulness.[1]

Qoheleth lived in such a world, one that seemed to be spinning out of control.[2] Not surprisingly, he came to hate life in such a universe. And yet he issued a call to seize the day, one that has been deemed the heart of his message.[3] Does this feature of his teaching make him a preacher of joy as some interpreters claim?[4] Or is this summons merely a way of making the most of a difficult situation that will soon become even worse?[5]

---

* The original appeared in Nuria Calduch-Benages, ed., *Wisdom for Life: Essays Offered to Honor Prof. Maurice Gilbert S.J. on the Occasion of his Eightieth Birthday* (BZAW 445. Berlin/ New York: Walter de Gruyter). Reprinted with permission.

The human condition, according to the primeval story of Adam and Eve, was characterized by a single word, *ʿāmāl*. A form of this word occurs seventy-five times in the Hebrew Bible, thirty-five of which are located in a single book consisting of twelve chapters. In that book, Ecclesiastes, ten of these uses appear in just six verses, 2:18-23, the same number as are found in the entire book of Job. Three occurrences in Proverbs and fourteen in Psalms make up the other uses in the Bible except for thirteen scattered in prophetic and historical books.[6] The importance of *ʿāmāl* for Qoheleth's thinking can hardly be exaggerated.[7] Hence this study of the above cluster and other isolated occurrences of the root *ʿml*.

THE NUANCES OF *ʿĀMĀL*

The basic sense of *ʿāmāl* suggests the onset of tiredness. The verb covers the activity that brings on weariness, and the noun represents both the result of labor, wealth in its various forms, and the toil itself. The adjective indicates a state of exhaustion. Companion words, those found in parallel cola, further clarify the odious features of *ʿāmāl*. They include *ʾāwen* (iniquity, sorrow), *ḥāmās* (violence), *shôd* (destruction), *sheqer* (lie), *kaʿas* (vexation), *mirmāh* (deceit), *ʿŏnî* (poor), *rēsh* (oppressed), *tōk* (oppression), *lāḥaṣ* (distress), and *shāw* (vanity). Together they indicate the activity that brings on exhaustion and the psychological state of distress.

Qoheleth does not associate *ʿāmāl* with any of these synonyms. He does choose forms of the verb *yāgaʿ* in 1:8 ("All words/things are tiresome . . .") and in 10:15 ("The toil of fools exhausts them so they do not know how to go to a city"), and the epilogist uses the verb *yegîʿat* in 12:12 ("Additionally, my son, be warned; there is no end to the making of many books, and much talking wearies the body").[8]

One reason for the absence of the usual synonyms for *ʿāmāl* in Ecclesiastes may be the peculiar discourse Qoheleth employs, where parallelism is seldom present. The explanation is probably more complex than this, however, as a comparison with the use of *ʿāmāl* in the book of Job shows.

For the author of the book of Job, *ʿāmāl* always describes the human condition as in Genesis 3.[9] The apparent exception, Job 3:20 ("Why does he give light to the *worker*, life to those bitter of soul?"), is better seen as complying with all the other uses of a form of *ʿāmāl* because of the parallelism between the one who toils and the unfavorable characterization of the worker as adversely affected by the expenditure of effort. Moreover, *'āmāl* is used along with synonyms such as *'āwen, shāw,* and *mirmāh.*

This triad indicates human misery through imagery derived from agriculture and from anthropology ("As I have seen, those who plow iniquity and sow trouble harvest it," 4:8; "conceiving trouble [*'āmāl*] and giving birth to sorrow [*'āwen*], their belly establishes deceit [*mirmāh*], 15:35, to which may be compared Ps 7:15, where the sequence in the same image is *'āwen, 'āmāl,* and *shēqer*).

The overwhelming use of *'āmāl* in the Psalter is like that in the book of Job. The word refers to trouble, a misery that gnaws at both flesh and mind. *'āmāl* can refer to unpleasant circumstances brought on by talk (Ps 10:7; cf. Prov 24:2), to mental perplexities (Ps 73:16), and even metaphorically to a disturbed existence (Ps 73:5). In one instance, *'āmāl* simply means toil (Ps 127:1), like Prov 16:26, and in Ps 105:44 it bears the extended sense of the product of human labor ("He gave them the territory of nations; they inherited the gain/property of peoples").

IS *'ĀMĀL* A NEUTRAL TERM?

In four instances, *'āmāl* is often taken to be neutral,[10] but the negative aspects of the word lurk in the background, for they imply expenditure of fruitless effort. In Jonah 4:10, God reminds the prophet that he, Jonah, had nothing to do with planting the vine that provided temporary relief from the blazing sun. Psalm 127:1 judges human construction projects to be empty apart from divine collaboration, and Prov 16:26 attributes labor to the appetite ("A worker's appetite toils for him, for his mouth urges him on"). Only Judges 5:26 lacks such negative undertones, although the use to which the worker's mallet was put by Jael is grim indeed.

'ĀMĀL IN ECCLESIASTES

Qoheleth never uses *'āmāl* to indicate misery as the human condition. Instead, he chooses the two exceptional senses in the book of Job, specifically toil and wealth.[11] For him, the human condition is *hebel,* which suggests transience, insubstantiality, and futility or absurdity.[12] Over and above the brevity of life and its irrationality, Qoheleth points to death[13] and the loss of control of possessions as exacerbating existence. He exposes this complaint in the context of an astonishing confession, at least for a sage. Life was the supreme good for the composers of the book of Proverbs and, it can be argued, even for the author of the book of Job. It was left to Qoheleth to declare hatred of life in general, not merely as a personal antipathy like that expressed by Job in 10:1 as a result of his extreme suffering. "I loathe my life" differs from the blanket statement by Qoheleth, which moves beyond the specific "my life" to "life itself."[14] In 2:18-23, *ʿāmāl* thematizes his dismay, and this concept is reinforced by three iterations that what he has just described is *hebel*.[15]

> And I loathed all my wealth for which I had labored under the sun because I must leave it to another who will succeed me. And who knows whether he will be wise or foolish; yet he will control all my earnings for which I worked ingeniously under the sun. This also is futile. So I turned my heart to despair concerning all the toil at which I had worked under the sun. For everyone whose wealth was acquired with wisdom, knowledge, and skill must give it as his portion to someone who did not work for it. This also is absurd and a grievous evil. For what accrues to a person in all his toiling and the striving of his heart at which he labors under the sun? All his days are painful and his occupation vexing; even at night his mind cannot rest. This also is absurd. (Eccl 2:18-23)

THE LARGER CONTEXT

Who speaks here? Qoheleth in the persona of the wisest of kings in the East, according to biblical lore.[16] This brief section leads up to the conclusion of the royal experiment in 2:24-26. What is that? The best option, Qoheleth opines, is to enjoy life. The problem is, however, that he also thinks such an alternative lies outside human control. Because pleasure is in the hands of an arbitrary deity, existence is tainted. Qoheleth's assessment is that everything is devoid of meaning and feeding on or shepherding the wind. The sages' fictional world has collapsed under Qoheleth's close scrutiny. Human deeds, however grandiose, amount to nothing substantial in a universe governed by an irrational deity.[17]

The unit under discussion moves from loathing, which picks up the same verb in 2:17, to a devaluation of everything, an assessment Qoheleth makes three times in this brief unit (2:19, 21, and 23). The reason for his hatred of possessions underlines Qoheleth's self-centered language,[18] which comes to light most conspicuously in the nine uses of *lî* (for myself) in 2:4-9. He must relinquish control of all he has acquired, and he has no idea whether or not the inheritor will be worthy of such goods. The distance separating this sentiment from that in Prov 13:22 is hardly explained by the actual successor to Solomon who in Ben Sira's words was "broad in folly and lacking in sense" (Sir 47:23).[19]

To emphasize his point, Qoheleth uses a particle of existence in introducing an example of absurdity.[20] By means of intelligence and skill, a person gathers possessions only to give them to someone else as his portion (*ḥeleq*) either during this life or at death. Such injustice elicits more than a mere "This also is *hebel*." Now Qoheleth adds "and grievous evil." Why? Because life's burden is constant; endless pain and vexation are capped by sleepless nights.

'INYAN AND 'ANAH

Qoheleth clearly attributes this heavy burden to God in 1:13 (". . . It is a sorry business God has bestowed on humans with which to afflict them").[21] The noun *'inyan* is unique to Qoheleth (2:23, 26; 3:10; 4:8; 5:2, 13, and 8:16). Its negative connotation is highlighted in 4:8 (". . . also this is *hebel* and unpleasant business"), although the addition of the adjective *rāʿ* in 5:15 shows that *'inyan* alone need not be construed negatively. The verb *'ānāh* has four possible senses: (1) to answer; (2) to be occupied with; (3) to afflict; and (4) to sing or chant.[22] Either the second or third meaning applies in 1:13. In light of the immediate sequel to 3:10, it seems likely that Qoheleth viewed the gift bestowed on humans as a heavy yoke. The meaning of *hʿlm* in 3:11 remains ambiguous; regardless of which sense an interpreter chooses—duration or the hidden—the gift does nobody any good as Qoheleth sees things.[23]

Why? The hidden culprit is death, a shadow hanging over everyone and coloring everything Qoheleth has to say. Death cancels the gains resulting from hard work and ingenuity. The word *yithrōn* is an economic term for the amount on the positive side of an accountant's ledger.[24] Qoheleth begins his teachings with a question: "What profit does a person have for all his toil at which he labors under the sun?" (1:3). In 2:11, he answers his own question. None. Here he uses forms of *maʿaśeh*[25] and *ʿāmāl* to indicate the total activity that yielded no surplus, just as he does in 3:9, once again phrased as an interrogative ("What profit does the doer have in that he works?"). Qoheleth varies the question in 5:15, prefaces it with a descriptive adjective ("This too is a severe malady"), and tacks on an observation that all his labor is for the wind.

Even if individual effort yielded nothing permanent, according to Qoheleth, it did offer momentary satisfaction. The word *ḥeleq* comes into play here.[26] The fictional king admits that he derived pleasure from all his expenditure of effort, "and this was my portion in all my wealth (or toil)" (2:10). Similarly, Qoheleth specifies eating, drinking, and experiencing good in one's work as the portion bestowed by God, a gift[27] that in 5:18-19 he calls both favorable and appropriate, good and beautiful. He makes the same point in 2:24, 3:13, and 8:15 without reference to portion. Unfortunately, every momentary pleasure stands under the judgment that "all human labor is for the mouth, and yet the appetite is never full" (6:7). Desire, he thinks, has the quality of Sheol, an open mouth that is never satisfied. Indeed, the specter of Sheol hovers over the advice in 9:7-10 that resembles what Siduri said to Gilgamesh and Enkidu.[28] In short, do your utmost to eke your portion of enjoyment out of daily existence during your brief, oh so brief, stay on earth.[29] The kinship with Egyptian Harper Songs is widely recognized, but literary dependence is unlikely. Carpe diem seems to have been a universal attitude among the young.

INJUSTICE

Qoheleth was troubled by something more than life's brevity or lack of meaning. The injustices he saw around him and the unfairness in daily life in general irked him, throwing into question the traditional belief in divine justice.[30] The link between *ʿāmāl* and retributive justice was well established. It stands out in Ps 140:10 ("May the trouble inflicted by their speech cover the heads of those around me").[31] Similarly, in a brief proverbial unit of Ps 7, the connection between *ʿāmāl* and retribution takes center stage (Ps 7:15-18). In addition to the image about being pregnant with trouble (v. 15), the psalmist appeals to an axiom: "the evil person who digs a hole will fall into it,[32] the *ʿāmāl* he caused recoiling on him, the *ḥāmās* descending on his head" (Ps 7:16-17). This connection did not escape the author of the book of Job (cf. 4:8 and 20:22), for whom misery could be viewed as divine discipline.[33]

CONCLUSION

Against this bleak background provided by *ʿāmāl, hebel,* and *ḥeleq,* and punctuated by hatred of life, every claim that Qoheleth's message was positive has a hollow ring. Even if *maʿaneh* in 5:19 means "keep one occupied with" as in later rabbinic texts,[34] the larger context makes it clear that Qoheleth thought only the lucky[35] fared well. "What," one may ask, "about those who could find no pleasure in watching others busy themselves with joys of the heart?" Moreover, even if young people are advised to enjoy life in 11:7, the words are doubly qualified, first by life's brevity and second by a future judgment. And finally, the inclusio at 12:8, coming as it does after the exquisite depiction of old age and death,[36] suggests that either Qoheleth persisted in his pessimism[37] or an editor thought he did.[38] In short, Qoheleth's hatred of life was no momentary phase but persisted to the end, notwithstanding the seven texts that soften the pessimism[39] for the lucky. For everyone else, God's favor[40] did not abound, only *ʿāmāl* and *hebel*.[41]

Notes

1. The relationship between human response and God's faithfulness gave rise to radically different views in the Bible. For some authors, YHWH's *ḥesed* trumped anything humans could do, whereas for others that loving kindness depended on loyal devotion on the part of worshipers. Given this uncertainty, efforts to sustain belief in divine justice within biblical literature took many forms, none of which was entirely satisfactory, on which see Crenshaw (2005).

2. See especially Seow (2001, 237–49) and Tamez (2006). The loss of political sovereignty, destruction of the cultic apparatus, collapse of the social fabric, and captive status were distant memories, but life under the Persian and Ptolemaic empires was far from ideal. Economic volatility, political oppression, vassalage, and excessive taxation were inescapably present realities (Crenshaw 2007, 285–99) and Seow (2008, 189–217).

3. Kaiser 1995, 66.

4. The language is Whybray's (1982, 87–98), but the claim that Qoheleth's message was optimistic is often made, e.g., by Gordis (1968), Krüger (2004), Lohfink (1990, 625–35), Lee (2005), and Schwienhorst-Schönberger (2004).

5. That grim future is signaled by the poetic description of old age and eventual death in Eccl 12:1–7 where the deterioration moves from a physical structure, a house, perhaps symbolic of the body, to the human body itself, on which see Koosed 2006. In accord with Qoheleth's observation that humans die but earth endures, the poem describes a robust nature in stark contrast with the death of mortals. Neither theory, deconstruction as put forth by Krüger (2004) nor a rhetoric of erasure, the apt term introduced by Berger (2001, 174), can negate the pessimism of Qoheleth's last words. Seow's assertion that apocalyptic imagery points to the end of the world is not supported by the continuation of funeral marches after the supposed end of time. If Qoheleth's language in this final poem derives from apocalyptic literature, as argued by Seow (1997, 376–82) and Janzen (2008, 465–83), it is muted almost beyond recognition.

6. Schwertner 1997 and Otzen 2001.

7. "Thus *ʿāmāl* occupies a central place in the intellectual world of the author as he tries to come to terms with the unfolding of human life" (Otzen, 2001). Fox (1999, 97–100) recognizes the importance of *ʿāmāl* for Qoheleth, as does de Jong (1992, 107–16), who uses it as a key to the structure of the book.

8. In context, the subject of the verb *yegiʿath* probably indicates oral recitation of written texts by students entrusted with studying and copying them. For recent discussion of the educational process in the ancient Near East, see Crenshaw 1998, Carr 2005, and van der Toorn 2007.

9. For my analysis of the book of Job, see Crenshaw 2011.

10. Otzen (1997, 197–98), but for a different view, see Fox (1999, 98). He writes that "Even in these verses, the noun *ʿāmāl* may mean 'misery' rather than 'toil.'"

11. Ginsberg (1950 and 1952) recognized the dual sense of *ʿāmāl* but probably exaggerated the number of instances in which the noun meant "wealth."

12. The rich nuances of *hebel* have been studied extensively. The direction of research is traced in considerable detail in a monograph by Miller (2002) and a suggestive article by Dor-Shav (2004, 67–87). The associated image of either chasing the wind or feeding on air presents a bleak picture of existence. Depending on which sapiential goal one emphasizes—the acquisition of knowledge or the forming of character—either absurdity or futility seems apt.

13. Imray 2009 examines Qoheleth's teaching as a philosophical response to Greek concepts of death. One can view death as the final process that began with the imposition of limits on human hubris that characterized the composers of the book of Proverbs insofar as they believed the intellect could virtually guarantee a good life, provided actions corresponded to the results of the inquiry.

14. In Crenshaw 2013, I lay a foundation for an approach to Qoheleth that emphasizes a rhetoric constructed from the levity of a tease and the gravity of the forlorn.

15. The significance of 1:12–3:15 (or 22) in the plan of the book has been recognized by several recent scholars and is chronicled by Schwienhorst-Schönberger 1997. Still, the key to unlocking the structure of Ecclesiastes has not been found despite the refrains that appear to set off individual units from what precedes and follows. A consensus does exist on the macrostructure of the book. It consists of a superscription in 1:1 and two epilogues, 12:9-12 and 12:13-14, an inclusio at 1:2 and 12:8, two nature poems, 1:4-11 and 11:8 (or 6)–12:7, and the corpus, 1:12–11:7.

16. The question is simple enough, but the answer is far from crystal clear. The initial speaker is replaced in 1:12 by a fictional king who soon vanishes, and the main speaker takes over only to be temporarily silenced in 7:27, then resumes speaking until silenced for good by one, if not two, new speakers in 12:9-14. On the basis of ancient instructions and proverbial collections with a prose framework, Fox (1977, 83–106) proposed that a narrator introduces a fictional speaker who reflects on his own past while presenting ideas that he holds in the present. The result is a distancing of the narrator from the unorthodox teachings of Qoheleth, and students are warned against adopting his dangerous views about reality. Instead, they are to

adhere to traditional fear of God and obedience. Although Qoheleth did advise hearers to fear God, his idea of fear differed greatly from that of the epilogist, and nowhere did Qoheleth advocate the keeping of commandments.

17. The disturbing depiction of YHWH in the Hebrew Bible is drawing much criticism today, on which see Miles (1995), Crenshaw (2001, 327–32), and Seibert (2009). The problem has even caught the eyes of philosophers who held a conference on the character of the God of the Bible (Bermann, Murray, and Rea, 2011).

18. Höffken (1985, 121–35) stresses Qoheleth's huge ego, largely on the basis of the nine uses of *lî* (for myself) in the royal experiment. Such self-interest prevails even when Qoheleth thinks about the value of having associates in 4:9-12, but this attitude is typical of sages because of their individualism. Similar clusters of personal references occur in Ruth 1:20-21, Jonah 4:2-3, Job 33:1-8 and 36:2-4 without indicating inflated egos.

19. Every effort to align specific incidents in Eccl 1:12–2:26; 4:13-16; and 9:13-16 with the biblical record of Solomon and his successor, Rehoboam, has failed. The rabbinic explanation for the differences among Song of Songs, Proverbs, and Ecclesiastes as products of youth, maturity, and senility respectively shows that these scholars had a sense of humor like that of the author of the Babylonian Debate between a Master and his Slave. Greenstein (2007, 55–65) examines Qoheleth in the light of this amusing text.

20. On *yesh*, see Schoors (1992, 151–52) and Crenshaw (2007, 10–12). The "high frequency" of this particle, its sixteen uses, may derive from Qoheleth's tendency to use anecdotal arguments from personal experience.

21. Some interpreters take *la'anôth* from *'ānāh*, "to busy oneself with, to occupy." The adjective *ra'* modifying *inyan* supports a negative reading of the infinitive. Fox (1999, 106) writes that "In 1:13 and 3:10, *la'anôth* may pun on the homonymous root *'NH*, 'to suffer.'"

22. Labuschagne (1997, 926) calls the usual distinctions in the four uses of *'NH* "anything but uncontested." Schoors (2004, 428) objects to the meaning "afflicts" for 1:13, insisting that Qoheleth nowhere says that God afflicts people, only that the deity gives difficult situations to deal with. Gordis (1968, 200) has the opposite opinion.

23. I remain convinced that *h'lm* in 3:11 refers to the hidden, like *ne'lam* in 12:12 (Crenshaw 1974, 23–55). The temporal emphasis dominates 3:1-8, but 3:9 shifts to the notion of profit. Qoheleth's denial that there is any profit is beautifully illustrated by the divine gift that does nobody any good. Emending the text to *h'ml* (Fox 2004, 23) accords with use in the book of Job but not with Qoheleth's understanding of the noun. Fox thinks the toil is mental.

24. On the socioeconomic context of Qoheleth, see Seow (1997, 21–33), Kugel (1989, 32–49), and Sneed (2012, 125–54).

25. Fox (1999, 102–103) thinks *ma'aśeh* refers to property in 5:5 like some uses of *'āmāl*. Divine intervention conflicts with Qoheleth's belief that God is remote and not involved in the nexus of cause and effect. This contradiction is but one of many in Qoheleth's thought.

26. Machinist (1995, 159–75) detects second-order thinking akin to Greek philosophy in Qoheleth's use of *ḥeleq, miqreh, 'ōlām,* and *ḥeshbon,* and Blenkinsopp (1995, 55–64) thinks Stoic influence lies behind the catalog of times.

27. Müller (1968, 507–21) discusses the importance of the verb *nāthan* in Qoheleth's discourse. Divine generosity is not questioned; its arbitrary nature tends to render human action irrelevant, ending in determinism (Rudman 2001).

28. Van der Toorn (2000, 23–30) examines the similarities between Qoheleth's teachings and ancient Near Eastern literature, especially the striking affinity with the Gilgamesh Epic, which was known in Syria and may have reached Qoheleth from this locale.

29. Alternatively, ". . . during your empty, meaningless stay under the sun." Gianto (1998, 473–79) compares Qoheleth to a text from Emar that mentions the brevity of existence and the unalterable fates fixed by the gods. The Egyptian Instruction of Papyrus Insinger has the refrain "The fate and fortune that come, it is the god who sends them."

30. If the expectation of divine judgment derives from him and not from an editor, as is the case in 12:14, Qoheleth seems to have been terribly conflicted over this issue.

31. The text is far from lucid here, but the psalmist seems to pray that his tormentors suffer the harm they have called down on him.

32. A proverbial saying in Eccl 10:8 voices the same opinion about retribution. Divine agency, if assumed, is definitely at odds with the remote deity, a situation that von Rad describes as an impenetrable barrier separating human thought from divine activity, resulting in loss of dialogue (1972, 230–32).

33. For the biblical understanding of suffering as God's way of disciplining those who veer from the expected religious path, see Crenshaw 2012.

34. Lohfink (1990, 625–35) refers to revelation by joy, but Schoors (2004, 431) writes, "This is an attractive idea, but, as said, the hi [phil] of *'nh* I does not make sense, and does not exist. Hence the theological idea of 'revelation by joy' based on this verb has no leg to stand on." The role of revelation in wisdom literature is treated in Crenshaw (2009, 41–62).

35. As is well known, the adjective *ṭôb* lacks a moral sense in Qoheleth's use, as does its opposite, *ḥōṭēʾ.*

36. See Gilbert's illuminating discussion of this poem (1981, 96–109), as well as the informative excursus by Fox (1999, 333–49).

37. Enns (2011, 49) notes that Qoheleth "strikes a tone of deep resignation," indeed that he "touches a more sensitive nerve: the trustworthiness, even goodness, of God" (122).

38. Holistic interpretations have created vanishing editors, but the realities of the text virtually require them, even if the nomenclature changes to transmitters who add a postscript. Even Fox (2004, 13) concedes the possibility of a pious gloss in 2:3 ("and to grasp folly").

39. Uehlinger's suggestion (1997, 234–35) that Qoheleth belongs to symposiastic philosophy, while intriguing, raises the question whether the pessimism of

Ecclesiastes would be at home at sumptuous banquets, however intellectual they purported to be. In this regard, Sirach seems more fitting as symposiastic literature.

40. Irony is certainly present in Ecclesiastes (Anderson 2000, 67–100; Backhaus 2000, 29–55; and Sharp 2004, 37–68), but discerning its presence is difficult. It is hugely ironic to call Qoheleth a sage when his teachings label everything *hebel*, even wisdom, and when the book ends by calling into question all his observations about life. Where does the irony fall? On his pessimism? On the statements about enjoyment? On divine judgment? On the claim that he spoke truthfully?

41. "It is as if *hebel* acts as a black hole or dark matter that sucks up any positive meaning left over for humanity. *Hebel* becomes the ultimate void and debit" (Sneed 1997, 308–309).

Bibliography

Anderson, W. H. U. "Ironic Correlations and Scepticism in the Joy Statements of Qoheleth," *SJOT* 14 (2000): 67–100.

Backhaus, F. J. "Kohelet und die Ironie," *BN* 101 (2000): 29–55.

Berger, B. L. "Qohelet and the Exigencies of the Absurd," *Biblical Interpretation* 9 (2001): 141–79.

Blenkinsopp, J. "Ecclesiastes 3:1-15: Another Interpretation," *JSOT* 20 (1995): 55–64.

Carr, D. *Writing on the Tablet of the Heart: Origins of Scripture and Literature*. New York: Oxford University Press, 2004.

Crenshaw, J. L. *Education in Ancient Israel: Across the Deadening Silence*. New York: Doubleday, 1998.

———. *Defending God: Biblical Responses to the Problem of Evil*. New York: Oxford University Press, 2005.

———. *Reading Job: A Literary and Theological Commentary*. Macon: Smyth & Helwys, 2010.

———. "The Eternal Gospel (Eccl 3:11)," J. L Crenshaw and J. Willis, eds., *Essays in Old Testament Ethics*. New York: KTAV, 1974, 23–55.

———. "The Reification of Divine Evil," *Perspectives in Religious Studies* 28 (2001): 327–32.

———. "Qoheleth's Quantitative Language," A. Berlejung and P. van Hecke, eds., *The Language of Qohelet in Context*. OLA 164; Leuven: Peeters, 2007, 1–22.

———. "Qoheleth in Historical Context," *Biblica* 88 (2007): 285–99.

———. "Sipping from the Cup of Wisdom," ed. P. K. Moser, ed., *Jesus and Philosophy: New Essays*. Cambridge, 2009, 41–62.

———. "Divine Discipline in Job 5:17-27, Proverbs 3:11-12, Deuteronomy 32:39 and Beyond," 178–89 in *Reading Job Intertextually*, K. Dell and W. Kynes, eds. New York: T & T Clark, 2012.

———. *The Ironic Wink: Qoheleth/Ecclesiastes*. Columbia: University of South Carolina Press, 2013.

Dor-Shav, E. "Ecclesiastes, Fleeting and Timeless," *Azure* 18 (2004): 67–87.

Enns, P. *Ecclesiastes*. Grand Rapids, 2011.

Fox, M. V. *A Time to Tear Down & a Time to Build Up*. Grand Rapids: Eerdmans, 1999.

————. *Ecclesiastes*. JPS Bible Commentary. Philadelphia: Jewish Publication Society, 2004.

————. "Frame-Narrative and Composition in the Book of Qohelet," *HUCA* 48 (1977): 83–106.

Gianto, A. "Human Destiny in Emar and Qohelet," *Qohelet in the Context of Wisdom*, A. Schoors, ed. Leuven: University Press, 1998, 473–79.

Gilbert, M. "La description de la viellesse en Qohelet XII,7, est-elle allegorique?" *VT Supplement Congress Volume Vienna 1980*. Leiden: Brill, 1981, 96–109.

Ginsberg, H. L. *Studies in Koheleth*. New York: Jewish Theological Seminary of America, 1950.

————. "Supplementary Studies in Kohelet," *Proceedings of the American Academy of Jewish Research* (1952): 35–62.

Gordis, R. *Kohelet—The Man and His World*. New York: Schocken, 1968.

Höffken, P. "Das EGO des Weisen," *ThZ* 4 (1985): 121–34.

Janzen, J. G. "Qohelet on 'Life under the Sun'," *CBQ* 70 (2008): 465–83.

Imray, K. "Qoheleth's Philosophies of Death." Ph.D. dissertation, Murdoch University, 2009.

Jong, S. de. "A Book on Labour: The Structuring Principles and the Main Theme of the Book of Qohelet," *JSOT* 54 (1992): 107–16.

Kaiser, O. "Die Botschaft des Buches Kohelet," *ETL* 71 (1995): 48–70.

Koosed, J. *(Per)mutations of Qohelet: Reading the Body in the Book*. New York/London: T & T Clark, 2006.

Krüger, T. *Qohelet*. Minneapolis: Fortress, 2004.

Kugel, J. "Qohelet and Money," *CBQ* 51 (1989): 32–49.

Labuschagne, C. J. "*'NH* to answer," *TLOT* 2 (1997): 926–30.

Lee, E. P. *The Meaning of Enjoyment in Qohelet's Theological Rhetoric*. BZAW 353. New York: Walter de Gruyter, 2005.

Lohfink, N. "Qoheleth 5:17-19—Revelation by Joy," *CBQ* 52 (1990): 625–35.

Machinist, P. "Fate, *miqreh*, and Reason: Some Reflections on Qohelet and Biblical Thought," Z. Zevit, ed., *Solving Riddles and Untying Knots*. Winona Lake: Eisenbrauns, 1995, 159–75.

Miles, J. *God: A Biography*. New York: Knopf, 1995.

Miller, D. B. *Symbol and Rhetoric in Ecclesiastes: The Place of Hebel in Qohelet's Work*. Academica 2. Atlanta, 2002.

Müller, H. P. "Wie sprach Qohälät von Gott?" *VT* 18 (1968): 507–21.

Otzen, B. "*ʾML,*" *TDOT* XI. Grand Rapids (2001): 196–202.

Rad, G. von. *Wisdom in Israel.* Nashville: Abingdon, 1972.

Rudman, D. *Determinism in the Book of Ecclesiastes.* JSOT SS 316. Sheffield: Sheffield Academic Press, 2001.

Schoors, A. *The Preacher Sought to Find Pleasing Words.* 2 volumes. Leuven: Peeters, 1992, 1994.

———, ed. *Qohelet in the Context of Wisdom.* Leuven: Peeters, 1998.

Schwienhorst-Schönberger, L. *Kohelet.* HthKAT. Freiburg: Herders, 2004.

Schwertner, S. "*ʾML toil,*" *TLOT* 2 (1997): 924–26.

Seibert, E. A. *Disturbing Divine Behavior. Troubling Old Testament Images of God.* Minneapolis: Fortress, 2009.

Seow, C. L. *Ecclesiastes.* New York, 1997.

———. "The Social World of Ecclesiastes," L. G. Perdue, ed., *Scribes, Sages & Seers.* Göttingen: 2008, 189–217.

———. "Theology When Everything Is Out of Control," *Interpretation* 55 (2001): 237-49.

Sharp, C. J. "Ironic Representation, Authorial Voice, and Meaning in Qohelet," *Biblical Interpretation* 12 (2004): 37–68.

Sneed, M. R. *The Politics of Pessimism in Ecclesiastes. A Social-Science Perspective.* Atlanta: Society of Biblical Literature, 2012.

———. "Qoheleth as 'Deconstructionist? 'It is I, the Lord, your Redeemer . . . who turns sages back and makes their knowledge nonsense' (Is 44:24-25)," *Old Testament Essays* 10 (1997): 303–31.

Tamez, E. *When the Horizons Close.* Eugene OR: Wipf & Stock, 2006.

Uehlinger, C. "Qohelet im Horizont altorientalischer Weisheitsliteratur," *Das Buch Kohelet,* ed. L. Schwienhorst-Schönberger. BZAW 254. New York: Walter de Gruyter, 1997, 155–247.

Van der Toorn, K. "Did Ecclesiastes Copy Gilgamesh?" *Biblical Review* 16 (2000): 23–30.

———. *Scribal Culture and the Making of the Hebrew Bible.* Cambridge: Harvard University Press, 2007.

Whybray, R. N. "Qoheleth, Preacher of Joy," *JSOT* 23 (1982): 87–98.

chapter five

THE JOURNEY FROM VOLUNTARY TO OBLIGATORY SILENCE*

Reflections on Psalm 39 and Qoheleth

The omniscient narrator in the prologue of the book of Job exonerated a scrupulous father from any spoken offense against YHWH, leaving open the possibility of rebellious thoughts. It did not take readers long to provide what the narrator neglected to do; in the eyes of some early rabbis, Job was guilty of thinking unseemliness of YHWH. In a delicious bit of irony, the narrator actually has Job harbor the fear that his children have gone astray and blessed[1] Elohim *in their thoughts* while in a sinful state. In Job's view, sin's pernicious tentacles extended beyond the deed to the thought that later expressed itself in action. The poet who composed Ps 39 determined to avoid both types of offense,[2] but in the end abandoned his voluntary silence for speech that ultimately echoes Job's plea to be left alone to die (Job 7:16; 10:20; cf. 9:27 and 14:6).

Warnings against loose speech abound in international wisdom.[3] The danger of being suspected of disloyalty to the ruling administration was real, as was punishment for false accusation and lies in general within a kinship society. Teachers compared a spoken word to an arrow that, once released, could not be recalled. They also warned that a spoken word could be carried

---

* The original appeared in Jon L. Berquist and Alice Hunt, eds., *Focusing Biblical Studies. The Crucial Nature of the Persian and Hellenistic Periods: Essays in Honor of Douglas A. Knight* (LHB/OTS 544. T & T Clark, 2012) 177–91. Reprinted with permission.

by a bird to unintended ears. In the imagination of teachers, the tongue's power over an individual resembled a ship's rudder. In each instance, a tiny instrument wielded control over something many times its size. The teachers' realism gave rise to such gems as the description of a gossiper who could not resist the latest tasty morsel.

In their zeal, however, teachers even sought to monitor the thought that lay behind words and deeds. Sometimes they attributed irreligious reasoning to practical atheists, whom they labeled "fools."[4] At other times, they adopted a pedagogy of uttering the unthinkable and thereby allowing untraditional views wider distribution in the same way some early rabbis employed the principle of uttering the impermissible and medieval philosophers introduced forbidden ideas into discourse as things to be rejected.[5] The introductory formula varied—"Do not say";[6] "Were it possible to say"; or "Heretics claim"—but the result was similar. Students widened their intellectual horizons by reflection on ideas that society found suspect.

The poet whose angst is exposed in Ps 39 chafed at the inescapable situation that this worldview created. Two realities impinged upon him: (1) the brevity of human existence and (2) the heavy hand of YHWH. The second of these two, punishment for sin, rendered the first one intolerable. The poet's provisional solution, a silence that was tantamount to withdrawing from life, brought further agitation. His extraordinary request for relief was fueled by his understanding of the human condition as *hebel*,[7] an assessment that placed him in a camp alongside Qoheleth. In the following close reading of Ps 39, we shall be attentive to intertextual associations in theme and in syntax, with special attention to Qoheleth.

PSALM 39:2-14

(2) I resolved that I would guard my way from sinning with my tongue; I would keep a muzzle to my mouth while the wicked one was in my presence. (3) I was completely silent; I refrained[8] from good but my pain intensified. (4) My mind was hot within me; A fire raged in my thoughts. I spoke out. (5) YHWH, tell me my end and what is the measure of my life; I want to know how fleeting I am. (6) Look, you have set my days at handbreadths, and my span is nothing in your sight; surely every person standing[9] is total emptiness. (7) Surely one walks as an image;[10] surely they hustle about—a breath;[11] He amasses but does not know who will gather in. (8) And now, Lord, what can I anticipate? My hope is in you.[12] (9) From every rebellion deliver me; lay not on me

the reproach of a fool. (10) I had been silent, not opening my mouth, for *you* did it.[13] (11) Remove your blow from me; I am dying from the rebuke of your hand. (12) With punishment for iniquity you chastise a person, and you consume his treasure like a moth. Surely everyone is a breath. (13) YHWH, hear my prayer, and listen to my outbursts; do not ignore my tears,[14] for I am a resident alien with you, a sojourner like all my ancestors.[15] (14) Look away from me so that I can smile before I die and am not.

Psalm 39 is unique in that it begins with the verb *ʾāmartî*. In the Psalter, the closest thing to it is Ps 82:6, which has *ʾanî - ʾāmartî ʾelōhîm ʾattem* ("I had thought you were gods") to indicate previous disposition in the same way *ʾāmartî* does in 39:2. The translation above is relatively straight-forward except for verse 6. I take *niṣṣāb* to suggest fixity, like one standing erect, but it may be a musical notation like *selâ* at the end of this verse and six verses later[16] or certainty about the human condition. The harsh tone and ambiguity of *kî ʾattâ ʿaśîtā* in the tenth verse prompted a later translator to render the clause in Greek less offensively, *ho poiēsas me* ("for you made me"). This slight change transformed an accusation into acknowledgment of YHWH as personal creator. The occasion for the poet's charge of heavy handedness on the part of the deity may be the silence referred to in verses 3-42. Hence the pluperfect translation in verse 10 rather than an improbable present tense.

Structure

The structure of the poem is unclear, for clues point to different ways of dividing its individual units. First, three vocatives (two uses of the Tetragrammaton and a single use of *ʾadonāi* suggest a tripartite prayer (vv. 5-7, 8-12, 13-14) that is introduced by verses 2-4. Second, the two refrains that conclude verses 6 and 12 and universalize the assessment of human existence as transience may indicate a two-part psalm with a final plea in verses 13-14. Whoever added the two *selâs* apparently viewed the poem as a composition comprising two units.

Both readings are predicated on the assumption that the poem was composed by a single author, but Otto Kaiser has reached an entirely dif-ferent conclusion on the basis of theme alone.[17] The concentration on *hebel* in verses 5-7 and 12 led him to postulate an older didactic poem that a redactor fashioned into a "school text" resembling Job 28, Qoh 3:1-8, Sir 24:1-22, and Wis Sol 2:1-9. By excising the first *kōl* and *niṣṣab* in verse 6, as well as *ʿal ʿāwôn* six verses later, Kaiser attributes greater uniformity to an original poem than its present form exhibits. The four uses of *'ak* in verses 6, 7, and 12 may reinforce his interpretation, if they are seen as isolating the short poem from its larger context.

Because the original poem that Kaiser has separated from the larger psalm lacks distinctive markers that point to a date, one could argue that it is a *late* insertion.[18] Its theme, life's transience, seems more at home in postexilic texts than in earlier ones. Viewing this unit about life's transience as a late insertion is subject to the objection that *dibbartî bilšônî* requires something other than *we'attâ*. The expression "and now" ordinarily marks strong transition,[19] whereas "I spoke out" should be followed by something that explains how the poet abandoned an earlier resolve to remain quiet. As the psalm stands now, the poet moves from the awareness of personal *hebel* to the generalization that everyone's existence is *hebel* before asking, "What can *I* expect?" in a world that lacks real substance.

Content

Psalm 39 is a supplication for relief from an unspecified affliction that is interpreted as punishment for an infraction of divine rule. The prayer consists of three separate petitions (the last one reinforced by cohortatives [vv. 13-14]) and is introduced by an autobiographical snippet. Whereas the usual lament introduced by *'ad matay* or *'ad 'ānâ* inquires about the duration of present suffering, this one asks about the number of days remaining before the grim reaper's scythe does its work.[20] In the absence of response, the psalmist determines to shorten those days by foregoing YHWH's presence.

The exposure of the poet's inner feelings[21] echoes that of Jeremiah, who also chafed from conduct that he considered inappropriate for YHWH. In both instances, adopting a policy of silence resulted in mental agitation that overcame the resolve to keep quiet. Two things about this personal revelation in verses 1-4 conceal more than they reveal. First, who is the evil one, and second, why did the poet abstain from good?

Apparently, the *rāšā'* is nearby, but why was refraining from speech an effective response to the presence of a wicked one? We know that sages wrestled with this issue, for they have preserved an answer in sayings juxtaposed to one another in Prov 26:4-5. Depending on the situation, one should either answer a fool to expose his stupidity or refuse to dignify a remark by responding. Was the poet afraid that he might say something that would encourage the *rāšā'*, perhaps an expression of envy for prosperous evildoers like that laid bare in Ps 73:3-14?[22] Or does the opening verb *'āmartî* in the sense of "resolve" point to cases like Pss 14:1 and 53:2 where this verb is followed by *belibbî* (*ô*)? In other words, is the psalmist afraid of voicing doubt that might strengthen practical atheists?

The second issue in the personal data that remains unclear is the statement that the poet refrained from good. One way of resolving the difficulty is to understand the expression as elliptical,[23] its meaning being "to do nothing," either good or bad. The verb would then have the sense of showing inactivity, as in Jdg 18:9 and 1 Kgs 22:3.[24] If the poet neither spoke nor did anything, there was less possibility of giving offense, for both words and deeds are often ambiguous. Another approach to the problem is to interpret the response to the presence of a wicked person against the background of the sages' warning against helping sinners. Charity, in other words, must be closely monitored lest one strengthen those bent on wrongdoing.

Curiously, the poet's good intentions only intensified the angst, creating a raging inferno within the mind and the seat of emotions. Humans, he learned, need something other than the instrument that effectively controls the mouths and behavior of domesticated animals. That discovery did not prevent a later teacher, Ben Sira, from using different symbolism in a prayer that a guard and a seal be placed on his mouth to prevent harmful speech (Sir 22:27–23:3). In addition, he requests that whips be set over his thoughts lest enemies exult over his misfortune.[25] Ben Sira's petition is immediately followed by a section in the Greek text identified as "discipline of the tongue" (Sir 23:7-15).

When the psalmist says he refrained from *ṭôb*, he obviously implies that he believed one capable of doing the good. That view was not universally shared, for a few thinkers considered goodness beyond the capacity of humans. In the reasoning of some, the mind is more devious than anything else (Jer 17:9a),[26] and consequently no one is able to do good (cf. Ps 62:10, "Surely humans are *hebel*, mortals a lie; on scales for weighing, together they weigh more than a breath" [*hebel*]; cf. Ps 116:11). Or is that opinion restricted to fools as in Ps 14:1? Apparently not, for this low view of humans is also attributed to YHWH in the next two verses. Such hyperbole stands in tension with the mention of the righteous (*bedôr ṣaddîq*) in verse 5, unless righteousness is judged to be less demanding than *ṭôb*. In that case, *ṭôb* would be a habitus and *ṣaddîq* a temporary achievement.

The first prayer that shatters the self-imposed silence seeks information that is hidden from most people: the precise time of their death. The poet chooses his language carefully, opting for the Hebrew noun *qēṣ* that Amos used to refer to the end of a nation. This desire to know one's ultimate destiny fueled an entire enterprise that promised secret knowledge about the future.[27] The psalmist bypasses these professionals and goes directly to YHWH. Others may have calculated human longevity as one hundred and twenty years[28] or as the more realistic seventy to eighty years, but the poet refuses to enter into a mythic explanation for a human life span. Instead, he shifts from duration to the quality of existence,[29] which he describes as total emptiness, a mere image devoid of substance despite every hustle and bustle. Ironically, he sees his own brief existence as nothing in YHWH's presence, presumably because the deity is not subject to time's erosive power.

The second prayer alternates between trust and accusation. The poet's only hope lies in the Lord, but this taskmaster exacts a heavy toll on mere humans. The language of painful discipline dominates this section, but so does that of death-dealing punishment. No wonder the poet boldly accuses the Lord even while explaining his earlier mutism. His emotions evoked the same extreme words, "For you did it," that the destruction of Jerusalem generated in the composer of Lam 1:21. Comparing YHWH to a destructive moth, the psalmist reduces existence to a single breath, a rare concrete sense of *hebel*.

The third prayer, or rather outburst (*HALOT*, 1443), uses the language of disenfranchisement to describe the poet's powerlessness. The resident alien and the sojourner, *gēr* and *tôšāb*,[30] were protected by provisions that were believed to have been established by YHWH. The powerful reminder that Abraham and all Israel's ancestors were but pilgrims on a brief journey invokes special consideration, the hospitality extended to visitors. Nevertheless, the poet abandons all hope and request that YHWH hasten the *qēṣ* by looking away.

Affinities with Other Psalms

The four occurrences of *'ak* in Ps 39 are two less than the six in Ps 62, where *hebel* is said to be the human essence in that an individual weighs less than a breath (Ps 62:10). In both psalms, the exclamatory particle *'ak* reinforces a low assessment of humankind, as if the judgment would not stand on its own. The psalmist who composed 144:4 compared people to a breath, but the weaker observation does not require any emphasis. Moreover, the initial statement in Ps 62:2 uses the same adjective *dûmiyyâ* that the poet uses in Ps 39:3 to characterize himself as silent. The sixth verse in Ps 62, nearly identical with verse 1, has the imperative *dōmmî* plus a reference to hope, like Ps 39:8. Verses 2-5 and 6-9, the two literary units in Ps 62 that *precede* the comment about human transience, are each set off by the musical notation *selâ*, unlike its appearance in Ps 39 *following* a refrain about humans as *hebel*.

The author of Ps 90 chose a different way to express the brevity of human existence. He compares people to grass that flourishes briefly and then dies. In his view, the irrevocable decree that relegates humans to dust in verse 3 becomes more oppressive in light of the seventy or eighty years allotted to humans, especially when YHWH's chastisement for offenses makes daily existence unbearable. The comparison of humans to a flower in Job 14:2 may be more elegant,[31] but flowers also wither and die. Both images, grass and flowers, are combined in Ps 103:15-17 and in Isa 40:6-8, which contrast their brief flourishing to YHWH's steadfast love and word respectively. In Isa 40:6-8, the divine breath changes vitality into its opposite, like the desert winds. The word for breath is *rûaḥ*, for *hebel* never applies to YHWH but does describe idols.

RESEMBLANCES TO QOHELETH

Whereas these texts move from human transience to divine immutability, Qoheleth emphasizes the anthropological angst resulting from life's brevity, anxiety made worse by its unfairness. Etymologically, the root *hebel* signifies "breath," breeze," or "vapor"; this concrete use occurs in the Bible only occasionally, e.g., Isa 57:13 (11 to *rûaḥ*) and Pss 39:12; 62:10.[32] In context with *rûaḥ*, it hovers in the background of Jer 10:14-15 (=51:17-18) but usually has a metaphorical sense, especially in polemic against the worship of idols and/or foreign gods.[33] Frequently, *hebel* indicates futility (Job 9:29; Ps 94:11; Isa 30:7; 49:4; Lam 4:17), a meaning that Qoheleth interchanges with the sense of ephemerality. Outside Qoheleth, *hebel* has this latter nuance in Job 7:16; Pss 39:6; 78:33; and 144:4.

Affinities between Ps 39 and Qoheleth go beyond a common theme, life as *hebel*. There are also some close syntactical relationships. Both authors refer to individuals who labor to accumulate things but cannot know who will gather them in. This particular problem expressed itself for Qoheleth in the context of inheritance (Qoh 2:18-23). He complains that he had used both wit and energy to acquire goods only to pass them along to a stranger who may lack intelligence altogether.

By dividing the consonants *bṣlm* differently in Ps 39:7, the picture changes from walking as an image to walking in a shadow,[34] which occurs in Qoheleth. For him a shadow prefigures the emptiness of life rather than providing relief from the hot sun.

Thus far the affinities between Ps 39 and Qoheleth have been striking. Three others, somewhat less persuasive, are worth considering. The psalmist worries about extinction with these words: *beṭerem 'ēlēk we'ēnennî* ("before I go and am no more").

Two things in this phrase recall Qoheleth: first, the verb for dying, which Qoheleth uses in its participial form *hôlēk*,[35] and second, the negative particle *'ēnennî* that denotes extinction.[36] The former is an abbreviated reference to going to be with dead ancestors, a euphemism for dying. The additional particle simply reflects the usual belief among Semites that a shadowy existence in Sheol was no real life. Hence the psalmist anticipates personal annihilation, at least on earth. The image of returning to dust is apt, for what distinguished a person no longer remains once the ravages of time have done their ruinous work. The third similarity between Ps 39 and Qoheleth is the rare use of the verb *ḥāšâ* for voluntary silence (Qoh 3:7; Ps 39:2).[37] Qoheleth does not move from a recognition of transience and rampant injustice to prayer. His response to the danger of loose speech is less extreme than that of the psalmist, although the occasion for guarding the tongue differs greatly. Qoheleth's justification for limited speaking is the distance separating Elohim from humans, not the fear of a human enemy. For the psalmist, suffering leads to a concept of *hebel* but does not generate a desire to enjoy life as it does for Qoheleth.[39]

Another significant difference is the way each thinker expresses inner resolve. The psalmist uses *'āmartî* alone, but Qoheleth adds *belibbî* to verbs of speaking. This linguistic expression occurs most often in Qoheleth and Psalms, although it can be found elsewhere.[40] The verbs range from *'āmar* and *dābar* to *hitbārēk* in Deut 29:18 ("Everyone who exalts himself inwardly, thinking 'I shall be safe although I follow my rebellious mind.'"). The usual *'āmar* and *dābar* plus the reference to the mind can be nuanced variously as "resolved," "prayed," "thought," "mused," and "imagined." Here is an example of each use.

> Gen 8:21—"YHWH resolved, 'I will never again destroy the earth because of humankind, for the human imagination is pernicious from youth' . . . ."
> Gen 24:45—"Before I had finished praying, Rebekah approached . . . ."
> 1 Sam 27:1—"David thought, 'I shall now perish by Saul's hand.'"
> Gen 17:17—"Abraham fell on his face; laughing, he mused, 'Can a child be born to one who is a hundred years old?'"
> Deut 7:17—"If you imagine, 'These nations are more numerous than we; how can we dispossess them?'"

About two thirds of these expressions occur in Genesis, Deuteronomy, Psalms, and Qoheleth. The latter's uses are noteworthy, given the brevity of the book when compared with the other three.

The unusual *ʿim lebābî ʿasîhâ* in Ps 77:7 introduces the idea of accompaniment, as if the mind joins the psalmist in the thought process ("I meditated with my mind"). On the basis of the Egyptian concept of communing with one's *ba* or soul, Michael V. Fox interprets Qoheleth's language about speaking *belēb* as conversation between two separate and independent entities.[41] He does this despite a solitary use of *debartî ʾanî ʿim libî* in Qoh 1:16. Fox's reading of Qoheleth rests on the assumption that the usual prepositional *be* has the sense of accompaniment rather than expressing location. If Qoheleth had wished to indicate dialogue between him and the mind as the seat of cognition, he could have done so by exclusive use of the preposition *ʿim* after verbs of speaking. That he did not do so suggests that he was not influenced by an Egyptian idiom when combining verbs of speech with *belibbî*.

Still, the personification of the *lēb*, at least metaphorically, does take place in the Hebrew Bible. According to Prov 14:10, the *lēb* possesses the power of perception, "knowing" its own bitterness, and Ps 27:8 attributes speech to it ("My heart says to you, 'Seek my face'"). In both instances, the cognitive aspect seems to give way to the emotive, and one cannot rule out a purely symbolic understanding of this language.

The contexts containing the language about speaking *belēb* are overwhelmingly negative. To many moderns, the fool is perhaps the most sympathetic one who engages in this practice ("The fool reasons: 'There is no god'" [Ps 14:1; 53:1]; "The fool boasts: 'I cannot be moved . . . God has forgotten; he hides his face[and] never looks; . . . You will not inquire'" [Ps 10:6, 11, 13]). The fiction of an omniscient narrator permits readers to grasp the innermost thoughts of others, especially when the intention is devious. Even a tendency to see oneself in the very best light is exposed in Esth 6:6 ("Haman thought: 'To whom would the king want to do a kindness more than to me?'").

A temporary suspension of justice encourages the wicked to presume an inactive deity ("Those who say, 'YHWH will do neither good nor evil'" [Zeph 1:12]). In the interest of humility, the newly freed Israelites are warned to give credit to YHWH. ("Do not boast: 'My strength and might acquired this wealth for me'" [Deut 8:17]. The most extreme instance of hubris in the Bible evokes this disparaging comment: "You thought: 'I will ascend to heaven above El's stars, set up my throne, sit in the mount of assembly in the abode of Saphon, mount the back of a cloud, [and] be like Eloyôn'" [Isa 14:13-14]). Nations, too, are reminded that they are subject to YHWH ("Who say: 'I am, and there is none besides me'" [Isa 47:10]; "Who think: 'Who will bring me down to earth?'" [Obad 3]).

A positive use of this expression is rare, like YHWH's determination to show a favorable face despite the inherent flaw in human nature. In Jer 5:24 the negative introduction does not rule out an attempt in a positive direction ("They do not say: 'Let us fear YHWH our God who gives rain . . .'"). One characteristic of the good person who makes a cameo appearance in Ps 15 is the inner acknowledgment of truth (*wedōbēr ʾemet bilbābô*, v. 2). The rare use of a participle in this expression implies that truthfulness is habitual, just as a similar one in Obad 3 suggests an arrogant state of mind.

Qoheleth uses the expression under discussion eight times. In 2:1, 15; 3:17, 18 it takes the form *ʾāmartî ʾanî belibbî*, changing to *debartî ʾanî belibbî* in the second of two occurrences in 2:15. In 1:16, as stated earlier, it has a different preposition, *ʿim* standing alone. In 9:1 the verb *ntn* is followed by the preposition *ʾel* (to), yielding, "For all this, I committed to my mind . . . ."[42] Similarly, 8:16 has "When I set my mind to know wisdom . . . ." As was true of Gen 27:41, in which Esau contemplated murder, the expression is not rigid, for there a subject falls between the verb and *belibbô*. Qoheleth varies the preposition, using the prefix *be* as well as free-standing *ʿim* and *ʾel*. He also prefaces the expression with a direct object following a causative or emphatic *kî*. In Qoheleth's case, the expression is self-revelatory, its autobiographical form differing from the others, which are instances of imaginary mind reading.[43]

CONCLUSION

At best, the preceding exercise in intertextuality[44] demonstrates that Qoheleth was not alone in viewing existence as *hebel* and that others took note of the lack of justice where reward for labor was concerned. Above all, a close reading of Ps 39 shows that at least one independent thinker who was in some ways like Qoheleth risked an intimacy with YHWH that exposed his weakness and temerity. The psalmist journeyed from voluntary to obligatory silence, in between these hoping in vain[45] to be granted the status of *gēr* and *tôšāb*. In the end, he opted for nonexistence but nonetheless it freed him from chastisement.[46]

Notes

1. The existence of antithetic meanings for the verb *bārak* in the prologue to the book of Job rests on the two instances in which the antagonist assures YHWH that an afflicted servant will curse him to his face. The other five uses of the verb (four in the prologue and one in the epilogue) are better explained as the usual "bless." Only two of these are considered problematic. The wife urges Job to bless God and die, just as a condemned Achan was instructed to give glory to God, and Job thinks his children may have sinned inadvertently and then blessed YHWH without having atoned for the offense. This understanding of his words is more charitable than the suspicion that they have deliberately transgressed.

2. In addition to the standard commentaries, the following special studies of Ps 39 address specific issues: Otto Kaiser, "Psalm 39," *Gottes und der Menschen Weisheit*, BZAW 261; Berlin/New York: de Gruyter, 1998) 71–83; Richard J. Clifford, "What Does the Psalmist Ask for in Psalms 39:5 and 90:12?" *JBL* 119 (2000): 59–66; W. A. M. Beuken, "Psalm 39," *Heythrop Journal* 19 (1978): 1–11; Ellen F. Davis, "Prisoner of Hope," *The Art of Reading Scripture*, ed. E. F. Davis and Richard B. Hays (Grand Rapids: Eerdmans, 2003) 300–305.

3. "Conceal your heart, control your mouth" (Ptahhotep 618); "A man may be ruined by his tongue/Beware and you will do well" (Ani 7, 8); "Do not sever your heart from your tongue . . ." (Amenemope 10, 16, cf. Insinger 25, 21); "Keep firm your heart, steady your heart, do not steer with your tongue; If a man's tongue is the boat's rudder/The Lord of All is yet its pilot" (Amenemope 18, 3-5). "You may trip over your foot in the house of a great man; you should not trip over your tongue" (Ankhsheshonq 10, 7). Similar advice can be found in Mesopotamian wisdom and in Ahiqar.

4. On the biblical attitude to those who acted as if God were not, see James L. Crenshaw, *Defending God: Biblical Responses to the Problem of Evil* (Oxford & New York: Oxford University Press, 2005) 27–40, 203–208.

5. James T. Robinson, *Samuel Ibn Tibbon's Commentary on Ecclesiastes*, Texts and Studies in Medieval and Early Modern Judaism 20 (Tübingen: Mohr Siebeck, 2007) 112–41 explains the way Ibn Tibbon used dialectic to good effect.

6. I examined the formula *'al tōmar* and its peculiar relationship to theodicy in "The Problem of Theodicy in Sirach: On Human Bondage," *JBL* 94 (1975): 49–64 (=*Urgent Advice and Probing Questions: Collected Writings on Old Testament Wisdom* [Macon: Mercer University Press, 1995] 155–74).

7. The search for the primary meaning of *hebel* continues in Dominic Rudman, "The Use of *hebel* as an Indicator of Chaos in Ecclesiastes," 121–41 in A. Berlejung and P. Van Hecke, eds., *The Language of Qohelet in Its Context: Essays in Honour of Prof. A. Schoors on the Occasion of His Seventieth Birthday*, OLA 164 (Leuven: Peeters, 2007). Ethan Dor-Shav, "Ecclesiastes, Fleeting and Timeless," *Azure* 18 (5765/2004): 67–87 opts for vapor or mist (74).

8. *Brown-Driver Briggs*, 364, lists "shew inactivity" as a meaning for the hiphil of *ḥāšâ*.

9. That is, even the person who can stand transfixed is actually no more than a vapor.

10. As MT stands, the picture is that of a fantasm, an image that quickly slips away. I understand the *bet* as essential (as an image).

11. The elliptical style of the poet reaches a high point here. Its meaning conveys the utter futility of human enterprises that ultimately amount to nothing, for possessions succumb to time just like people.

12. "This double expression of existential complaint offers an exact frame to the core verse, 'My hope is in thee' (v. 8b) . . . this core verse functions like the prow of a ship in high seas" (330–31 in Samuel Terrien, *The Psalms: Strophic Structure and Theological Commentary* [Grand Rapids: Eerdmans, 2003]).

13. Although some interpreters understand this verse as present, it seems better to take it as the poet's reflecting back on a previous condition and offering a justification for silence, one that points straight to YHWH.

14. According to Berakot 32b, supplication moves on an ascending scale (prayer, crying aloud, tears). The last of these, tears, can pass through any door, for the gates of tears are always open. The psalmist, however, is less sanguine than some rabbis.

15. Robert Alter, *The Book of Psalms* (New York/London: W. W. Norton & Company, 2007) 140 sees this verse as an "instance of the so-called breakup pattern in which a hendiadys ('sojourner and settler' meaning 'resident alien') is split up with each of the component terms set into one of the two parallel versets."

16. Amos Hakam, *The Bible: Psalms with the Jerusalem Commentary*, vol. 1 (Jerusalem: Mosad Harav Kook, 2003) 308, n. 4 attributes this view to some commentators, although he thinks *nisʾab* means "certain, established."

17. Kaiser, "Psalm 39." He also relies heavily on uniformity of consonants in each colon.

18. Any attempt to ascertain the date of a biblical psalm requires decisions about so many unknowns as to render the conclusion highly tenuous, on which see James L. Crenshaw, *The Psalms: An Introduction* (Grand Rapids: Eerdmans, 2001) and "Foreword: The Book of Psalms and Its Interpreters," xix–xliv in Sigmund Mowinckel, *The Psalms in Israel's Worship* (Grand Rapids: Eerdmans, 2004).

19. H. A. Brongers, "Bemerkungenwerken zum Gebrauch des adverbialen *weʿattāh* im Alten Testament," *VT* 15 (1965): 289–99.

20. John Goldingay, *Psalms: Psalms 1–41*, vol. 1, Baker Commentary on the Old Testament Wisdom and Psalms (Grand Rapids: Baker Academic, 2006) 557–58 implausibly translated *hôdîʿenî* by "acknowledge" and thinks the poet is asking for strength to accept a short life.

21. Alter, *The Book of Psalms*, 137 thinks the dominance of triadic versets, as opposed to the usual dyadic, expresses a powerful psychological tension, introducing an element of surprise and destabilizing what has gone before it.

22. The numerous studies of this psalm have not exhausted its riches, on which see James L. Crenshaw, *The Psalms*, 109–27.

23. This is not the only instance of ellipsis in the psalm (cf. v. 6, "they hustle—a breath," and vv. 2a and 5b). On the basis of *mēhamôn* in Ps 37:16 and *hehāmôn* in 1 Chr 29:16, one could construe *yehemāyûn* as a distortion of an original reference to wealth.

24. Alter, *The Book of Psalms*, views the *mem* on *miṭṭôb* as one of deprivation, but this interpretation is unlikely since the silence is voluntary.

25. As late as 1Q412 15, the poet advises doors of protection for the tongue, and the epistle of James compares the tongue to a fire and considers it an instrument of poison (vv. 6-8), a small member that controls humans the way rudders guide ships. Here, too, the idea of bits in the mouths of horses is mentioned in the context of keeping the tongue in check.

26. James L. Crenshaw, "Deceitful Minds and Theological Dogma: Jer. 17:5-11," in *Prophets, Sages & Poets* (St. Louis: Chalice, 2006) 73–82, 222–24 (=*Utopia and Dystopia in Prophetic Literature*, ed. Ehud Ben Zvi [Helsinki: Finnish Exegetical Society; Göttingen: Vandenhoeck & Reuprecht, 2006] 105–21); and P. J. Tomson, "'There Is No One Who Is Righteous, not even One,': Kohelet 7, 20 in Pauline and Early Jewish Interpretation," 183–202 in *The Language of Qohelet in Its Context*.

27. Practitioners of various divinatory techniques sought to read the future and in doing so to gain both prestige and monetary profit. Apocalyptic literature takes a much wider sweep by focusing on changes of universal magnitude.

28. A text from Emar, Enlil, and Namzitarra, reckons life to be 120 years (cf. Gen 6:3). Like Qoheleth, this author sees life as fleeting; the closing lines read that "the days of man are approaching, day to day they verily decrease, year after year they verily decrease. One hundred twenty years are the years of mankind—verily it is their bane" (J. Klein, "The 'Bane' of Humanity: A Lifespan of One Hundred Twenty Years," *Acta Sumerologica* 12 [1990]: 57–70).

29. This shift mirrors that from silence to speech, perhaps also from trust to sharp attack.

30. 1 Chr 29:15 brings together several ideas that appear in Ps 39, specifically resident alien and sojourner, all our ancestors, days like a shadow, and absence of hope. The Epistle of Hebrews 11:13 applies the category of sojourners to a long list of biblical heroes. According to Lev 25:23, the earth belongs to YHWH, its inhabitants being sojourners and resident aliens.

31. See James L. Crenshaw, "Flirting with the Language of Prayer (Job 14:13-17," *Worship and the Hebrew Bible: Essays in Honor of John T. Willis*, ed. Patrick Graham, Rick Marrs, and Steven McKenzie, JSOT SS 284 (Sheffield: JSOT Press, 1999) 110–23 (=*Prophets, Sages & Poets*, 6–13, 201–203).

32. Rudman, "The Use of *hebel* as an Indicator of Chaos in Ecclesiastes," 121–22 and 133 does not include Ps 39:12, limiting the concrete use to two, and even then, he writes, "a figurative use is evident."

33. Deut 32:21 has *hebel* in parallelism with *lōʾ ʾēl*, suggesting that idols have no real vitality. Several examples of *hebel* emphasize the powerlessness of idols (Jer 10:3, 8, 15; 14:22; 16:19; Jonah 2:9). According to 2 Kgs 17:15, Israelites who turned to *hahebel* became worthless themselves (*wayyehbālû*).

34. The *mem* thus becomes the participial prefix to the verb *hālak*. Other interpreters think the word *beṣelem* derives from a root *ṣlm* and means shadow.

35. The exquisite poem in 1:4-11 begins with the clause *dôr hōlēl wedôr bāʾ* ("a generation dies [literally 'goes'] and another comes"). Similarly 6:4 says that the stillbirth "comes in futility and departs, its name covered by darkness."

36. On this negative particle, see James L. Crenshaw, "Qoheleth's Quantitative Language," 1–22 in *The Language of Qohelet in Its Context*; Antoon Schoors, *The Preacher Sought to Find Pleasing Words: A Study in the Language of Qohelet*, OLA 41 (Leuven: Peeters, 1992) 151f.; and Bo Isaksson, *Studies in the Language of Qoheleth with Special Emphasis on the Verbal System*, AUU: Studia Semitica Upsalensia, 10 (Uppsala, 1987) 172–74.

37. Goldingay, *Psalms*, vol. 1, 556 writes that "*ʿālam* never occurs to describe voluntary silence except as an attribute to YHWH's servant who is silent under attack (Isa 53:7), though Job also apparently kept silence for a week (2:13). The parallel verb *ḥāšâ* is likewise never used to describe voluntary silence except in Ecclesiastes' meditation (3:7)." The relevance of Job 2:13 escapes me, for it does not use the verb *ʿālam*.

38. Antoon Schoors, "God in Qoheleth," 251–70 in R. Brandscheidt and T. Mende, eds., *Schöpfungsplan und Heilsgeschichte: Festschrift für E. Haag* (Trier) and "Theodicy in Qoheleth," 375–409 in *Theodicy in the World of the Bible*, A. Laato and J. C. De Moor, eds. (Leiden/Boston: Brill, 2003).

39. The role of joy in Qoheleth is widely debated, with Norman Whybray and Norbert Lohfink leading the way to a positive understanding of joy as a divine gift. Others, like me, cannot reconcile the prevailing mood of the book and its haunting refrains that emphasize life's emptiness with anything approximating joy. For the opposite view, see Whybray, "Qoheleth, Preacher of Joy," *JSOT* 23 (1982): 87–98; Lohfink, "Qoheleth 5, 17-19—Revelation by Joy," *CBQ* 52 (1990): 625–35; and Ludger Schwienhorst-Schönberger, "Gottes Antwort in der Freude: Zur theologie göttlicher Gegenwart im Buch Kohelet," *Bibel und Kirche* 54 (1999): 156–63. On the problem, see Hans-Peter Müller, "Theonome skepsis und Lebensfreude—Zu Koh 1, 12-3, 15," *BZ* 30 (1986): 1–19.

40. Gen 8:21; 17:17; 24:45; 27:41; Deut 7:17; 8:17; 9:4; 15:9; 18:21; 1 Sam 27:1; 1 Kgs 12:26; Pss 10:6, 11, 13; 14:1; 53:2; 77:6; Qoh 1:16; 2:1, 15; 3:17, 18; Isa 14:13; 47:8, 10, Jer 5:24; 13:22, Zeph 1:12; Ob 3; Est 6:6. Qoh 9:l has *natattî ʾel libbî*.

41. *A Time to Tear Down & a Time to Build Up: A Rereading of Ecclesiastes* (Grand Rapids: Eerdmans, 1999) 176. ("Note how this heart is treated as a distinct 'person' in 1:17 and 7:25," presumably in addition to 2:1.) In his discussion of the heart in Qoheleth's thought, Fox refers to a similar concept in the Egyptian "Memphite Theology" (77–78).

42. Arguing that this and related expressions (*nātan lelibbî*) imply intentional movement, Pierre Van Hecke, "The Verbs *raʾâ* and *šemaʿ* in the Book of Qohelet: A Cognitive-Semantic Perspective," 203–20 (here 215, n. 51) in *The Language of Qohelet in Its Context* considers it less likely that listening, a passive state, is meant. He overlooks the possibility that listening as an intellectual activity is highly intentional.

43. The extent of detachment in Qoheleth has assumed fresh perspective as a result of Fox's interpretation of the frame narrative as a device that distinguishes a speaker, Qoheleth, from the narrator who keeps at a safe distance because of Qoheleth's radical teaching.

44. The claim that the historical paradigm has been replaced by a literary one may be exaggerated, for even the current interest in reception history combines both history and literature. The extensive intertextual studies by André Robert in the first half of the twentieth century were inspired by an interest in the influence of earlier literature on successive generations, not by Julia Kristeva.

45. Hope, that is, can be sustained only as long as there is life. The psalmist's final words of death and non-being emphatically authenticate the claim that human existence is fleeting, like breath itself.

46. In this analysis of Ps 39, I have omitted the superscription that mentions Jeduthun, like Ps 62, which also distinguishes words and thoughts (v. 5). According to 2 Chr 5:12, Jeduthun, a Levite singer along with Asaph and Heman, was present when Solomon dedicated the temple.

chapter six

QOHELETH, FLAWED GENIUS*

If some people are unable, for whatever reason, to heed Qoheleth's advice to enjoy life, and if death threatens to cut short the pleasure others find, is there a serious flaw in his fundamental teaching? The epilogues in 12:9-14 appear to suggest exactly that. They comprise two triads of verses (12:9-11 and 12:12-14) that give important information about the speaker and either offer a summary of his insights or suggest an alternative teaching to what has appeared before.[1]

A GUIDE TO READERS

Apparently someone thought readers of the body of the book would need guidance in a number of matters: who was Qoheleth, whom did he teach, what was his method of working, what was the effect of his teaching, did he go too far, and did he leave out anything significant?

The first question was easily answered. He was a wise man, a *ḥākām*. The word that functions both as a noun and an adjective often simply refers to a person who possessed expertise in any number of crafts or who was especially astute.[2] Sometimes, however, *ḥākām* indicates professional status in a guild, as here. Both uses, the singular form in 12:9 and the plural in 12:11, refer to Qoheleth's membership in an elite class of sages.[3]

---

* The original appeared in James L. Crenshaw, *Qoheleth: The Ironic Wink* (Columbia: University of South Carolina Press, 2013) 93–107, 143–48. Reprinted with permission.

Identification in this exclusive group suggests that people should listen to what he has to say.

We note that this biographical comment is silent about the earlier claim of kingship, and it does not repeat the Solomonic fiction. Instead, it merely associates the author with sages whose sayings were treasured and therefore preserved in writing like those in the book of Proverbs.

The second question, "Whom did he teach?" provokes a surprising response. Rather than young boys, the expected answer given the usual student body in the ancient Near East[4] and presumably in Israel, the word *hāʿām* appears. Qoheleth taught the people, it states, as if to say that he resembled a peripatetic philosopher in Greek society. His teachings, that is, were aimed at ordinary adults rather than children.[5] We see here, then, a democratizing tendency in education.

How did he go about this innovative endeavor? Just like all effective instructors, he listened carefully to others, engaged in rigorous research, arranged arguments for maximum effect, and hunted for the most appealing vocabulary that did not require him to sacrifice the truth.[6] A combination of logos, ethos, and pathos may be implied.[7] He valued rational thinking, backed by his own integrity of character and motivated by strong conviction that gave his word a mesmerizing effect of emptiness, like the universe itself.

This last point is a deduction based on the necessity to put a positive spin on his teachings. Truth is painful at times, and what Qoheleth taught was especially disturbing. That is why the comparison of his teachings to nails and goads was felt to be necessary. Just as goads inflict pain on domestic animals, Qoheleth's words bring dismay. Still, the goads work to make oxen behave in a desired way, and are therefore beneficial at least to humans. Moreover, Qoheleth's insights into the nature of reality are believed to be reliable, like securely planted nails that will not give way under heavy pressure.

The obscure point about collections deriving from one shepherd is capable of at least three interpretations. (1) It may be a metaphor for the divine source of such collections. In the ancient Near East the epithet shepherd often refers to a deity,[8] just as it does in the Bible.[9] Against this reading, however, is the probability that biblical wise men reached their conclusions on their own without disclosure of hidden secrets from God.[10] (2) The expression "one shepherd" may indicate Solomonic authorship. This interpretation, too, seems unlikely because of the wide divergence of Qoheleth's teachings from those attributed to Solomon in the book of

Proverbs. (3) The more likely meaning of the phrase about a shepherd takes *'eḥād* ("one") to indicate "any."[11] The point would be that goads used by any shepherd were a necessary evil. Similarly, Qoheleth's words stung the hearer while embodying useful information. It was disturbing to be reminded that all human achievements amount to a huge zero and that God is indifferent to goodness.[12]

What, then, was the firmly planted nail? Was it the knowledge that everything under the sun was *hebel* or that we should eat, drink, and be merry? Perhaps the metaphor should not be pressed beyond the mere assertion that Qoheleth's words were at the same time painful and useful. There seems to be no doubt that the point was taken to mean something akin to the perennial town/gown conflict. That seems to be the purpose of the sharp warning in 12:12 ("Beyond these, my son, be warned: the making of many scrolls has no end, and much learning is weariness to the flesh").[13]

We need not restrict ourselves to ancient Greece to witness the fear of untraditional teachings, although the death sentence imposed on Socrates shows how far even a highly cultured society will go to protect the innocent from what is thought to be dangerous. In the ecclesial community, the treatment of Galileo centuries ago and its modern corollary, the demonizing of Darwin, reveal the tenacity of a refusal to let the intellect roam freely in the quest for truth. So does the contemporary hue and cry over sex education for children. Sadly, some parts of the Bible sanction this limiting of intellectual pursuits, most notably Ben Sira's warning against investigating areas that have not been commanded.

> Do not seek what is too difficult for you nor investigate things beyond your power. Ponder what has been commanded, because the hidden is not your concern. Do not meddle in matters beyond your ken, for more than you can understand has been shown you. Conceit has led many astray. Wrong thinking has impaired their judgment. (Sir 3:21-24)

We do not know what kind of speculation Ben Sira disliked, although several possibilities come to mind. He may have viewed the probing of questions like those in the book of Job dangerous and unproductive. Alternatively, he may have considered speculation about the end times and astral influences a waste of time and energy.[14] The context suggests yet another possibility: he may have thought that the mere pursuit of the unknown led to intellectual pride. Whatever his reasons, Ben Sira veered from the position of the unknown composer of Prov 25:2 who wrote that "God's glory is to conceal things, but the glory of kings is to search them out."

Once the exploration of the unknown was pronounced off limits to young thinkers, it was a tiny step to the stifling of intellectual pursuits altogether. That is precisely the attitude that the author of 2 Esdras, also called 4 Ezra, highlights.[15] Remarkably, this resistance to asking difficult questions is attributed to the angel Uriel who has become the divine spokesman.[16]

The angel's argument rests on the undeniable fact that the human intellect often comes up against things that are destined to remain hidden, and that a similar limitation prevents people from accomplishing everything they set out to do. The limits that Uriel mentions involve simple things that we encounter every day as well as things outside the spatial and temporal realms.

> Go, weigh for me the weight of fire, or measure for me a blast of wind, or call back for me the day that is past . . . . How many dwellings are in the heart of the sea, or how many streams are at the source of the deep, or how many streams are above the firmament, or which are the exits of Hades, or which are the entrances of paradise? (2 Esd 4:5, 7)[17]

In short, the angel discourages Ezra from probing deeply into the ways by which God governs the world. Neither the delay in implementing justice nor the specific time frame for setting things right is, according to Uriel, a legitimate subject of investigation. Ezra is expected to trust God even in the face of apparent neglect of the covenanted people. Such suppressing of intellectual curiosity inevitably leads to suspicion of doubt, which comes to expression in Wisdom of Solomon: "Because he is found by those who do not put him to the test, and manifests himself to those who do not distrust him" (Wis 1:2).

Complete trust is expected regardless of circumstances. To question the divine ways, which implies an element of doubt, is said to make one incapable of understanding sacred mysteries. The author of the epistle of James applies this idea to explain why prayer sometimes fails: "But ask in faith, never doubting, for the one who doubts is like a wave of the sea, driven and tossed by the wind, for the doubter, being double-minded and unstable in every way, must not expect to receive anything from the Lord" (Jas 1:6-8).

Something else stands out in Qoheleth's disclaimer about the fruit of intellectual endeavors. Suddenly, the audience shifts from the people (*hā'ām*) to young boys, the probable students addressed in Prov 1–9 by a teacher who may also be their real parent. The references to both mother and father make it likely that the setting is the family, even if "my son" means "my student." In light of the fact that scribal schools consisted largely of children of the teacher, the instructions and sayings may be perfectly at home there. Understandably, the strong verb "be warned" in this context carries a serious message that students ignore at their peril.[18]

Neither point in the warning has anything really new. Scribes both far and near busily occupied themselves with the task of producing literature. The written word took several forms and appeared in different media: cuneiform writing (wedge-shaped symbols), primarily on clay tablets in Mesopotamia and at Ugarit; hieroglyphics and demotic writing (cursive) on papyrus in Egypt; and alphabetic Hebrew and Aramaic in Israel on leather, occasionally on copper and stone too. The extensive library at Qumran in the vicinity of the Dead Sea provides definitive evidence of the truth in the claim that the production of written texts was endless.

Curiously, the brief anecdote in 4:13-16 about a ruler who came from poverty or imprisonment to the throne, reminiscent of the fictional story of Joseph's rise to a seat of authority, uses both the verb for being advised or warned (*hizzāhēr*) and the expression *ʾēn qēṣ* ("there was no end to"). In that context, however, *ḥākām* has the usual sense of expertise, in this case, at statecraft, which neither poverty nor imprisonment had dulled. Even more surprisingly, youth is not viewed as an impediment to wise rule and advanced years do not automatically guarantee wisdom. This attitude toward the young is closer to Greek thought than to Hebraic.

The effect of cutting off debate is to render opponents silent. The victory, however, is Pyrrhic. That is the force of the summation in verse 13a. "End of the matter; everything has been heard."[19] What a bold claim. Precious little in Qoheleth's teaching reads like a closed book.

Matters are left tentative, issues unresolved, as if challenging hearers and readers to carry the argument further. True, Qoheleth makes absolutist claims about everything being *hebel*, but he often examines competing perceptions without tipping his hand about his preference. For him, there was no end, for each answer opened up another question, or two.

Has everything been heard? What wise man or woman would dare make such an assertion? And if "heard" has the sense of "obeying" as is frequently the case, the sentence is surely an exaggeration. Qoheleth has not made disciples of everyone, and there is little evidence that his views have ruled the day.[20] Quite the contrary, for the author of Wisdom of Solomon raises a powerful protest over the expression of *carpe diem* that characterizes Qoheleth's teaching. This sharp polemic against living for the moment shows how easy it is to misrepresent an opponent's view. Nowhere does Qoheleth voice such crass violence in the cause of self-indulgence as that articulated in Wis 2:10-12: "Let us oppress the righteous poor man; let us not spare the poor widow, or regard the gray hairs of the aged. But let our might be our law of right, for what is weak proves itself to be useless." Enjoyment for Qoheleth was made possible, if at all, by hard work and divine favor. It had nothing to do with oppressing defenseless members of society.

Did Qoheleth go too far? From the perspective of whoever wrote the imperative, "Fear God and keep his commandments," and claimed that these two activities were the sum total of humanity,[21] we may deduce that at least one person believed Qoheleth had wandered far beyond the essential knowledge about how one should behave. Instead of probing the secrets of the world around us, we should, so this individual believed, concentrate on religious duty.[22]

It is not as if Qoheleth neglected the first of these. Avoiding anything that would anger God was, he thought, in one's best interest. Fearing God was thus an absolute necessity. Moreover, the expression "fear God" seems to have carried a basic sense of dread. In Qoheleth's view, fearing God resembles the awe inherent to experiencing the numinous, a simultaneous attraction to and revulsion of the holy that Rudolf Otto named "mysterium tremendum et fascinans."[23] The prophet Isaiah illustrates the feeling exactly when reacting to an experience of holiness: "Woe is me, I am lost . . . for my eyes have seen the King, the LORD of hosts" (Isa 6:5).

The second imperative, "keep his commandments," goes beyond anything that Qoheleth taught. He is completely silent about the Mosaic legislation. In this matter, Qoheleth differed radically from Ben Sira, who identified the speculation about personified Wisdom with the law handed down by Moses.[24] Neither Ben Sira nor Qoheleth, however, mentions specific commandments. Ben Sira does refer to the obligation to support the priests who administered the cult, and it is possible to posit certain Mosaic teachings as the motivation for some of Ben Sira's remarks about parental respect and charitable giving, but other reasons for both are readily available. It is much more difficult to find anything in Qoheleth's teaching that was motivated by the commandments.

Qoheleth seems to have been fond of universal claims; he held an all-or-nothing attitude. The conclusion that fearing God and keeping the commandments somehow comprised the entirety of humanity ("the whole of man") accords with the tendency to universalize. What does this mean? Every duty imposed on a person from outside, or the complete potential open to anyone who acts autonomously rather than from external compulsion? Voluntary action comes closer to Qoheleth's views elsewhere in the book, for he rejects the comforting belief that God rewards the obedient worshiper.

If the remarks about a divine judgment in the body of the book come from Qoheleth, they provide a reason for adding the twofold imperative about fearing God and keeping the commandments. At some unknown time a shift occurs in which the old view of death as God's judgment on individuals is challenged by belief in a universal assize when all people will be held responsible for their actions. In the book of Joel this judgment day is believed to be a time when the nations who have persecuted the Judeans will be punished severely.

In due time, the final judgment is projected onto the stage of eternity and individualized. The two concepts, immediate judgment at death and a delayed judgment until some future moment when all will face their Maker, continue in New Testament times. The parable about the rich man and Lazarus reflects the idea of an immediate judgment at death, while the Apostle Paul thinks in terms of a day of universal judgment at a date to be determined by God alone.

As everyone knows, the very thought of being judged for one's deeds acted as a powerful motive for disciplined behavior. In case anyone lacked the knowledge about what that constituted, the answer was available: "Be religious and observe the teachings attributed to Moses." The word for commandments, miṣwôth, probably has this restricted meaning, although it could be more general. In that case, it refers to the mandates issued by wise teachers, of whom Qoheleth was one. Even a limited understanding of the Hebrew word poses difficulty, for it is unlikely that this editor intended readers to observe the whole body of ritual enjoined in the Bible. Lacking further instruction, how would readers have kept this command? We do not know.

The final epilogue concludes by elaborating on this imagined judgment: "Surely God will bring every work into judgment, concerning every secret, good or bad." With this warning, the earlier advice that Qoheleth gives about following the desires of eyes and mind is exposed for what it is, like all deeds in the last judgment. Unlike God's work, which has been shown to be mysterious and even painful, at least for some people, human deeds are subject to scrutiny by a higher power. This idea is not lost to Ben Sira, who warns his students that the Lord will reveal their secrets and overthrow them before the whole congregation (Sir 1:30). A moment's reflection exposes the dilemma presented by the prospect of bringing every deed to light. If Qoheleth is right that God is actually indifferent to human aspirations to live a virtuous life, why this sudden turnaround? Either he has changed his mind about divine arbitrariness or someone else is the author of the epilogue. Furthermore, if God treats everyone without regard to conduct, how can anyone prepare for a day of judgment? A consistent God who made known the divine will for humans would enable them to clean up their act so that airing their deeds would not be shameful.

Regardless of the real nature of the epilogues—a framing device or editorial glosses—they illustrate the dramatic impact of Qoheleth's teachings. He has either exposed the true limits of wisdom or he has shown its transformative power. For many interpreters, Qoheleth exemplifies wisdom's bankruptcy,[25] its inability to answer ultimate questions. In him, the mind has come up against the unknown and unknowable. To be sure, the intellect is capable of answering many questions, as Qoheleth clearly demonstrates. Nevertheless, it can do no more than touch the outermost edges of the hidden mysteries of God.[26] Unaided, the intellect leaves humans at the mercy of a power over which they have no control. Their vulnerability makes them receptive to an alternative belief system. That is why revelation fares so well in the ancient world. Answers are available, according to this worldview. One need only listen for a divine voice.

For other interpreters, Qoheleth demonstrates wisdom's resiliency, its openness to alternative views.[27] From this perspective, wisdom opens new vistas, all the while correcting itself in the light of fresh discoveries and failed explanations. Far from exhibiting the weakness of the intellect, Qoheleth reveals its crowning achievement. Always ready to alter his views, Qoheleth pursued questions and let the answers correct all preconceived notions.[28] This latter point is nicely illustrated by his brief story about a poor but wise man.

POOR BUT WISE (QOH 9:13-16)

The sages who composed the sayings that make up the several collections in the book of Proverbs constructed a fictional world in which intellectual prowess and resolve of will were thought to guarantee success. The latter was measured by tangible qualities such as wealth, health, progeny, and status. By acquiring the virtues of timing, eloquence, patience, and integrity, individuals believed they could influence their destiny for good. Those who refused to shape character in this way were said to have brought misfortune upon themselves. The wise who promoted this optimistic literary construct were divided over the means by which action produced favorable or unfavorable results. Sometimes their sayings imply that deeds carry within themselves appropriate consequences, while at other times they seem to attribute both reward and punishment to deity. On rare occasions, they suggest that the divine role is merely that of facilitator, like a midwife who assists the delivery of an infant.[29]

All three modes of matching deed and consequence rest on an assumption that human beings and deity are fundamentally alike. Without a principle of similarity,[30] there could be no knowledge of divinity apart from special disclosure. Such revelation could only initiate from above, since analogy from human thoughts and actions would inevitably abort. The supreme fiction of an orderly universe in which justice prevails arises out of this belief in a correspondence between human and divine character, it being taken for granted that deity valued truth and justice in the same way good people did.

What happens, however, when this comforting view that women and men are made in the divine image (*beṣelem ʾelōhîm*) is shattered by the conviction that the deity is responsible for shameful acts that are more accurately described as bestial than as humane?[31] That is precisely the situation in which Job finds himself when confronted by a deity he no longer recognizes. It is also the context for Qoheleth's philosophical search for a more permanent and tangible meaning in life than *hebel*. The shifting worldview either precipitated a crisis or served as catalyst for the creation of a more reliable perspective on the world.[32] Either way, the era may correctly be called axial.[33] The social causes for the vanishing dream among sages are complex, as we can gather from an incident that made a lingering impact on Qoheleth.

Shaking the Foundations

> This also I have observed[34]—wisdom[35] under the sun, and personally significant. A tiny village, sparsely populated, yet a great king came to it, surrounded it, and built mighty siege-works[36] against it. There was found[37] in it a poor man [but] wise, and he could have rescued[38] the city by means of his wisdom but no one thought about that poor man. I say: "Wisdom is superior to strength, although the wisdom of the poor [man] was scorned, his words unheard." (Qoh 9:13-16)

An accusative of specification, *ḥokmāh* ("wisdom") calls attention to the particular anomaly being introduced. The introductory *gam* implies that it does not stand alone ("this *also*"), but it is unclear just what antecedent instances of wisdom Qoheleth has in mind. The immediate context[39] offers two very different insights: (1) the fastest runner does not always win a race, nor does the strongest person necessarily prevail in battle; and (2) wise, understanding, and informed people do not always receive bread, riches, and favor. The reason: chance may come into play, rendering null and void the qualities on which humans rely for favorable outcomes. The images of fish and fowl being caught in a loathsome net or trap signify a grim outcome for humans.

Hence Qoheleth's language of personal observation brings home the earlier point and makes smooth transition to the familiar threat posed by unchecked power. Thematic words highlight sage and wisdom, here discovered in the unlikeliest of places. A peasant[40] possesses wisdom; the ultimate position of *ḥākām* almost invites readers to imagine an adversative (poor *but* wise). In his case, the acquisition of wisdom has not yielded its anticipated harvest.[41] Wise and therefore prosperous has become poor *but* wise. Contrasting words, great and small, describe competing factions and build up certain expectations with respect to who will win this conflict.

A great king is the subject of at least three verbs in succession. Although normal Hebrew syntax implies that the fourth verb has the same subject as the preceding three verbs, exceptions do occur.[42] Furthermore, Qoheleth's linguistic usage frequently goes its own way. One may therefore read *ûmāṣā'* as impersonal ("one found"), which makes more narrative sense than thinking that the king who was overseeing the siege could somehow have discovered an intelligent commoner residing inside the wall of the town, and moreover that his advice would have swayed a king to spare a city he was determined to pillage.[43]

Does the poor but wise man do anything, or is he merely acted upon? One's reading of the verb indicating an act of saving reflects a decision about which of the two antecedent points this story illustrates. A potential understanding of the verb ("he could have rescued") accentuates the statement that intelligence does not necessarily produce beneficial results. An actual reading ("he saved") emphasizes the observation that the swift and strong are not always assured victory.[44] If the poor but wise man delivered the city under siege, the populace was singularly ungrateful, and if no one remembered him, how could Qoheleth have heard of the incident? Moreover, Qoheleth's memory would negate the denial that anyone remembered him, unless the story is more personal than meets the eye.[45] If the city fell to the great king, the people's failure to think about a possible rescuer illustrates the fatal flaw of sages: dependence on others' acceptance of their wisdom. Notably, the adjective *ḥākām* is lacking in the end, where only "that poor man" appears.

Qoheleth's personalization of his anecdote, "therefore I said," reasserts conventional belief that intelligence is superior to strength only to controvert it with the reminder that the peasant's wisdom was despised and his advice went unheeded. The two "better than" proverbs that follow this anecdote contrast shouts of a ruler among fools with the words of the wise that are quietly heeded (and spoken?) and declare wisdom to be better than implements of war, although like a little fire in proverbial lore,[46] a single errant one can destroy a lot of good. Throughout this section, "time and affliction" hover in the background, like nets and traps.

The requirement of verisimilitude has guided the analysis of Qoheleth's example-story to this point. In all likelihood, however, it is a product of his fertile imagination,[47] just like that in 4:13-16, where another poor but wise youth is deemed better than an old but foolish king who does not know how to be instructed any longer. This "rags to riches" story remotely recalls elements of the narrative about Joseph, although the stress now falls on fading loyalty. Here too conventional wisdom is turned on its head, for age is no longer associated with sagacity nor youthfulness with lack of understanding.

With a single stroke of the pen the rhetoric in 9:13-16 becomes one of erasure;[48] expectations vanish like smoke or mist (*hebel*). A tiny village that has every right to rest securely like Laish in Judg 18:7 found itself at the mercy of a king bent on breaching its defenses, and a commoner stood out as one possessing extraordinary intelligence of a tactical nature. While the deity may be able to frustrate best-laid plans for battle, the determining force in the story about a poor but wise man is chance, and its essential characteristic is lethal.

Perhaps this brief anecdote illustrates the point I wish to make about an Axial Age better than anything else in Qoheleth's profound reflections about the nature of things, for it concerns beliefs about the good life and about power. It is precisely here that the greatest threat to the sapiential view of the world rests. The abuse of power and its effect on the innocent bring to naught every hope for security, the necessary precondition for successful living. Once the deity is no longer thought to exercise control over the course of human events, lawlessness naturally follows. Catastrophic disasters like the destruction of Jerusalem threaten long-held convictions about a just deity and lead to a new concept of divinity as remote and hidden, if not altogether alien.[49]

A corollary of this sea change in the concept of deity is agnosticism, which has serious implications for the traditional view of reward and punishment. The disappearance of universal moral order undermines wisdom's *raison d'etre*. In earlier times the deity's glory is said to have consisted in concealing things (or words), a king's glory in finding them out. In such a world, sages imagine themselves in the service of, and even in the role of, royalty. With Qoheleth, that exalted position is reduced to a farce (1:12–2:26).[50] In this new context, life's grandeur has faded, leaving loathsome back-breaking toil and its meager yield (2:18a).[51]

Two words, *ḥinnām* ("without cause") and *hebel*, signify this fundamental transformation in viewing the world. One derives from the prose introduction to the book of Job and the other is Qoheleth's favorite expression for reality. The first, *ḥinnām*, explodes the comfortable assumption that the universe operates according to a calculable moral principle. In its place, the adversary substitutes an absence of cause, in other words, gratuitous action devoid of any discernible reason. The second, *hebel*, robs human conduct of any gain in the final analysis, rendering life totally futile and frequently absurd.[52]

It is not necessary to document the traditional understanding of reality that the authors of Job and Qoheleth undercut by these two important concepts, disinterested righteousness (*ḥinnām*) and futility (*hebel*). It is embodied in the sacred texts that were gradually emerging in exilic times, especially the Deuteronomic interpretation of causation that pervades priestly, prophetic, and apocalyptic literature as well as the book of Proverbs and the lament tradition. Its most succinct expression occurs in Ps 37:25: "I have been young and also [am] old, but I have not seen the righteous forsaken or his offspring searching for bread." A proper society, by this standard, is one in which the deity enforces a strict system of measured cause and effect. In the psalmist's mind, this is exactly the kind of moral order sustained by the sovereign whom his poetry honors.

Such a simplistic interpretation of human events pronounces judgment on the poor for ignoring instruction (Prov 13:18) and on the sick for religious offense, as Job's friends do. Obedience to divine instruction brings blessing, hence wealth (Prov 10:22); disobedience brings curse, according to this way of thinking. It applies both to society and to individuals, at least in official narratives that record the nation's history. Its power rests in a persuasive logic that appeals to utopian dreams, easily reinforced by "testimonials" accumulated over time in which the theory seems to work.[53]

Now and again astute thinkers broke free from this type of reasoning enough to acknowledge an occasional wise person among the poor ("A rich man may consider himself intelligent but a perceptive poor man finds him out," Prov 28:11). More commonly, popular wisdom emphasized the vulnerability of the poor and the ease by which they were either ignored or treated contemptuously (Prov 18:23). Therefore, kindness to the poor was viewed with favor inasmuch as the creator had fashioned both the affluent and the impoverished (Prov 14:31; 17:5; 19:17; 22:2).

The radical thinker Qoheleth questioned the very premises of traditional wisdom when insisting that despite claims to the contrary a *ḥākām* simply cannot know (8:17). Although a proper time for everything exists, in Qoheleth's estimation, the deity has made it impossible for anyone to discover it (3:11).[54] Wisdom may have an advantage over folly, but it is only relative. In the end, wisdom yields no lasting profit because death cancels all supposed gain. Everything therefore is futile and shepherding wind (1:14b). The decisive factor governing human lives is chance, another name for a distant deity's arbitrary conduct that is wholly oblivious to a moral norm.

Societal Changes

What social realities contributed to Qoheleth's dismantling of the sages' traditional understanding of theology and anthropology? Answers to this question vary, but three things stand out above the rest, one economic, another political, and a third institutional.[55] In chapter 2 I discussed Qoheleth's historical context. Here I emphasize the social implications of foreign hegemony and the resulting second-class citizenship into which his compatriots had been thrown by a world that seemed to be spinning out of control. Three words capture the social factors succinctly: affluence, revenue, and inheritance.

A. Affluence. An unprecedented economic volatility may explain Qoheleth's lingering concern for profit, together with his anecdotal references to a miser, a loser at investing, and the hidden costs of an increase in possessions. In a society where money answers everything, the primary goal was to manage wealth wisely. The singular advantages of a monetary economy included, among other things, the availability of disposable funds, a type of liquidity that was unknown under pastoral nomadism and subsistence farming. The radical changes introduced by Persian and Ptolemaic rulers[56] presented rare opportunities to acquire vast sums of money but also to lose heavily in an unpredictable market. The resulting shifts in class and the social turmoil created by reversals of fortune brought secondary effects as well, particularly changes in status. In general, three distinct levels existed in Yehud: (1) the affluent, (2) a retainer class, and (3) the peasantry. Belonging to the first group were the higher rank within the priesthood, some scribes, wealthy landowners, tax "farmers" and collectors, and foreign officials. The lower clergy and ordinary scribes made up the majority of the second level, and day laborers who toiled to eke out a living comprised the third. A certain restlessness characterized all three. The rich, never satisfied, feared the loss of their treasures; the middle class hungered for more; and, lacking any champion, the peasantry recognized their vulnerability on many fronts.

B. Revenue. The depoliticization of the priestly class greatly reduced their power from that of Ezra roughly two centuries earlier.[57] Their waning influence can be measured by Qoheleth's virtual silence about them and their responsibilities during the era when the temple cult was believed to have assured divine blessing for an entire people. Like prophets, about whom he says nothing, priests and sages alike depended on esteem among citizens for status. Disenfranchisement and depoliticization brought alienation[58] and relative deprivation, disturbing the natural rhythm of society.

This disenchantment, a rupture in the symbolic universe to which Qoheleth bears witness, was precipitated by governmental policy inaugurated by Persian rulers and continued during Ptolemaic times. Throughout the provinces, spies rendered the articulation of any seditious thought a virtual death sentence. An elaborate bureaucracy involving supervisors, each with a more authoritative boss, extended all the way to the king himself. Their responsibility mainly involved the gathering of revenues, often achieved by farming out taxes to others who increased the official tax burden for personal gain. The potential for abuse of privilege was huge.

Qoheleth's lament that justice was absent from the judiciary reveals corruption at the core. Royal grants to favorites, the military, and temple personnel were handed out arbitrarily. Proprietary rights over one's portion were threatened by those on a higher rung of the social ladder. The heavy levy of taxes was felt most keenly by peasants, especially in years of drought or diseases that reduced the yield from grain fields and olive orchards. A bad year might require peasants to borrow seed money for the next year's planting, often at an exorbitant rate of interest, and failure to repay debt frequently turned them or their children into slaves until the slate was clean.[59]

In addition, the requirement to fulfill military duty when the foreign ruler conscripted the populace threatened those who could ill afford a temporary or, worse, permanent loss of valuable workers in the fields and vineyards.

C. Inheritance. Naturally, the most exposed institution was the family. Although Qoheleth says little about it,[60] he often refers to the practice of transferring possessions to an heir at death. His remarks about this process lack any hint of satisfaction over being able to ease the lot of succeeding generations. Worse still, they imply that individuals cannot know whether recipients of largesse will be deserving or not. Qoheleth's language contains not the slightest indication of intimate knowledge within the confines of a household, unlike the prose conclusion to the book of Job. For Qoheleth, the inability to hold on to hard-earned possessions is conclusive evidence of life's utter absurdity.

The major figure within households receives no praise from Qoheleth, who urges her counterpart to enjoy life with "a woman whom you love." This curious language leaves the object of pleasure unclear, whether one's wife or more probably a lover like the girl in Song of Songs.[61] The unflattering assessment of women in 7:26-29 contrasts markedly with the glowing praise in Prov 31:10-31. Qoheleth does not say that all women are more bitter than death, for he describes a particular type of woman.[62] Even if in 7:26 he quotes a proverbial saying, the validity of which he questions, Qoheleth nevertheless proceeds to pronounce a wholly negative judgment on women and an almost equally absolute assessment of men. As we have seen, such a low opinion of human nature in general is well known in the Bible and in ancient Near Eastern literature.[63] Sadly, misogyny raised its ugly head in much of the literature of the ancient Near East and became even more obnoxious in Greco-Roman texts.

A Remote Deity and Its Consequences

It is noteworthy that Qoheleth never personifies wisdom. In this regard, he follows the author of the book of Job, whose distancing of deity invites mediation.[64] Accordingly, the poetic dialogue introduces three mysterious figures who Job hopes will come to his assistance (a mediator, a witness, and a redeemer), and Elihu refers to additional ones, an angel and a messenger. Qoheleth's deity is even more remote, but the gulf between creator and creatures is unbroken.[65] For him, "God is in heaven and you are on earth, therefore let your words be few" (5:1b). With respect to power, divine or human, Qoheleth's primary concern assumes a defensive stance, a caution grounded in precedent.

Unlike the teachers in the book of Proverbs, Qoheleth never uses "my son" with reference to his audience.[66] Its only occurrence is in the second epilogue. His heightened egotism[67] and general aloofness have led some interpreters to think of him as unmarried, and his compassion for oppressed members of society has been questioned. Although a vibrant intellectual group is reflected in his remarks about hermeneutics, he acknowledges that intellectual pursuits take a heavy toll and ultimately are not worth the effort. Why then does he take such pains to develop a vocabulary that enables him to engage in philosophical reflection about the meaning of human existence?[68] Why, too, does he begin to think about the cognitive process? In him readers are far removed from village life presumed in the older collections in the book of Proverbs. Strangely, however, he offers little evidence of residing in an urban environment and even less proclivity for religious practice while living in the city that boasts a functioning temple and cultic personnel.

In short, Qoheleth's *hebel* thinking helped bring about the complete destruction of a sacred canopy already gravely threatened by *ḥinnām* reasoning in the book of Job. The combination of economic, political, and familial circumstances enabled Qoheleth to achieve a significant breakthrough with respect to the limits of knowledge. His rhetorical "who knows?" and "no one knows" and "one cannot find" reminded listeners and later readers of human vulnerability before death and a remote, arbitrary deity.[69] His world evoked a concession that everything under the sun was *hebel*, even the momentary pleasures available to a lucky few. For them, too, the darkness of Sheol awaited, symbolized by chance, his word for fate. The plight of the oppressed, for whom there were no comforters, was actually universal.

Attempts to Counter ḥinnām and hebel Thinking

Such a world devoid of the comfort of a merciful deity was intolerable to the sages who followed. Ben Sira went to great lengths to highlight divine compassion. His incorporation of Israel's narrative tradition made it possible to document divine mercy in sacred memory. To minimize the impact of Qoheleth's concept of a remote deity, he took up the earlier myth of personified *ḥokmāh*, which he nationalized while simultaneously opening it up to all people through linkage to the story of creation. His identification of *ḥokmāh* with the Mosaic Torah was an extraordinary claim that Israel's intellectual legacy had universal application. At the same time, as we have seen, Ben Sira freely used arguments of Stoic philosophy to defend divine justice, specifically the existence of opposites in nature that assured a principle of exact reward and retribution. Above all, however, he replaced Qoheleth's agnosticism with fervent praise.[70]

The unknown author of Wisdom of Solomon, thoroughly Hellenized and writing in elevated Greek like the prologue to Sirach, adopted rhetoric to defend Israel's deity against charges of cruelty to Egyptians. In doing so, he used the story of the exodus as pivot, showing how in it the same natural elements were harmful to Egyptians and beneficial to the people they had wrongly enslaved. Within a mercy dialogue[71] he argued that Israel's God acted with restraint, giving the Egyptians ample opportunity to repent, and with a punishment characterized by measure for measure. This author even added an erotic dimension to speculation about *ḥokmāh* already present in Prov 8:22-31 and Sir 4:18; 14:20-27, but now linked to King Solomon who had taken her as wife.

Whereas Ben Sira had considered death less odious than Qoheleth viewed it, the author of Wisdom of Solomon could not pretend that it was inconsequential. The demise of a child was for him a wrenching dilemma, but his belief in the soul's immortality and his trust in God's goodness eased the pain of premature death.[72] His reflections on theodicy involved both philosophy and psychology, while eventually introducing an eschatological response.[73]

The new circumstances made it possible for these two authors to reconstruct a sacred canopy, thereby returning to the original enchanted world. Perhaps the heady days under the High Priest Simon II and the overall resurgence of the priesthood played a role for Ben Sira, as did his membership in an increasingly important scribal profession. The author of Wisdom of Solomon lived in a wholly different context, the Alexandrian. His concerns, which are tangential to those surfacing as a direct result of thinking characterized by *ḥinnām* and *hebel*, are introduced by a distortion of Qoheleth's own words. The wish to capture the present moment was by no means unique to Qoheleth; it has a strong presence in Egyptian literature. One hazards a guess that the social reality he experienced was not restricted to Jerusalem.

The wisdom literature from Qumran took up Qoheleth's emphasis on the deity's remoteness, which it labels "the mystery that is to be," while combining this idea with an apocalyptic expectation, where mediation through a host of angelic beings eased the tension arising from apparent divine inaction.[74]

Israelite sages, like their counterparts in Egypt and Mesopotamia, shaped a worldview in which the intellect possessed the capacity to open up the means of securing the good life. That elevation of human potential was brought down through a combination of rigid doctrine and historical circumstances. The removal of the sacred canopy was largely the work of radical ideas that are summed up in two words: *ḥinnām* and *hebel.* In this situation of anomie, new social conditions brought unrest at every level of citizenry. Affluence, political instability under foreign rule, and the imperiled family evoked a sense of utter futility. The breakdown of utopian views presented a rare opportunity for those who practice wisdom to demonstrate its potential for achieving a breakthrough. Qoheleth did precisely that, although his emphasis on life's meaninglessness, the deity's remoteness, and the limits of knowledge was unacceptable to later sages like Ben Sira and the author of Wisdom of Solomon. The dream of prosperity was not easily abandoned, even for a society that yielded an anecdote about a poor *but* wise man.

Notes

1. For some interpreters, Fox and Shields, for example, Qoheleth exemplifies dangerous teachings that the framing narrative warns against. Others think the first epilogue is admiring, if realistic, about the effects of such unorthodox thoughts, and that the second epilogue seeks to direct readers' attention to more traditional views.

2. Expertise in weaving, design, jewel-making and so forth is called wisdom. There is also a shady side to wisdom, counsel that brings death (the crafty serpent in the Garden of Eden; Jonadab who advised Amnon on how to seduce his half-sister, Tamar; and Hushai, who persuaded Absalom to delay his attack on a fleeing David).

3. R. N. Whybray, *The Intellectual Tradition in the Old Testament*, BZAW 135 (Berlin/New York: de Gruyter, 1974) thinks the wise were wealthy landholders.

4. Girls were not normally given scribal training. The teachings in Proverbs specifically apply to boys or young men.

5. Both the book of Job and Ecclesiastes were probably written for advanced students or for adults with an intellectual bent.

6. Crenshaw, *Education in Ancient Israel.*

7. Although the rhetoric is Greek, it nevertheless has utility in describing aspects of Hebrew literature.

8. In "A Dispute between a Man and his Ba," death is compared to the scent of lotus blossoms and myrrh, longing for home while in a lengthy captivity, recovery from illness, and a smooth pathway (*AEL*, vol. 1, 168). It is no surprise, then, that death can be called "shepherd."

9. The Twenty-third Psalm has made the metaphor of God as shepherd familiar to many. William L. Holladay, *The Psalms through Three Thousand Years: Prayerbook of a Cloud of Witnesses* (Minneapolis: Fortress, 1993) discusses the reasons for this rise in the popularity of Ps 23 in the late nineteenth and early twentieth centuries.

10. In contrast with the Mesopotamian tradition about the seven wise men from primordial times who received divine secrets that they transmitted to humans.

11. Fox, *Ecclesiastes*, 84, translates as follows: "The words of sages are like goads/ and [those of] the masters of collections are like implanted nails, stuck in by a shepherd."

12. That is also the difficulty that Job complains about.

13. Is this an attack on Qoheleth for adding his teachings to a growing canon (Proverbs and Job), or does it indicate concern over works, some of which eventually were labeled Apocrypha and Pseudepigrapha?

14. Ignorance about the future invariably presents an opportunity for people to profit by claiming special insight, whether from studying the stars and constellations or from immediate revelation. The modern "Left Behind" series of publications reveals the persistence of this phenomenon.

15. Michael E. Stone, *Fourth Ezra* (Minneapolis: Fortress, 1990) stresses the transforming visions in this powerful cry of distress.

16. One way to shield Yahweh from objectionable acts and ideas is to shift the blame to lesser figures like Uriel and Satan.

17. See my "Impossible Questions, Sayings, and Tasks," 265–78 in *Urgent Advice and Probing Questions*.

18. The danger was both immediate—punishment by a teacher—and punishment in later life—the consequence of wrong thinking.

19. Note that the word is "heard," not "said."

20. Too many alternatives were being offered those willing to think for themselves, including mystery religions.

21. The "whole of a human being" is ambiguous. Franz Delitzsch, *Commentary on the Song of Songs and Ecclesiastes* (Edinburgh: T & T Clark, 1877) 200 writes, ". . . these two stars do not turn the night into day."

22. As implied by the King James Version.

23. *The Idea of the Holy* (New York: Oxford, 1958).

24. In Sir 24:33 he seems to think of his own teachings as inspired prophecy. In other words, he mediates revelation in the same way personified Wisdom does.

25. Hartmut Gese, "The Crisis of Wisdom in Koheleth," 141–53 in Crenshaw, ed., *Theodicy in the Old Testament*, IRT 4 (Philadelphia/London: Fortress and SPCK, 1983) and Shields, *The End of Wisdom* (Winona Lake: Eisenbrauns, 2006).

26. Michael Fishbane, *Garments of Torah* (Bloomington IN: Indiana University Press, 1989).

27. Above all, Krüger, *Qoheleth*.

28. Berger, "Qohelet and the Exigencies of the Absurd," uses the apt phrase "a rhetoric of erasure." Gary D. Salyer, *Vain Rhetoric: Private Insight and Public Debate in Ecclesiastes* (Sheffield: Academic Press, 2001) prefers "vain rhetoric." The reason: "I" discourses imply their own limitation and invite dialogic dissension with their major premises and conclusions (390).

29. Klaus Koch, "Gibt es ein Vergeltungsdogma im Alten Testament?" *ZThK* 52 (1955): 1–42 (abridged ET in James L. Crenshaw, ed., *Theodicy in the Old Testament*, 57–87) stated the issue in extreme terms by which deeds carry within themselves the appropriate consequences. Scholars have responded by assigning a much larger role to Yahweh in the nexus between cause and effect than Koch envisioned.

30. Karel van der Toorn, "Sources in Heaven: Revelation as a Scholarly Construct in Second Temple Judaism," 265–77 has explained the rise of revelation and elitism as a product of the breakdown of the principle of similarity between gods and humans. Joyce Rilett Wood, in "When Gods Were Men," 285–98 (in *From Babel to Baylon: Essays on Biblical History and Literature in Honor of Brian Peckham*, ed. J. R. Wood et al. [London: T & T Clark, 20016]) thinks editors began in the mid-sixth century BCE to make a sharp distinction between humans and deity that was nonexistent until then. She writes that "gods and goddesses of the ancient world, whether Near Eastern or east Mediterranean, were created in our image, so that an almost perfect parallel can be drawn between them and us" (285).

31. Attempts to paint a more attractive picture of Yahweh reveal the depth of concern to negate the effect of questionable conduct attributed to the deity. These efforts are discussed in my *Defending God.*

32. Hartmut Gese, "The Crisis of Wisdom in Koheleth," and Martin Rose, "De la <<Crise de la Sagesse>> a la <<Sagesse de la Crise>>."

33. William S. Morrow, *Protest Against God: The Eclipse of a Biblical Tradition,* HBM 4 (Sheffield: Sheffield Phoenix Press, 2006) associates the distancing of deity with an Axial Age, roughly exilic and early postexilic times when Yahweh came to be viewed as both remote and unfathomable.

34. Baruch A. Levine, "The Appeal to Personal Experience in the Wisdom of Qoheleth," distinguishes three uses of the verb *ra'ah* in Qoheleth's discourse: (1) seeing as observation of events and phenomena; (2) seeing as reflecting on the meaning of "happenings"; and (3) seeing as perceiving, realizing.

35. No textual basis for deleting *ḥokmāh* ("wisdom") exists. It may function as an accusative of specification emphasizing the anomaly to be discussed (Jouon-Muraoka, 126g).

36. Qoh 7:26 refers to snares, and in 9:12 the singular form occurs. Two manuscripts have a word that differs orthographically in the letter "*r*," easily confused with "*d*" (cf. LXX, Symmachus, Peshitta, and Vulgate).

37. According to regular syntax of Hebrew, the sequence of verbs should have the same subject, the first change coming with "and he delivered." For an impersonal reading ("one found"), see GKC 144d.

38. The verb for deliverance can be understood as either actual or potential. For unrealized possibility in verbs, see *GKC* 106p.

39. The commentaries (e.g., Krüger, Seow, Schwienhorst-Schönberger, Fox, Crenshaw) address the difficulties involved in ascertaining discrete literary units in Qoheleth's observations.

40. In biblical Hebrew, *misken* ("poor man," "commoner") is limited to Ecclesiastes, where it occurs four times (4:13; 9:15 [bis] 9:16).

41. In 7:15 Qoheleth calls attention to such miscarriage of justice that he has personally observed. From this he concludes that it is a mistake to strive for membership with the devout or even to be particularly astute.

42. Bo Isaksson, *Studies in the Language of Qoheleth with Special Emphasis on the Verbal System* and Antoon Schoors, *The Preacher Sought to Find Pleasing Words.* Isakkson reads *ûmillaṭ* as "he might have saved the city," but Schoors refuses to exclude either interpretation, actual or potential.

43. One could think of an unmentioned person coming upon the poor man and bringing him into the king's presence or some other such explanation that the narrative leaves in the dark.

44. Opposite interpretations are given, for example by Krüger, *Qoheleth,* 178–80 and Seow, *Ecclesiastes,* 308–11. The former opts for an actual deliverance of the city; the latter prefers a potential reading of the verb.

45. In that case, Qoheleth would have been the commoner. Samuel Ibn Tibbon interpreted this story as "a journey of the soul," an allegory with universal application.

46. "Do not disdain a small document, a small fire, a small soldier" ("The Instruction of 'Ankhsheshonq,'" 16, 25).

47. Levine, "The Appeal to Personal Experience in the Wisdom of Qoheleth," 340 disagrees. For him the story was based on Qoheleth's personal observation that caused him to ponder its significance.

48. Berger, "Qohelet and the Exigencies of the Absurd," 174.

49. Hans Peter Müller, "Der unheimliche Gast. Zum Denken Kohelets," *ZThK* 84 (1987): 440–64 and "Neige der althebräischen <<Weisheit>>. Zum Denken Qohäläts," *ZAW* 90 (1978): 238–64.

50. Roberto Vignolo, "Wisdom, Prayer and Kingly Pattern: Theology, Anthropology, Spirituality of Wis 9," 255–82 in *Deuterocanonical and Cognate Literature: Yearbook 2005: The Book of Wisdom in Modern Research,* ed. Angelo Passaro and Giuseppe Bellia (Berlin & New York: de Gruyter, 2005).

51. In the royal fiction, the king is described as personally involved in the toil that produced buildings, gardens, canals, and so forth. Qoheleth claims to have arrived at the view that his work and its fruit are loathsome in the final analysis.

52. Ethan Dor-Shav, "Ecclesiastes, Fleeting and Timeless," 67–87, captures the vibrancy of Qoheleth's use of *hebel.*

53. James L. Crenshaw, "Deceitful Minds and Theological Dogma."

54. I remain convinced that *haʿelem* ("the hidden") is a superior reading to the MT *hāʿōlām* ("eternity"), Qoheleth's primary concern being the unfathomable nature of the cognitive gift.

55. On Qoheleth's environment see Seow, "The Social World of Ecclesiastes" and my "Qoheleth in Historical Context," *Biblica* 88 (2007): 285–99. For a social-scientific approach, see Mark Sneed, "The Social Location of the Book of Qoheleth," *HebSt* 39 (1998): 41–51 and *The Politics of Pessimism in Ecclesiastes: A Social Science Perspective* (Atlanta: SBL, 2012). According to Sneed, Qoheleth resisted the excessive rationalism of earlier sages who claimed to know much about God and his ways. In doing so, he returned to a concept of a truly unknowable God, one who is capricious and holy. Qoheleth's pessimism enabled his compatriots to cope in a world in which the deity failed to live up to expectations.

56. Seow's defense of a date for Qoheleth during the Persian era, based largely on linguistic grounds, has failed to persuade recent commentators, in part because language is not like a meteor that flashes for a brief moment and then burns itself up. Even if a cluster of vocabulary items identical to Qoheleth's use first appeared in the late fifth and early fourth centuries BCE, its immediate disappearance is wholly unlikely. For Seow's argument, see "Linguistic Evidence and the Dating of Qohelet," *JBL* 115 (1996): 643–66. Robert Harrison, *Qoheleth in Socio-Historical Perspective*, Ph.D. diss., Duke University, 1991 defends a Hellenistic date, accepted by most interpreters. The broader context has been studied recently by Christoph Uehlinger, "Qohelet im Horizont mesopotamischer, levantinischer und ägyptischer Weisheitsliteratur der persischen und hellenistischen Zeit," 155–247 in *Das Buch Kohelet: Studien zur Struktur, Geschichte, Rezeption und Theologie*, ed. Ludger Schwienhorst-Schönberger, BZAW 254 (Berlin & New York: de Gruyter, 1997) and Reinhold Bohlen, "Kohelet in Kontext hellenistischer Kultur," 249–73 in *Das Buch Kohelet*.

57. Seow's use of Nehemiah's memoir to document international trade at an early date could be pushed back to texts from the time of Isaiah or Ezekiel. The desire to possess more things hardly began in Qoheleth's day, even if the later minting of coins facilitated commerce.

58. Frank Crüsemann, "The Unchangeable World: The 'Crisis of Wisdom' in Koheleth," 57–77 in *The God of the Lowly*, ed. Willy Schottroff and W. Stegemann (Maryknoll NY: Orbis, 1984) depicts Qoheleth's alienation from the less privileged members of society.

59. "The increase of indenture of persons is a consequence of problems of self-sufficiency in the household economy and is typically related to the growth of commerce and production outside traditional family or 'lineage' modes of production" (Carol Meyers, *Discovering Eve: Ancient Israelite Women in Context* [New York and Oxford: Oxford University, 1988] 192). In harsh times when money was in high demand, interest rates escalated. The records from Egypt reveal instances of extraordinary rates of interest on loans in cash, in at least one case reaching 120% per annum.

60. Similar reticence has characterized biblical interpreters for the most part, recently overcome by the joint venture of Carol Meyers, Joseph Blenkinsopp, John J. Collins, and Leo G. Perdue (*Families in Ancient Israel* [Louisville: Westminster/John Knox, 1997]).

61. The expression "Enjoy life with the woman you love" is similar to "and I found more bitter than death the woman who is a snare, whose heart is a net, whose hands are bonds" (Qoh 7:26) in that the references to woman require further

elucidation. One expects the *ʾishshāh* ("wife") in Qoh 9:9 to end with the second person pronominal suffix, indicating possession.

62. Thomas Krüger, "'Frau Weisheit' in Koh 7, 26?" *Biblica* 73 (1992): 394–403 introduces the idea of personified Wisdom to recent interpretations of the verse as a popular proverb that Qoheleth refutes (e.g., Norbert Lohfink, "War Kohelet ein Frauenfiend?" 259–87 in *La Sagesse de l'Ancien Testament*, ed. Maurice Gilbert [BETL 51; Leuven: University Press, 1979]).

63. "Enlil, king of the gods, who created teeming mankind, Majestic Ea, who pinched off their clay, The Queen who fashioned them, Mistress Mami, Gave twisted words to the human race, They endowed them in perpetuity with lies and falsehood." ("The Babylonian Theodicy")

64. Only Job 28:12-28 even remotely resembles speculation about a feminine embodiment of divine perception, on which see *Job 28: Cognition in Context*.

65. "The way of wisdom provides no guarantee, and projects no reciprocity in the human-divine encounter" (Levine, "The Appeal to Personal Experience in the Wisdom of Qoheleth," 344).

66. The second epilogue does adopt this usual type of addressing listeners (12:12). It has an ancient pedigree ("The Instruction of Suruppak," 31; *COS* 569).

67. Peter Höffken, "Das EGO des Weisen."

68. Peter Machinist, "Fate, *miqreh*, and Reason," and Martin Rose, "Qohelet als Philosophe und Theologe."

69. Hans Peter Müller, "Wie sprach Qohälät von Gott?"; Antoon Schoors, "God in Qoheleth," 251–70; and Schoors, "Theodicy in Qohelet," 375–409 in *Theodicy in the World of the Bible*.

70. Johannes Marböck, *Weisheit im Wandel: Untersuchungen zur Weisheitstheologie bei Ben Sira*, BBB 37 (Bonn: Hanstein, 1971).

71. Moyna McGlynn, *Divine Judgment and Divine Benevolence in the Book of Wisdom*, WUNT 139 (Tübingen: Mohr Siebeck, 2001) 25–53.

72. Michael Kolarcik, *The Ambiguity of Death in the Book of Wisdom 1–6: A Study of Literary Structure and Interpretation*, An Bib 127 (Rome: Pontifical Biblical Institute, 1991).

73. James L. Crenshaw, "The Problem of Theodicy in Sirach," and Collins, *Jewish Wisdom in the Hellenistic Age*, 133–232.

74. Matthew J. Goff, *Discerning Wisdom*.

chapter seven

THE SAGES ON REMEMBERING AND FORGETTING

INTRODUCTION

For the Judean sages death was final. Hence the importance of leaving a favorable memorial after the body had turned to dust. In an ideal universe, those with flawless reputations could count on their names being pronounced in blessing,[1] while their opposites with tainted reputations were destined for annihilation (Prov 10:7, *zēker ṣaddîq librākāh wešēm rešaʿ ʿim yirqāb*).

Unfortunately, such a universe did not exist; at the very least, it was contested. Qoheleth makes explicit what is painfully exemplified by the righteous servant Job: that even good people are often cursed, while everyone is subjected to a single fate—to die and be forgotten (Qoh 9:5, *weʾēn ʿōd lāhem śākār kî niškaḥ zikrām*).[2] In a word, the dead need not entertain thoughts of reward.

The optimism was contested but not altogether refuted. Ben Sira parades a list of names that have survived for centuries as examples for the faithful. In his mind, memory played a crucial role in moral formation (Sir 7:36, *bkl m syk zkr ʾhrt wl wlm ʾl tsht*). But not just any memory. For him, the pondering of one's final moment served as a catalyst for ethical behavior,[3] which ruled out rejoicing over the death of others, presumably persons who had wronged you. Why? Because another's demise is a powerful reminder that the grim reaper's scythe is inescapable (Sir 8:7, *'l tthll l gw zkr klnw nspym*). The pronoun "we" in Ben Sira's language personalizes the gathering to one's ancestors. In this instance, the object of remembering is the knowledge of a future event;[4] the verb *zākar* thus covers a vast sweep of chronology: past, present, and future.

FORGETTING

What about forgetting? The pedagogical setting of the sages responsible for the book of Proverbs,[5] whether within the household or in a more formal classroom of future professional scribes,[6] ought to have encouraged free use of warnings against forgetfulness. In an oral culture where few could read and write, memory flourished. But only among those who listened attentively, hence the many encouragements to pay attention.

In two places the parental voice[7] warns the son (*benî*) not to forget what is being laid out before him (Prov 3:1; 4:5). In this context, words pregnant with meaning abound. In 3:1 the emphasis falls on authority; *tôrātî* and *miṣwōtay* are the sages' equivalent of divine commands.[8] Such authoritative decrees need to be committed to memory. The other verse moves in an entirely different direction. Here the priority falls on purchasing something of great value. That unnamed entity is called "wisdom and understanding."

Given the personification of wisdom in the parental teachings, in Ben Sira, and in Wisdom of Solomon, it is tempting to think the bridal price lies behind the twofold use of the verb *qānāh*.[9] In that case, the son would be told to buy wisdom for a bride. This bold idea takes hold in Deutero-canonical and extra-canonical wisdom literature.[10]

Wisdom as wife was but one option, as Prov 2:17 makes abundantly clear. Folly always lurked in the shadows.[11] Much practice had equipped Folly with remarkable eloquence, which the learned sage calls the product of a smooth tongue (Prov 2:16). There was truth in her seductive *bon mot*: "Stolen water is sweet, and bread eaten in secret is pleasant" (Prov 9:17). Faithfulness, however, was not her strong suit. Seeking adventure and novelty, she is said to forget her marital vows and break away from a covenant with God (Prov 2:17).

Forgetfulness was not limited to those who worshiped Yahweh. The Queen Mother who is portrayed as counselor to prince Lemuel in Prov 31:1-9 warns him against excessive drinking of intoxicants. Why? Because according to royal ideology in the ancient Near East[12] he has the responsibility to see that the voiceless poor have access to justice. Strong drink, like erotic excess, will make him forget these duties (Prov 31:3-5).

The connection between wine and forgetting is highlighted in 1 Esdr 3:20-23. The poignancy of this court page's description of wine's power was not deemed sufficient to win the contest, but who can deny its veracity? Wine in excess makes one forget sorrow and debt, permits one to feel rich, forgetting kings and satraps and even ties forged from friendship and genetic bonds. Worse still, on waking from a drunken stupor the person remembers nothing that took place in the interval. The fourfold use of the negated verb "to remember" (twice in the singular [*ou memnetai*] and twice in the plural [*ou memnentai*]) universalizes the point.[13]

The description in Prov 23:29-35 of the drunkard's woes does not mention the loss of memory, but its realism suggests that a momentary blotting out of sorrow and debt is nothing compared to the permanent sorrow that clings to one who must have another drink. Something worse than temporary forgetting has taken place: a complete break with reality, an inability to feel blows.

A. Forgetting as a Good Thing

Loss of memory is not always bad. Recognizing this fact, Lemuel's mother tells her son to "give strong drink to the dying and wine to the bitter of soul" (Prov 31:6). The reason: so they can forget their poverty, no longer remembering their misery (Prov 31:7). In one sense, everyone is dying. What does the participle *'ōbēd* mean beyond this truism?

The context supports two different interpretations. The "dying" may refer to those individuals who have been sentenced to die by the royal court.[14] Alternatively, the "perishing" may indicate those who find themselves on the margins of existence,[15] too poor to obtain a hearing in places of power where sentences are handed down. The latter reading seems to be implied by what follows: "Speak up for the dumb, for the legal cause (*din*) of all who are passing away; speak up, judge rightly; adjudicate for the weak and poor" (Prov 31:8-9). The repetition of *petaḥ pîkā* and *din* reveals the urgency of this maternal advice.

B. Forgetting in the Book of Job

Now Job saw himself as an *'ōbēd*, a loyal *'ebed* whom God had wronged. What does the poet who composed the book of Job say about remembering and forgetting? Each of Job's friends comments on remembering. Eliphaz reminds Job to think about[16] what he considers an undeniable truth: that no innocent person ever perished (Jb 4:7a). In 18:17, Bildad focuses on evil people, whose memory, he says, is erased from earth. Zophar's remark in 11:16 turns out to be prophetic, at least the second half of the observation: "For you will forget your misery; you will remember it like water that passes by."[17]

Elihu calls on Job to remember to praise God's works (36:24), something in his present condition he would find difficult. Only Zophar and Bildad mention forgetting. The latter friend associates forgetting God with the perishing, those whose hope dies (8:13) because they have chosen the wrong paths. The speaker in 28:4 refers to forgotten miners,[18] and God alludes to the forgetful stork (39:15). Job, too, has little to say about loss of memory, other than chafing over his guests' forgetfulness (19:14) and, more important, uttering an oath ("If I forget my murmuring [*śiaḥ*] . . .").[19]

C. Remembering in the Book of Job

Job does say something profound about remembering, and it concerns God. What confounds Job is the thought that the creator is bent on destroying the work of divine hands. "Remember that you made me like clay; will you turn me to dust again?" (10:9). The prophetic image of the divine potter destroying a blemished pot[20] and beginning anew is not applicable to one who has been highly praised by both narrator and Yahweh. The deity is hardly the healer who binds up wounds,[21] at least as Job sees things.

More promising, although only for a fleeting moment of imagined relief, is Job's wish that God would temporarily hide him in Sheol until the divine anger has eased.[22] Then when Job's life is no longer in jeopardy, God would set a time and remember him (14:13). At this point sober reality sets in and Job thinks God destroys human hope (14:19). So much for the nostalgic picture of the deity longing for the work of his hands (14:15).

Although Job's active imagination provides momentary relief, he cannot escape a heavy burden, one imposed on him by God without cause (*ḥinnām*).[23] No wonder he calls on God to remember that his life is no more substantial than wind (*rûaḥ*, 7:7). The comparison of human existence to a breeze has a long pedigree in the ancient Near East, although the noun is usually *hebel* and its equivalents.[24] In the Bible the notion surfaces most acutely in a few psalms[25] and in Qoheleth, for whom it has become a refrain with universal application.

D. Memory in Qoheleth

Qoheleth never refers to his opus as an avenue to immortality the way some Egyptian writers did.[26] Nevertheless, the scroll was precisely that. A certain irony abounds in that he thought a veil of forgetfulness was draped over all the deceased, whether wise or foolish, stillbirths or successful births (Qoh 2:16; 6:4). And the failure to remember was not due to chronological remoteness, for he believed that even those persons who had just died were soon forgotten (Qoh 1:11).

Qoheleth's obsession with economic gain[27] produced the secondary thematic refrain in 1:3 ("What profit accrues to anyone in all his toil at which he labors under the sun?"). That desire for something to show for one's work had fueled earlier sapiential instruction, and it had been reinforced by an almost unfailing conviction that human effort, coupled with virtue, would pay off in the end.[28] That belief was contradicted, at least for Qoheleth, by the many instances in which persistent effort yielded nothing but misery. A single destiny befell everyone, and with death came the eradication of memory, presumably that of the corpse and that of its survivors (Qoh 9:5). With death also came the cessation of any reward (Qoh 9:5b, "The dead know nothing, have no more reward, for their memory is forgotten"). Forgotten, that is, along with all their emotions: love, hate, and envy (Qoh 9:6).[29]

One example of the calamitous results of forgetfulness struck Qoheleth as huge. A poor but wise man could have saved a small village from the threat of a foreign invader, but nobody remembered to consult that poor man (Qoh 9:13-16). Viewed differently, the story illustrates the lack of gratitude displayed by villagers who had been rescued from destruction.[30]

In Qoh 8:10 the current state of the text presents difficulties in determining exactly what is being said. If the reading in the Masoretic Text (*weyistakkehû*) is preferred over the Septuagint's "praise," Qoheleth complains that good people's actions are forgotten while the wicked are buried with honor. On this interpretation, Qoheleth contrasts two kinds of individuals. The immediate sequel is limited to evildoers, and this concentration on a single group may suggest that the Septuagint has the best reading.[31]

Less consequential but nonetheless self-revelatory is the chance remark in Qoh 7:22 about habitual cursing of others. Qoheleth observes that people should not take umbrage when a servant curses the master. Why? Because those being reviled remember the numerous times they have cursed others. The language for remembering is different (*yāda' libekā*), but frequency has left a permanent imprint like oral recitation (cf. Qoh 8:5).

Death was never far from Qoheleth's thinking, but that did not prevent him from appreciating the sweetness of sunlight. Was his exhortation to rejoice as long as life lasts the result of the sentence hanging over all? Was it a desperate attempt to taste nectar before the approach of an eternity of darkness as in Isa 22:13? Is the *waw* in Qoh 11:8b adversative or conjunctive? Much hinges on how one answers this question.

If conjunctive, the verb *yizkōr* ("Let him remember" or "he should remember")[32] only slightly diminishes the force of the previous jussive (*yismaḥ*, "let him rejoice"). Support for this optimistic assessment of Qoheleth's teaching has been found in the linguistically similar 5:19, where one finds "For he will not long remember days of his life for God *ma'aneh* with the rejoicing of his mind."[33] The untranslated participle can mean "keeps one occupied with," which fits nicely with the reference to joys.

Viewing the *waw* in 11:8b as adversative yields a translation of the participle more in line with the thematic refrain with which Qoheleth's words open and close (1:2; 12:8). On this reading, *ma'aneh* derives from *'ānāh*, "to afflict." Accordingly, the joys one can recall are constant irritants, reminders that death brings them to an end.[34]

Of one thing Qoheleth is certain. The ability to rejoice in one's lot (*ḥeleq*) lies outside human control. It follows that, contrary to the dominant view in the Bible, God does not micromanage the universe, unfailingly rewarding virtue and punishing vice. For Qoheleth, that axiom has lost its power. In its place is the certainty that chance (*miqreh*) governs everything. Significantly, the comment about enjoyment in 5:17-18 is set within the context of commiseration over grievous evils (5:12; 6:1). Clearly, not everyone was able to rejoice, and Qoheleth's advice, if positive, applied only to a few.[35]

However one interprets the participle *ma'aneh* in 5:19 and the *waw* in 11:8, the ending in the latter verse surely qualifies the rejoicing. It is difficult to get excited about happiness that opens into *kōl šebbā hābel.* Similarly, the imperative *semaḥ* in 11:9 and the six imperatives that follow in 11:9-10 conclude with *hābel.* In addition, the thematic third one flaunts traditional teaching when encouraging young people to walk in the ways of their hearts and in the desires of their eyes (cf. Num 15:39).[36]

Does Qoheleth's last use of the verb *zākar* fall within conventional theology when urging the hearer, "Remember your *bôre'eykā* in your youthful days"? If the *waw* on *zekor* continues the *semaḥ* in 11:9, it is interrupted by the remark about youth being *hābel.* Here too the question about adversative or conjunctive *waw* arises. But what is to be remembered? Even if the unusual form for creator can be explained linguistically,[37] the notion itself seems strange. Qoheleth thinks God made everything appropriate for its time (3:11), but the piety behind such an interpretation of *bôre'eykā* strikes me as foreign to his thought.[38]

The sentiment expressed there is matched in the story about the pious Tobit. In Tob 4:5 he tells his son to "remember the Lord our God all your days." He then proceeds to offer a sort of ethical code, one of two testaments in the book (Tob 4:5-21; 11:6-10).[39] Tobit's own devotion to Yahweh is stressed in Tob 1:12 ("Because I remembered God with all my heart"). The father's advice to remember God is repeated in the longer account of Sinaiticus (GII), but this verse (4:9) is part of a section that impedes the flow of the story, comes too soon, and repeats what comes more naturally in Tob 14:3-11.[40]

Remembering God with reference to the future does not present a serious problem (cf. Sir 7:36; 8:7). The text from Ben Sira suggests a different reading of *bôreʾeykā*, one that best accords with Qoheleth's thinking elsewhere and that is more in tune with the coded language in Qoh 12:1-7.[41] Two possibilities seem most obvious, either "your grave" (*bôrekā*) or "your well" (*beʾerekā*). Qoheleth's preoccupation with death favors the first; his appreciation for the love of one's life favors the second (cf. Prov 5:15, 18). Nevertheless, a third option cannot be ruled out. Aqiba explains the saying of Akabya ben Mahalel in Abot 3:1 as follows: "Know whence you came (*bʾrk*, your source), whither you are going (*bwrk*, your grave), and before whom you are destined to give an accounting (*bwrʾyk*, your creator).[42]

CONCLUSION

What the sages said about forgetting varied from the trivial to deep emotional distress, from a divine comment on storks' forgetfulness to Job's determination not to forget a legitimate complaint against God. It concerns parents' pleas for their teachings to take hold in their children as well as the erasure of disturbing recollections. More tellingly, it laments a terrible fact, that the memory of the deceased will be permanently wiped out. Because they cared deeply about reputation, sages had a great deal to say about memory. It was the only known substitute for immortality,[43] and an active consideration of one's ultimate destiny—the building of character. Knowing that life was nothing more than wind forced individuals to ask existential questions about their origin and destiny. Memory thus encouraged grateful persons to praise the creator but also pressed them to plead to be remembered on high.

Notes

1. See J. Scharbert, "*brk*," TDOT 2:299–300 and W. Schottroff, "*zkr*," to remember," TLOT 1:381–88. The basic meaning of *zākar* is "to remember," but it also connotes active consideration and thinking about persons or situations that recall impressions of them (H. Eising, TDOT 4:66).

2. The verb *sakah* means letting something that is spatially distant slip from the mind but also overlooking something that lies before the eyes (W. Schottroff, "*škh* to forget," TLOT 3:13–23). It functions theologically as the explanation for Israel's troubles (the nation has forgotten Yahweh) but also appears in laments (do not forget us).

3. Presumably, Ben Sira thinks the expectation of judgment in the form of premature dying protects an individual from engaging in wrongful acts. On the basis of Qoh 12:14, something more than an early death may be envisioned in some circles ("For God will bring every deed into judgment, concerning everything hidden, whether good or evil").

4. M. Gilbert, "La description de la vieillesse en Qohelet xii 1-7. est elle allégorique?" *Congress Volume Vienna 1980*, ed. J. A. Emerton, VTS 32 (Leiden: Brill, 1981) 101.

5. K. Dell, *The Book of Proverbs in Social and Theological Context* (Cambridge: University of Cambridge Press, 2006) thinks the primary concerns of proverbial material, ethics and education, "give wisdom literature an entrance into the heartland of Israelite concern."

6. J. L. Crenshaw, *Education in Ancient Israel: Across the Deadening Silence* (New York: Doubleday, 1998); D. M. Carr, *Writing on the Tablet of the Heart: Origins of Scripture and Literature* (New York: Oxford University Press, 2005); and K. van der Toorn, *Scribal Culture and the Making of the Hebrew Bible* (Cambridge MA: Harvard University Press, 2007).

7. The brilliant study by C. A. Newsom, "Woman and the Discourse of Patriarchal Wisdom: A Study of Proverbs 1–9," 142–60 in *Gender and Difference in Ancient Israel*, ed. P. L. Day (Minneapolis: Fortress Press, 1989) has not been surpassed.

8. For defense of this statement, see my article, "Wisdom and Authority: Sapiential Rhetoric and Its Warrants," 326–43 in Crenshaw, *Urgent Advice and Probing Questions* (Macon GA: Mercer University Press, 1995, originally in VTS 32:10–29).

9. M. V. Fox, *Proverbs 1–9* (New York: Doubleday, 2000) 173–74 notes that, contrary to its use in Mishnaic Hebrew, *qānāh* is never used in the Bible for the bridal price.

10. Sir 4:11-19; 14:20-27; Wis Sol 7–8.

11. Personified Folly may antedate the personification of Wisdom. The two figures make excellent contrasts in parental instruction.

12. L. Kalugila, *The Wise King*, ConBOT 15 (Lund: GWK Gleerup, 1980) and N. Lohfink, "Poverty in the Laws of the Ancient Near East and the Bible," Theological Studies 52 (1991): 34–50.

13. The three speeches are analyzed in my article, "The Contest of Darius' Guards in 1 Esdras 3:1–5:3," 222–34 in *Urgent Advice and Probing Questions*.

14. The legal terms, however, are weighted toward decrees for the well-being of the weak.

15. The advice stops short of advocating for taking steps to remove the causes of poverty. For that reason, it has been called cynical and sarcastic by B. K. Waltke, *The Book of Proverbs: Chapters 15–31* (Grand Rapids: Eerdmans, 2005) 508–509.

16. The axiomatic nature of the object of the verb *zakar* implies that an act of remembering occurs in the thought process.

17. Although in his restored condition Job may be able to think his troubles have vanished like departing waters, forgetting what he has endured is something altogether different.

18. On this poem, see *Job 28: Cognition in Context*, ed. E. van Wolde (Leiden: Brill, 2003), especially the article by E. L. Greenstein, "The Poem on Wisdom in Job 28 in Its Conceptual and Literary Contexts," 253–80.

19. In Job's use the noun *siaḥ* has shifted from positive meditation to bitter complaint.

20. The beginning anew in Jeremiah's eyes involves removing the stony heart and replacing it with one more attentive to Yahweh's will (Jer 31:31-34).

21. J. L. Crenshaw, "Divine Discipline in Job 5:17-18, Proverbs 3:11-12, Deuteronomy 32:39, and Beyond," 178–89 in *Reading Job Intertextually*, ed. K. Dell and W. Kynes (New York: T & T Clark, 2013).

22. What Job imagines is "a new and different God," one who does not have to be summoned but will take the initiative to call Job, no longer despising the work of divine hands but longing for it "with the same intensity that equals the human quest to be with God" (S. E. Balentine, *Job* [Macon GA: Smyth & Helwys, 2006] 220).

23. On *hinnam* in the book of Job, see my article, "Sipping from the Cup of Wisdom," 41–62 in *Jesus and Philosophy: New Essays* (Cambridge: Cambridge University Press, 2009).

24. K. Seybold, "*hebhel/habhal,*" TDOT 3:313–14.

25. Pss 39:7, 62:10; 144:4; and cf. 78:33.

26. "Man decays, his corpse is dust/All his kin have perished;/But a book makes him remembered/Through the mouth of its reciter" (M. Lichtheim, *Ancient Egyptian Literature*, vol. 2 [Berkeley: University of California Press, 1976] 177).

27. Two things stand in the way of human gain, according to T. Krüger: (1) the changing of the times that sets a duration on any possible gain and (2) the limited accessibility of possible profit that depends on the favor or lack of favor of time and circumstance (*Qoheleth* [Minneapolis: Fortress Press, 2004] 78).

28. The adverb "almost" needs to be emphasized, for sages were aware that there were exceptions to an exact correspondence between conduct and reward or retribution.

29. In the case of Qoh 9:6, the pronominal ending "their" locates the emotional states in humans. The issue is less clear in 9:2 because of a missing indicator

("whether love or hate no one knows; everything before them is *hebel*" [following LXX, Syriac, and Vulgate]). Divine indifference was not a foreign concept to Qoheleth.

30. For opposing interpretations, see M. V. Fox, *A Time to Tear Down & a Time to Build Up* (Grand Rapids: Eerdmans, 1999) 298–300 (rescue accomplished) and C. L. Seow, *Ecclesiastes* (New York: Doubleday, 1997) 310–11 (rescue could have occurred but did not).

31. A. Schoors, *Ecclesiastes* (Leuven: Peeters, 2013) 622 does not exaggerate when saying: "This is an extremely difficult verse." He thinks the wicked are praised for their hypocritical devotion (626).

32. Schoors, *Ecclesiastes*, 787 opts for a conjunctive "and."

33. N. Lohfink, "Qoheleth 5:17-19—Revelation by Joy," *CBQ* 52 (1990): 625–35.

34. J. L. Crenshaw, "Qoheleth's Hatred of Life: A Passing Phase or an Enduring Sentiment?" 119–31 in *Wisdom for Life (FS M. Gilbert)*, M. Calduch-Benages, ed., BZAW 445 (Berlin/Boston: de Gruyter, 2014).

35. The author of 2 Esdras (4 Maccabees) has his hero complain bitterly about the huge gulf between the number of those who are destined for salvation and the masses who are damned.

36. Ben Sira differs from Qoheleth on this issue (cf. Sir 5:2). L. Schwienhorst-Schönberger, *Kohelet* (Freiburg: Herder, 2004) 529 thinks of Sir 5:2 as a light warning about misunderstanding Qoheleth's call to rejoice.

37. Seow, *Ecclesiastes*, 351 explains the unusual form as the result of confusion in late Hebrew of III Alep and III Weak roots, not as a plural of majesty.

38. Schoors, *Ecclesiastes*, 796 concurs ("It remains difficult to see here the presence of the Creator, who is never mentioned with this term in the book, and it also remains difficult to give a place to God's judgment in Qoheleth's thought").

39. A somewhat later testamentary injunction "that almost encapsulates Tob 4:5-21" can be found in Test of Job 45:1-3 according to C.A. Moore, *Tobit* (New York: Doubleday, 1996) 165.

40. Moore, *Tobit*, 165.

41. On the imagery in Qoheleth's closing poem, see Fox, *A Time to Tear Down & a Time to Build Up*, 338–49.

42. J. L. Crenshaw, "Three Things You Must Know To Escape the Clutches of the Evil One," 1–14 in *Testimonies of Vocation*, W. E. Rogers, ed. (Greenville: Furman University, 2011) mines this text for what it contributes to vocational choice.

43. On the origin of belief in resurrection, see my "Love Is Stronger than Death: Intimations of Life Beyond the Grave," 53–78 in *Resurrection*, ed. J. H. Charlesworth (New York: T & T Clark, 2006).

chapter eight

DIVINE VULNERABILITY: REFLECTIONS ON GENESIS 22*

The Offering of Isaac

The seductive power and simple artistry of the story about the binding of Isaac almost compensate for its disturbing features. Yet when its drama and narrative craft are exhausted, some things linger to trouble readers. Those who believe the tale is divinely inspired are confronted with a portrayal of the deity from which they rightly recoil.[1] Others who view the story as a product of creative imagination are struck by the psychological damage it can do, especially to children.[2] There seems to be no escaping the harmful effect of this harrowing tale. The Danish philosopher Soren Kierkegaard realized that the story impugns either God's character or Abraham's.[3] That left him with an untenable position: hoping to solve the dilemma by transforming the father into a monster, at least in Isaac's eyes. Alternatively, from that day Abraham's eyes were darkened, he grew old, and never knew joy again. Estrangement would surely have followed, as I tried to capture when writing the following poem.[4]

Estrangement
The familiar voice that bids me go to an unknown mountain

---

* The original appeared in Isaac Kalimi, ed. *Bridging Between Sister Religions: Studies of Jewish and Christian Scriptures Offered in Honor of Prof. John T. Townsend* (BRLJ 51. Leiden: Brill, 2016) 19–30. Reprinted with permission.

pierces my heart but stays the knife in a trembling hand.
The deed's undone,
yet the unspeakable lingers between me and Sarah,
Isaac and his dad,
the three of us and that voice, suddenly alien.

Who can deny the artistry of the story about the supreme test for father
and son, perhaps also for the God they worshiped, if the particle of entreaty
attached to the divine imperative provides a hint of compassion. "Take,
I beg of you, your only son whom you love, Isaac, and go to the land of
Moriah and offer him as a burnt sacrifice on one of the mountains that I
will make known to you."[5] Never mind that God seems to have forgotten
that Abraham has another son, Ishmael, as well as a servant Eliezer who was,
according to ancient custom, like a son to the patriarch.

Perfect symmetry balances five uses of Elohim with five YHWHs, the
latter sometimes part of a traditional formula such as "angel of YHWH,"
and three signs of the direct object in connection with the journey and
an equal number when preparing for the sacrifice.[6] Unless one follows
the Septuagint or the Vulgate, the symmetry is broken when Elohim calls
Abraham only once but the heavenly messenger addresses him twice by
name in a manner that will be replicated when YHWH speaks to Moses
from the burning bush. Inverted sentence order occurs at the outset, placing the onus of the test on Elohim, not on an alien deity or a subordinate
like the Adversary who will play a major role in a similar test, this time
with Job as the victim of divine malfeasance.[7] Information intended for
readers is withheld from Abraham: "This is a test." They are not told what
the outcome of the test will be. When the weather channel tests its system
by emitting a jarring alarm, we are quickly assured that there is nothing
ominous involved. Ancient readers were less fortunate; they were kept in
the dark until the last second, forcing them to ask, "Will Abraham actually
turn his beloved son into ashes?" Everything up to this moment suggests
that he will do so.

We see a thing of beauty in the short story with an almost perfect
pattern, a chiasm of frame, command, journey, the binding of Isaac, command, journey, frame. The narrative has anticipation, increasing tension
("the place that I will make known to you," "Abraham said to the lads,
'You stay here with the ass; I and the boy will go yonder; we will worship
and return to you'"). It also has pained dialogue between father and son,
with a daring request for clarification. Was Isaac's invocation, "My father,"
a desire to reclaim the status of son once he has been lumped together with

the lads as "the boy"? Was the inquiry, "Where is the victim?" somehow connected with this change in address? And is Abraham's response ambiguous except in *hinnēnî* ("Here I am") as if attentive both to God and to Isaac? The syntax permits "my son" to be either appositive or vocative. In other words, Abraham may be saying, "My son, God will provide the victim," or he may say, "God will provide the victim, namely you." The haunting refrain, "The two of them journeyed together," leaves unexpressed what has been called the most poignant and eloquent silence in all of world literature.[8] The two instances of the refrain form an inclusio but do not give way to a third when Abraham and his two servants return to Beersheba where Abraham must face his wife alone and tell her what he has been doing for nearly a week. Sarah has not been privy to Abraham's plans for their beloved son, although Midrash Tanhuma has Abraham on departing tell Sarah he is taking Isaac to be educated at a distant location.[9] No wonder rabbinic speculation includes the tragic ending that Sarah lets out six shrieks and dies, or that Pseudo-Jonathan has Satan inform her that Isaac has been slain.[10]

The literary critic Eric Auerbach characterized the story as fraught with background, in contrast to Greek storytelling, specifically in Homer's account of Odysseus's scar, where foregrounding occurs.[11] Its "bare bones" language is broken only by terms of endearment ("your son, Isaac, whom you love" and "his father Abraham"). Huge gaps openly invite readers to activate the imagination, which they readily have done. How old was Isaac? "Thirty-seven," a number based on Gen 17:17 and 23:1. He was therefore strong enough to resist had he chosen to do so. How did Abraham respond to God? By engaging in dialogue. It went something like this: "Which son? I have two sons." The one you love. "I love both of them." Isaac. (Let us not forget Eliezer. Abraham could have said, "I have three sons.") Alternatively, because only Abraham and Isaac saw God in a cloud forming a column from heaven to earth, the servants were not worthy of being offered up to YHWH.[12]

The initial words, "after these things," link the story with what precedes, but how wide is the net? Intertextual association with Genesis 12, the call of Abraham to leave parents and homeland, which is tantamount to sacrificing them symbolically, requires us to spread the net widely. When the angel commends Abraham for being willing to offer up his son, it repeats the threefold promise from the earlier experience. Obedience will lead to blessing, progeny, and land now in the hands of Canaanites. In a sense, he has been asked to give up both past and future, with only a precarious present existence far from home. One could translate "After these words" as in Targum Pseudo-Jonathan. What words? According to this text, Ishmael and Isaac argued with one another about who was more worthy to receive the inheritance. Isaac claimed to be willing to give up his members were God to require it. Hence the divine test.[13]

More telling than Genesis 12 is the immediate context. Thematic links lead readers back to the story about a jealous Sarah who persuades her spineless husband to drive a rival wife and her son into the desert where they will surely die from exposure. Although Abraham expresses dismay over the likelihood that both Hagar and Ishmael will die in the desert, God shows no such compassion until the ordeal has almost run its course. Still, both patriarch and matriarch are complicit in what seems to entail the death of two people. What father can be so heartless? The story does not suggest that he was worried about his ignorance concerning their fate. Yet this is the man who is asked in the very next episode of Genesis to kill his only remaining son, as far as he knows. Will a seriously flawed Abraham sully the narrative that follows? Why does he acquiesce in a monstrous test?

Where is the chutzpah as manifest in the plea for the doomed citizens of Sodom and Gomorrah?[14] Why does he not argue with God that he has suppressed his feelings for Isaac out of a greater desire to be obedient? Surely he loves Isaac more than he cares for strangers in condemned cities. Is Hermann Gunkel right that Abraham demonstrates his love for his son by carrying the fire and the knife?[15] The sole clause of apposition, "whom you love," reverberates in the silence that is broken only by footsteps for three long days, symbolic of the eleventh hour.[16] We can imagine a journey characterized by downcast eyes except to see the mountain designated for the site of immolation. And yet, seeing is thematic for both Genesis 21 and 22. Although divine accompaniment is implied by the promise to make known the place for the burnt offering, readers are not told when or how that information was disclosed to Abraham. We are left with the question, "Was the knowledge gained by God ("Now I know") worth the terrible cost of such a test?"[17]

Some small compensation may be found in the many artistic renderings of the agony experienced by father and son, however eager Abraham may have been to obey and however willingly Isaac may have presented the throat, as in rabbinic speculation.[18] Who can ever forget the depiction of Abraham's suffering by Rembrandt once he had a son?[19] What a contrast with the earlier painting of 1635 that emphasized the patriarch's eagerness to obey God at any cost. Now twenty years later, a face is etched in pain while a comforting arm cradles Isaac to shield his eyes from the knife that a moment before had been poised to slit the throat.[20] The many paintings of the story in the catacombs and the thousands of artistic renderings to the present day suggest that artists have seen the story as a test of their own ability to depict pathos on such a grand scale.

Beauty alone cannot justify this storytelling. Nor can the sacrifice of one's son be defended as the ethical norm, as Jon Levenson does when rejecting Kierkegaard's interpretation of the deed as a "teleological suspension of the ethical" by a Knight of Faith.[21] Human sacrifice, even if normal during patriarchal days, was horrifying in the same way genocide and slavery were. We do not know whether the requirement in Exod 22:29a to offer up one's firstborn son in the same way sheep and oxen were to be slaughtered was ever implemented.[22] According to Jeremiah, such a thought never entered YHWH's mind. We can certainly say that the killing of one's offspring was abominable even if thought to be divinely authorized. In this regard, Immanuel Kant is right.[23] The argument even exists today in legal defense of the criminally insane; it is called command hallucination, the belief that God orders someone to kill another human being.[24] No one in his or her right mind could take such a command seriously. Then was Abraham mistaken as in Genesis Rabbah 56:8 where God says, "I did not command you to sacrifice your son but to take him up to a mountain"?[25]

Nor can the episode be justified by its "happy outcome," whether by following the story line or by assuming that Abraham actually slew Isaac and angels carried the body either to Sheol or to the garden of Eden, where the dew of heaven revived him and for three years he was nursed back to health by angels. As Shalom Spiegel has shown in exquisite detail, the tradition about the ashes of Isaac antedates the death of Jesus and requires the belief that Isaac really died.[26] After all, he is strangely absent on the return journey, and he is not mentioned in connection with his mother's funeral. That he died is not the opinion of the mother of the seven martyred sons in 2 Maccabees 7 who chides father Abraham with the words, "Yours were the trials, mine the performances."[27] Nor was it the view of those who said the ram's blood was as if that of Isaac, or the ram's name was Isaac.[28] Still, if Isaac actually died at his father's hand, Christians had no claim to superiority over their Jewish brothers and sisters, for both looked to the redemptive power of a slain hero. In both theological traditions, there could be no redemption without spilled blood.

It did not help that in some circles people believed YHWH killed and made alive, wounded and bound up,[29] as stated in Deut 32:39, or that the author of Exodus called YHWH both warrior and healer. We must consider what Karel van der Toorn has called the principle of similitude, of similarity between God and mortals.[30] Humans have always depicted the deity in their own image, or, as Robert Wright has shown in *The Evolution of God*, used images that convey their deepest desire.[31] In short, for children of the Enlightenment God is a literary construct. The problem arises when this fabrication is viewed as absolute, demanding a bended knee. The result is vividly illustrated in Jack Miles's scintillating book, *God: A Biography*.[32] A shadow side of the deity resembling the demonic emerges and eventuates in the Satan as a means of salvaging divine character. Defending God is a fruitless enterprise, as I have shown in an exhaustive treatment of the biblical and extra-biblical data.[33]

Any discussion of the shadow side of God leads to the book of Job, especially the prose introduction and conclusion, with its obvious intertextual links to Genesis 22. Sara Japhet[34] and Andreas Michel[35] have laid bare the semantic affinities between the two stories about a divine test: they include, among other things, "stretch forth your hand," "offer up a whole burnt offering," the imperative "take," the lifting up of the eyes from afar, the expression "after these things," and "my servant" as the designation for both Abraham and Job. A much-maligned Job thought he was undergoing a test from which he would emerge successfully "like gold refined in fire" (Job 23:10). Enthusiasts like the composer of Ps 26 asked to be subjected to a divine test, and testing was mutual. Humans put God to the test, even on occasion prodded by YHWH to do so as in the case of King Ahaz, who is told to make the test as deep as Sheol or as high as heaven (Isa 7:11). In the eyes of the prophet Isaiah, nothing was impossible for God.

Regrettably, God as described in the Bible could not be trusted to be consistent, as the incidents involving Ishmael and Isaac reveal. In the former case the deity showed a compassionate side, but in the latter instance a hostile demeanor. Which God does Abraham encounter, the one who rescued Ishmael and Hagar or the one who commanded the patriarch to undergo an agonizing three days? Amazingly, the Bible celebrates this ambiguity in a liturgy emphasizing the thirteen divine attributes: "YHWH, merciful, compassionate, kind, long-suffering . . . but also punishing sinners to the third and fourth generation" (Exod 34:6-7).

One can say that the biblical description of a flawed deity is mirrored in a perverse humankind, a concept that reaches its highest point in Jer 17:9a ("The human mind is wholly sick; who can fathom it?"). How else could it be? Deceitful minds only produce corrupt theological dogma,[36] a biblical insight that seems to have been lost on inerrantists and extremists everywhere. Jewish lore about the *yētser hārā'* and the Christian model prayer arise from the recognition that a fundamental flaw exists in human beings. Does a flaw exist in God too? Some have thought so, for it is difficult to imagine that a benevolent God would create an evil inclination and lead good people into temptation.

When we pause long enough to ask what could possibly justify the monstrous test, answers fail to ease our angst. Some have said that it aims to build character, a conviction that has been converted into a proverb ("Whom God loves, he chastens, just as a father disciplines the child he loves," Prov 3:11). The church theologian Irenaeus used this argument of soul building to explain adversity, the suffering that tests the human spirit. Unfortunately, there is precious little soul building here, and only for Abraham. One could argue that for him the experience was soul wrenching rather than soul building.

Then what about Isaac? Does not Jewish tradition say that three tears fell from Abraham's eyes into those of Isaac, or that the tears of the angels melted the knife in Abraham's hand?[37] Nowhere is Isaac explicitly offered an opportunity to exhibit courage except in rabbinic imagination where he asks to be bound securely lest his body tremble and the sacrifice be ruined.[38] And Sarah? She is completely excluded from any possibility of improving her character, which has been sorely tested in the story leading up to Genesis 21, where, no longer victim, she instigates extreme suffering on a rival wife and son.

This line of thought leads to the question, "Who is the central character in the story involving Abraham and Isaac?" In Jewish readings Isaac takes center stage, with Abraham standing nearby, but in Christian readings Abraham is the hero. Perhaps God is a close rival to the human characters in both traditions. Who gets left out? Sarah, by implication, but the ram that was caught in the thorns receives no credit for paying the ultimate price by being in the wrong place at the wrong time. The silence about the real victim has persisted until quite recently, and the voices seem to fall on deaf ears for the most part.

For some readers, the story is justified in that it chronicles the transition from sacrificing the firstborn to the time when a substitute was accepted. This interpretation may be correct, although the point is a subtle one, never made explicitly.[39] No one can miss the implication of the angel's remarks: the thought is tantamount to the deed; however, Isaac has already been saved, so the ram cannot be considered a substitute for him.

Now if it is true that the story is a creation of a flawed human being, and if people have created God in their own image, does it not follow that the deity is vulnerable like the ones after whom the majestic Being is modeled? Does the mere hint that Elohim recognizes the enormity of the ordeal facing Abraham suggest divine vulnerability? Perhaps. I have expressed that idea in a reflection on Genesis 1.[40]

> The Tear
> Had God known the course of those first words, he would ne'er have spoken,
> ripping night from day,
> land from sea, you from me.
> Instead, God shattered eternity's silence and then cried, a tear falling
> from divine eyes into mine, exploding in a shriek of eternity.

According to the Bible, the act of creation did not arise from loneliness but from self-emptying love, which exposes God to human willfulness. No one has seen this truth more clearly than Abraham Joshua Heschel, who talked about divine pathos, turning Aristotle's concept on its head.[41] YHWH is the most moved mover, not the unmoved mover, according to Heschel's apt turn of phrase. Christians, too, invoke a similar theological argument, that a self-sacrifice on the deity's part is the means of restoring an estranged humanity to its divine source. Here the dual nature of God is laid bare: he wounds but binds up, kills but brings to life. In this instance, however, the victim is paradoxically none other than the one who afflicts. It follows that the monstrous test of Abraham has cosmic significance insofar as it discloses the character of God as intrinsically vulnerable.

One thing becomes clear from Gen 22. It leaves no room for presuming that God presents a smiling countenance to exemplary humans. Closer to the truth is the pained recognition at the end of Ps 88 and Lam 5 that YHWH has utterly abandoned and rejected his people. Loneliness on the part of humankind and suffering on God's part naturally follow. Thus the two poets have authentically described the human condition. Experience has taught them that the comforting message of theism is hardly that; indeed it only increases angst. They have projected their own vulnerability onto the heavens. Kindred spirits went even further. The author of the book of Job perceived that genuine religious devotion asks nothing in return, is truly without cause, against logic. Qoheleth is even more radical, insisting that ultimately life is empty, short, and futile.[42] Human vulnerability, that is, matches divine vulnerability. So a monstrous test faces moderns too, one that leaves them alone on a journey into oblivion. At journey's end, we have no guarantee of being met by a solicitous angel with words of blessing. Like Greek tragedy, the story tugs at the heart, asking how far mortals are capable of going while serving the Eternal One. For ancients, the question was, "Will they sacrifice what is most precious, the fruit of their bodies even when not as payment for the 'sin of their souls,' to use the language of Micah?" For us, the question has taken a different turn: "Will silent heavens require us to slay our belief in transcendence?"[43]

In this context, it is easy to solve the problem presented by the unflattering picture of God. We can admire the artistry of the story, lifting up its capacity to energize the imagination and celebrating the supreme sacrifice of the human spirit for what is thought to be a noble end. We can even convince ourselves that we need a sense of awe that is grounded in the sublime, without which life would be impoverished. For some believers, however, more is required. They must accept the story line and say that the divine experiment depended on Abraham's willingness to obey God regardless of the consequences. And that means that the patriarch's checkered history of partial obedience exposed divine vulnerability at its core.

In the final analysis, we are faced with a heart-rending story, whether the product of the human imagination or divine inspiration, and its lingering effect haunts Christians who try to understand the passion narrative and Jews for whom a contemporary form of the binding of Isaac has been a horrific nightmare. It is thus possible to say that humans today are subjected to a monumental test, whether to sacrifice belief in God or to take a leap of faith in the faint hope that our ancestors have not been completely blind and deaf to a deeper reality, divine vulnerability.[44]

Notes

1. Not everyone is offended by acts attributed to God that, committed by humans, would be immoral and even criminal. The extremes to which defenders of the deity will go are on exhibit in several essays in *Divine Evil: The Moral Character of the God of Abraham*, ed. M. Bergman, M. Murray, and M. C. Rea (Oxford: Oxford University Press, 2011). I prefer the biblical questioning of God in the book of Job and Psalms of Lament, or the radical honesty of Qoheleth. See my "Qohelet and Scriptural Authority," 17–41 in *Scriptural Authority in Early Judaism and Ancient Christianity*, ed. I Kalimi, T. Nicklas, and G. G. Xeravits, DCLS 16 (Berlin & New York: De Gruyter, 2013).

2. P. Höffken, "Genesis 22 als Religionspädagogisches Problem," 221–37 in *Frömmigkeit und Freiheit: Theologische, ethische, und seelsorgerliche Anfragen*, ed. F. Wintzer, H. Schröer, und J. Heide (Rheinbach-Merzbach: CMZ Verlag, 1995).

3. *Fear and Trembling* (Garden City NY: Doubleday & Co., 1941). Kierkegaard's different scenarios for the impact of this ordeal on father and son utilize various modes of a mother's weaning an infant from breast milk. The total effect is mesmerizing.

4. *Dust and Ashes* (Eugene OR: Wipf & Stock, 2010) 17. The combination of sources, Elohist and Yahwist, becomes complicated once the angel of YHWH appears. I take the words "from me" to imply that the angel is thought of as speaking in YHWH's voice. The book of Jubilees attributes the test of Abraham to Mastema, not Elohim (17:15–18:19), while Pseudo-Philo blames jealous angels (*Liber Antiquitatum Biblicarum* 32:1-4).

5. As early as Rashi, the particle of entreaty in Gen 22:1 was interpreted as softening the harsh imperative, hence my translation "Take, I beg of you . . . ."

6. On the narrative artistry of this story, see my "A Monstrous Test: Genesis 22," 9–29 in *A Whirlpool of Torment: Israelite Traditions of God as an Oppressive Presence* (Minneapolis: Fortress Press, 1984, reprinted by SBL, 2008) and *Defending God: Biblical Responses to the Problem of Evil* (Oxford: Oxford University Press, 2005) 57–65, 214–16. Note 9, p. 214 gives a bibliography of the different approaches to Genesis 22. A much longer one is found in J. Ebach, *Gott im Wort: Drei Studien zur biblischen Exegese und Hermeneutik* (Neukirchen/Vluyn: Neukirchener Verlag, 1997) 5–7.

7. In the final analysis, this means of distancing YHWH from malicious conduct fails in that the Adversary can only act by permission of the one who rules over the heavenly beings. For my understanding of this text, see Crenshaw, *Reading Job: A Literary and Theological Commentary* (Macon GA: Smyth & Helwys, 2011).

8. E. A. Speiser, *Genesis* (Garden City NY: Doubleday & Co., 1964) 164. First readers, too, wait in stunned silence as father and son walk that lonely road

9. Abraham said to Sarah, "There is a place far from here where they educate boys; I will take him there and educate him. She replied: Go in peace."

10. Leviticus Rabbah 20:2 and Pseudo-Jonathan on Gen 22:20. I. Kalimi, "The Binding of Isaac in Rabbinic Literature and Thought," *Review of Rabbinic Judaism* 13 (2010): 27 notes that the rabbis did not explain the discrepancy between Abraham's return to Beersheba and Sarah's death at Hebron. Kalimi wonders if they meant that she left Beersheba on learning what Abraham had done.

11. *Mimesis* (Princeton: Princeton University Press, 1953). That Auerbach's judgment about Hebrew narrative does not apply to every biblical text was recognized long before Robert Alter's criticism in *The Art of Biblical Narrative* (New York: Basic Books, 1981).

12. G. Vermes, *Scripture and Tradition in Judaism* (Leiden: E. J. Brill, 1961) 196 describes this Cambridge fragment of the Tosefta of the Palestinian Targum as "foreign to the most ancient version of the narrative."

13. Kalimi, "Binding," 9. E. F. Davis, "Self-Consciousness and Conversation: Reading Genesis 22," *Bulletin for Biblical Research* 1 (1991): 27–40 writes that the Rabbis "teach us to read with the heart of the mystic, intoxicated with God, utterly bound and utterly free, whose suffering is transformed and obedience is completed in love" (40).

14. On this text, see my article, "The Sojourner Has Come to Play the Judge: Theodicy on Trial," 83–92 in *God in the Fray: A Tribute to Walter Brueggemann*, ed. T. Linafelt and T. K. Beal (Minneapolis: Fortress Press, 1998).

15. *Genesis*, 8th ed. (Göttingen: Vandenhoeck & Ruprecht, 1969) 237.

16. G. M. Landes, "The 'Three Days and Three Nights' Motif in Jonah 2:1," *JBL* 86 (1967): 446–50.

17. J. L. Mays, "'Now I Know': An Exposition of Genesis 22:1-19 and Matthew 26:36-46," *Theology Today* 58 (January 2002): 519–25 calls these two tests "a clarifying experience for God" (520).

18. See R. M. Jensen, "The Offering of Isaac in Jewish and Christian Tradition. Image and Text," *Biblical Interpretation* 11 (1994): 85–110.

19. Rembrandt's marriage to Saska resulted in four children. The first three, two daughters and a son, died shortly after birth (their son, Rombartus, lived slightly more than two months, their two daughters, both named Cornelia, lived only two weeks). Their fourth child, Titus, named after Rembrandt's sister Titia, died in the plague at nearly twenty-seven years old, just over a year before Rembrandt's death in 1669.

20. In this painting, Isaac is not bound, the angel holds both Abraham's arms while conveying a message canceling the original command, and both father and son are open-mouthed as if struck by the angel's words and the radiance of the light above the three figures. J. I. Durham, *The Biblical Rembrandt: Human Painter in a Landscape of Faith* (Macon GA: Mercer University Press, 2004) 103 comments, "He has put himself on Mount Moriah. And anyone really seeing this painting in the Hermitage has been right there with him." On these two paintings and the very different one of Abraham and Isaac from 1645, see G. von Rad, *Das Opfer des Abraham* (Mainz: Kaiser Verlag, 1971) 86–94.

21. *The Death and Resurrection of the Beloved Son: The Transformation of Child Sacrifice in Judaism and Christianity* (New Haven: Yale University Press, 1993). Levenson's criticism highlights the problem of imposing modern views on ancient literature, very much in vogue today because of its injurious effect on many. T. E. Fretheim, *Abraham: Trials of Family and Faith* (Columbia: University of South Carolina Press, 2007) is not entirely convinced by Levenson's argument. Fretheim mines the story for its theological profundity while recognizing its dangers to the mentally unstable as well as the fear it generates in children.

22. After all, the prophet Micah pondered that possibility: "Shall I give my first-born for my transgression, the fruit of my body for my own sin?" (Mic 6:7b). He offers a better alternative, which he thinks has been communicated by God: "Doing justice, loving kindness, and walking humbly with your God" (v. 8).

23. Kant's concern was that the command was contrary to moral law and therefore a deception, definitely not coming from God. To this, B. Dov Lerner objects that the philosopher ignored God's promise and covenant. Lerner also accuses Kierkegaard of refusing to take seriously the possibility of the miraculous. See Lerner, "Saving the *Akedah* from the Philosophers," *The Jewish Bible Quarterly* 27 (1999): 168–69.

24. Dealing with schizophrenia is still in its infancy. How does one assign blame when the voices are real?

25. In short, rather than *šḥṭ* (to slaughter), God uses the verb *ʿlh* which means "to go up" and by extension "a burnt offering," that which ascends to God.

26. *The Last Trial* (New York: Schocken Books, 1967).

27. Technically, the performances in this "martyr legend" belonged to the seven sons, although their mother is described as urging them to face death courageously and therefore would have suffered unimaginable psychological stress. The emphasis on resurrection conveniently hides that element of the story.

28. Kalimi, "Binding," 25.

29. J. L. Crenshaw, "Divine Discipline in Job 5:17-18, Proverbs 3:11-12, Deuteronomy 32:29, and Beyond," 178–89 in *Reading Job Intertextually*, ed. K. Dell and W. Kynes (London: Bloomsbury T & T Clark, 2013).

30. "Sources in Heaven: Revelation as a Scholarly Construct in Second Temple Judaism," 265–77 in *Kein Land für sich allein: Studien zum Kulturkontakt in Kanaan, Israel/Palästina und Ebirnari für Manfred Weippert zum 65. Geburtstag* ed., U. Hübner und E. A. Knauf (Göttingen: Vandenhoeck & Ruprecht, 2002).

31. New York: Little, Brown and Company, 2009.

32. New York: Knopf, 1995.

33. Crenshaw, *Defending God*.

34. "The Trial of Abraham and the Test of Job: How Do They Differ?" *Henoch* 16 (1994): 153–72. B. N. Fisk, "Offering Isaac Again and Again: Pseudo-Philo's use of the Aqedah as Intertext," *CBQ* 62 (2000): 481–507 argues that the net should be spread wider to include stories about Jephthah, Deborah, and Balaam.

35. "Ijob und Abraham. Zur Rezeption von Gen 22 in Ijob 1-2 und 42:7-17," 73–97 in *Gott, Mensch, Sprache: Schülerfestschrift für Walter Gross zum 60. Geburtstag*, ATSAT 58 (St. Ottilien: Eos Verlag, 2001).

36. J. L. Crenshaw, "Deceitful Minds and Theological Dogma: Jer 17:5-11," 105–21 in *Utopia and Dystopia in Prophetic Literature*, ed. E. Ben Zvi (Helsinki: Finnish Exegetical Society; Göttingen: Vandenhoeck & Ruprecht, 2006).

37. Genesis Rabbah 56:7.

38. Genesis Rabbah 56:8.

39. Davis, "Self-Consciousness," 31–32 rejects it. Her reasons: (1) the absence of any suggestion that the command accords with established custom; (2) the lack of historical reference; (3) silence about any struggle by Abraham for ethical discernment; and (4) God's failure to repudiate human sacrifice.

40. Crenshaw, *Dust and Ashes*, 19.

41. *The Prophets* (New York: Harper & Row, 1962).

42. See J. L. Crenshaw, *Qoheleth: The Ironic Wink* (Columbia: University of South Carolina Press, 2013).

43. For many Westerners, science has replaced God. In this new world, poetry, music, and art no longer are believed to connect humans with a transcendent realm.

44. I thank my friend and colleague Ellen Davis for reading an earlier version of this essay and making helpful comments for its improvement. She, too, emphasizes divine vulnerability when interpreting Gen 22:1-19.

Other available titles from SMYTH&HELWYS.

#Connect
Reaching Youth Across the Digital Divide
Brian Foreman

Reaching our youth across the digital divide is a struggle for parents, ministers, and other adults who work with Generation Z—today's teenagers. *#Connect* leads readers into the technological landscape, encourages conversations with teenagers, and reminds us all to be the presence of Christ in every facet of our lives. *978-1-57312-693-9 120 pages/pb* **$13.00**

Atonement in the Apocalypse
An Exposé of the Defeat of Evil
Robert W. Canoy

Revelation calls believers to see themselves through the unique lens of redemptive atonement and to live and model daily that they see themselves in the present moment as redeemed people. Having thus seen themselves, believers likewise are directed to see and to relate to others in this world the very way that God has seen them from eternity.

978-1-57312-946-6 218 pages/pb **$22.00**

Beginnings
A Reverend and a Rabbi Talk About the Stories of Genesis
Michael Smith and Rami Shapiro

Editor Aaron Herschel Shapiro declares that stories "must be retold—not just repeated, but reinvented, reimagined, and reexperienced" to remain vital in the world. Mike and Rami continue their conversations from the *Mount and Mountain* books, exploring the places where their traditions intersect and diverge, listening to each other as they respond to the stories of Genesis. *978-1-57312-772-1 202 pages/pb* **$18.00**

Bugles in the Afternoon
Dealing with Discouragement and Disillusionment in Ministry
Judson Edwards

In *Bugles in the Afternoon*, Edwards writes, "My long experience in the church has convinced me that most ministers—both professional and lay—spend time under the juniper tree. Those ministers who have served more than ten years and not been depressed, discouraged, or disillusioned can hold their annual convention in a phone booth."

978-1-57312-865-0 148 pages/pb **$16.00**

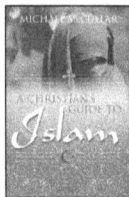

A Christian's Guide to Islam
Michael D. McCullar

A *Christian's Guide to Islam* provides a brief but accurate guide to Muslim formation, history, structure, beliefs, practices, and goals. It explores to what degree the tenets of Islam have been misinterpreted, corrupted, or abused over the centuries.

978-1-57312-512-3 128 pages/pb **$16.00**

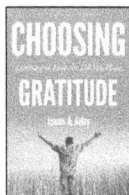

Choosing Gratitude
Learning to Love the Life You Have

James A. Autry

Autry reminds us that gratitude is a choice, a spiritual—not social—process. He suggests that if we cultivate gratitude as a way of being, we may not change the world and its ills, but we can change our response to the world. If we fill our lives with moments of gratitude, we will indeed love the life we have.

978-1-57312-614-4 144 pages/pb **$15.00**

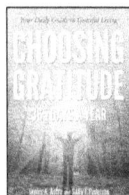

Choosing Gratitude 365 Days a Year
Your Daily Guide to Grateful Living

James A. Autry and Sally J. Pederson

Filled with quotes, poems, and the inspired voices of both Pederson and Autry, in a society consumed by fears of not having "enough"—money, possessions, security, and so on—this book suggests that if we cultivate gratitude as a way of being, we may not change the world and its ills, but we can change our response to the world.

978-1-57312-689-2 210 pages/pb **$18.00**

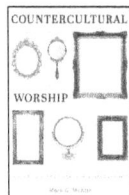

Countercultural Worship
A Plea to Evangelicals in a Secular Age

Mark G. McKim

Evangelical worship, McKim argues, has drifted far from both its biblical roots and historic origins, leaving evangelicals in danger of becoming mere chaplains to the wider culture, oblivious to the contradictions between what the secular culture says is real and important and what Scripture says is real and important.

978-1-57312-873-5 174 pages/pb **$19.00**

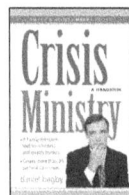

Crisis Ministry: A Handbook
Daniel G. Bagby

Covering more than 25 crisis pastoral care situations, this book provides a brief, practical guide for church leaders and other caregivers responding to stressful situations in the lives of parishioners. It tells how to resource caregiving professionals in the community who can help people in distress.

978-1-57312-370-9 154 pages/pb **$15.00**

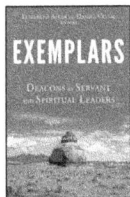

Exemplars
Deacons as Servant and Spiritual Leaders
Elizabeth Allen and Daniel Vestal, eds.

Who Do Deacons Need to Be? What Do Deacons Need to Know? What Do Deacons Need to Do? These three questions form the basis for *Exemplars: Deacons as Servant and Spiritual Leaders*. They are designed to encourage robust conversation within diaconates as well as between deacons, clergy, and other laity.   978-1-57312-876-6 128 pages/pb **$15.00**

The Exile and Beyond (All the Bible series)
Wayne Ballard

The Exile and Beyond brings to life the sacred literature of Israel and Judah that comprises the exilic and postexilic communities of faith. It covers Ezekiel, Isaiah, Haggai, Zechariah, Malachi, 1 & 2 Chronicles, Ezra, Nehemiah, Joel, Jonah, Song of Songs, Esther, and Daniel.   978-1-57312-759-2 196 pages/pb **$16.00**

Fierce Love
Desperate Measures for Desperate Times
Jeanie Miley

Fierce Love is about learning to see yourself and know yourself as a conduit of love, operating from a full heart instead of trying to find someone to whom you can hook up your emotional hose and fill up your empty heart.   978-1-57312-810-0 276 pages/pb **$18.00**

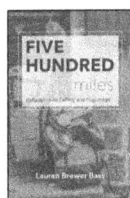

Five Hundred Miles
Reflections on Calling and Pilgrimage
Lauren Brewer Bass

Spain's Camino de Santiago, the Way of St. James, has been a cherished pilgrimage path for centuries, visited by countless people searching for healing, solace, purpose, and hope. These stories from her five-hundred-mile-walk is Lauren Brewer Bass's honest look at the often winding, always surprising journey of a calling.   978-1-57312-812-4 142 pages/pb **$16.00**

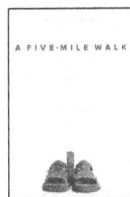

A Five-Mile Walk
Exploring Themes in the Experience of Christian Faith and Discipleship
Michael B. Brown

Sometimes the Christian journey is a stroll along quiet shores. Other times it is an uphill climb on narrow, snow-covered mountain paths. Usually, it is simply walking in the direction of wholeness, one step after another, sometimes even two steps forward and one step back.

978-1-57312-852-0 196 pages/pb **$18.00**

Glimpses from State Street
Wayne Ballard

As a collection of devotionals, *Glimpses from State Street* provides a wealth of insights and new ways to consider and develop our fellowship with Christ. It also serves as a window into the relationship between a small town pastor and a welcoming congregation.

978-1-57312-841-4 158 pages/pb **$15.00**

God's Servants, the Prophets
Bryan Bibb

God's Servants, the Prophets covers the Israelite and Judean prophetic literature from the preexilic period. It includes Amos, Hosea, Isaiah, Micah, Zephaniah, Nahum, Habakkuk, Jeremiah, and Obadiah.

978-1-57312-758-5 208 pages/pb **$16.00**

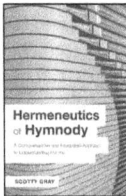

Hermeneutics of Hymnody
A Comprehensive and Integrated Approach to Understanding Hymns
Scotty Gray

Scotty Gray's *Hermeneutics of Hymnody* is a comprehensive and integrated approach to understanding hymns. It is unique in its holistic and interrelated exploration of seven of the broad facets of this most basic forms of Christian literature. A chapter is devoted to each and relates that facet to all of the others.

978-157312-767-7 432 pages/pb **$28.00**

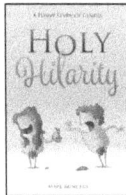

Holy Hilarity
A Funny Study of Genesis
Mark Roncace

In this fun, meaningful, and practical study of Genesis, Mark Roncace brings readers fifty-three short chapters of wit and amusing observations about the biblical stories, followed by five thought-provoking questions for individual reflection or group discussion. Humorous, yet reverent, this refreshing approach to Bible study invites us, whatever our background, to wrestle with the issues in the text and discover the ways those issues intersect our own messy lives. It's seriously entertaining.

978-157312-892-6 230 pages/pb **$17.00**

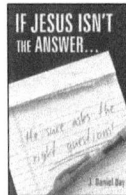

If Jesus Isn't the Answer . . . He Sure Asks the Right Questions!
J. Daniel Day

Taking eleven of Jesus' questions as its core, Day invites readers into their own conversation with Jesus. Equal parts testimony, theological instruction, pastoral counseling, and autobiography, the book is ultimately an invitation to honest Christian discipleship.

978-1-57312-797-4 148 pages/pb **$16.00**

To order call **1-800-747-3016** or visit **www.helwys.com**

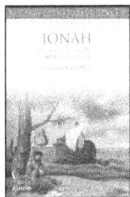

Jonah (Annual Bible Study series)
Reluctant Prophet, Merciful God

Taylor Sandlin

The book of Jonah invites readers to ask important questions about who God is and who God calls us to be in response. Along with the prophet, we ask questions such as What kind of God is the God of Israel? and Who falls within the sphere of God's care? Most importantly, perhaps, we find ourselves asking How will I respond when I discover that God loves the people I love to hate? These sessions invite readers to wrestle with these questions and others like them as we discover God's mercy for both the worst of sinners and the most reluctant of prophets.

Teaching Guide 978-1-57312-910-7 164 pages/pb **$14.00**

Study Guide 978-1-57312-911-4 96 pages/pb **$6.00**

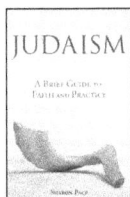

Judaism
A Brief Guide to Faith and Practice

Sharon Pace

Sharon Pace's newest book is a sensitive and comprehensive introduction to Judaism. How does belief in the One God and a universal morality shape the way in which Jews see the world? How does one find meaning in life and the courage to endure suffering? How does one mark joy and forge community ties?

978-1-57312-644-1 144 pages/pb **$16.00**

Live the Stories
50 Interactive Children's Sermons

Andrew Noe

Live the Stories provides church leaders a practical guide to teaching children during the worship service through play—and invites the rest of the congregation to join the fun. Noe's lessons allow children to play, laugh, and act out the stories of our faith and turn the sanctuary into a living testimony to what God has done in the past, is doing in the present, and will do in the future. As they learn the stories and grow, our children will develop in their faith.

978-1-57312-943-5 128 pages/pb **$14.00**

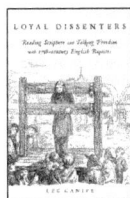

Loyal Dissenters
Reading Scripture and Talking Freedom with 17th-century English Baptists

Lee Canipe

When Baptists in 17th-century England wanted to talk about freedom, they unfailingly began by reading the Bible—and what they found in Scripture inspired their compelling (and, ultimately, successful) arguments for religious liberty. In an age of widespread anxiety, suspicion, and hostility, these early Baptists refused to worship God in keeping with the king's command.

978-1-57312-872-8 178 pages/pb **$19.00**

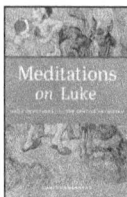

Meditations on Luke
Daily Devotions from the Gentile Physician
Chris Cadenhead

Readers searching for a fresh encounter with Scripture can delve into *Meditations on Luke*, a collection of daily devotions intended to guide the reader through the book of Luke, which gives us some of the most memorable stories in all of Scripture. The Scripture, response, and prayer will guide readers' own meditations as they listen and respond to God's voice, coming to us through Luke's Gospel. *978-1-57312-947-3 328 pages/pb* **$22.00**

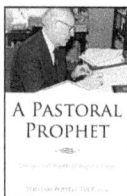

A Pastoral Prophet
Sermons and Prayers of Wayne E. Oates
William Powell Tuck, ed.

Read these sermons and prayers and look directly into the heart of Wayne Oates. He was a consummate counselor, theologian, and writer, but first of all he was a pastor. . . . He gave voice to our deepest hurts, then followed with words we long to hear: you are not alone.

—Kay Shurden
Associate Professor Emeritus, Clinical Education,
Mercer University School of Medicine, Macon, Georgia
978-157312-955-8 160 pages/pb **$18.00**

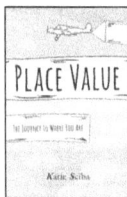

Place Value
The Journey to Where You Are
Katie Sciba

Does a place have value? Can a place change us? Is it possible for God to use the place you are in to form you? From Victoria, Texas to Indonesia, Belize, Australia, and beyond, Katie Sciba's wanderlust serves as a framework to understand your own places of deep emotion and how God may have been weaving redemption around you all along.

978-157312-829-2 138 pages/pb **$15.00**

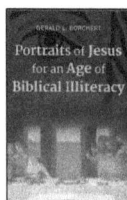

Portraits of Jesus
for an Age of Biblical Illiteracy
Gerald L. Borchert

Despite our era of communication and information overload, biblical illiteracy is widespread. In *Portraits of Jesus*, Gerald L. Borchert assists both ministers and laypeople with a return to what the New Testament writers say about this stunning Jesus who shocked the world and called a small company of believers into an electrifying transformation.

978-157312-940-4 212 pages/pb **$20.00**

Preaching that Connects

Charles B. Bugg and Alan Redditt

How does the minister stay focused on the holy when the daily demands of the church seem relentless? How do we come to a preaching event with a sense that God is working in us and through us? In *Preaching that Connects*, Charles Bugg and Alan Redditt explore the balancing act of a minister's authority as preacher, sharing what the congregation needs to hear, and the communal role as pastor, listening to God alongside congregants. 978-157312-887-2 128 pages/pb **$15.00**

Reading Isaiah
(Reading the Old Testament series)
A Literary and Theological Commentary

Hyun Chul Paul Kim

While closely exegeting key issues of each chapter, this commentary also explores interpretive relevance and significance between ancient texts and the modern world. Engaging with theological messages of the book of Isaiah as a unified whole, the commentary will both illuminate and inspire readers to wrestle with its theological implications for today's church and society.

978-1-57312-925-1 352 pages/pb **$33.00**

Reading Jeremiah
(Reading the Old Testament series)
A Literary and Theological Commentary

Corrine Carvalho

Reflecting the ways that communal tragedy permeates communal identity, the book of Jeremiah as literary text embodies the confusion, disorientation, and search for meaning that all such tragedy elicits. Just as the fall of Jerusalem fractured the Judean community and undercut every foundation on which it built its identity, so too the book itself (or more properly, the scroll) jumbles images, genres, and perspectives. 978-1-57312-924-4 186 pages/pb **$32.00**

Ruth & Esther (Smyth & Helwys Bible Commentary)

Kandy Queen-Sutherland

Ruth and Esther are the only two women for whom books of the Hebrew Bible are named. This distinction in itself sets the books apart from other biblical texts that bear male names, address the community through its male members, recall the workings of God and human history through a predominately male perspective, and look to the future through male heirs. These books are particularly stories of survival. The story of Ruth focuses on the survival of a family; Esther focuses on the survival of a people. 978-1-57312-891-9 544 pages/hc **$60.00**

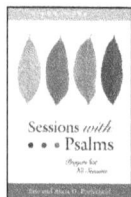

Sessions with Psalms (Sessions Bible Studies series)
Prayers for All Seasons
Eric and Alicia D. Porterfield

Useful to seminar leaders during preparation and group discussion, as well as in individual Bible study, *Sessions with Psalms* is a ten-session study designed to explore what it looks like for the words of the psalms to become the words of our prayers. Each session is followed by a thought-provoking page of questions.   *978-1-57312-768-4 136 pages/pb* **$14.00**

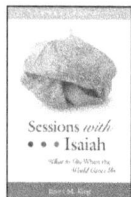

Sessions with Isaiah (Sessions Bible Studies series)
What to Do When the World Caves In
James M. King

The book of Isaiah begins in the years of national stress when, under various kings, Israel was surrounded by more powerful neighbors and foolishly sought foreign alliances rather than dependence on Yahweh. It continues with the natural result of that unfaithfulness: conquest by the great power in the region, Babylon, and the captivity of many of Israel's best and brightest in that foreign land. The book concludes anticipating their return to the land of promise and strong admonitions about the people's conduct—but we also hear God's reassuring messages of comfort and restoration, offered to all who repent.

978-1-57312-942-8 130 pages/pb **$14.00**

Stained-Glass Millennials
Rob Lee

We've heard the narrative that millennials are done with the institutional church; they've packed up and left. This book is an alternative to that story and chronicles the journey of millennials who are investing their lives in the institution because they believe in the church's resurrecting power. Through anecdotes and interviews, Rob Lee takes readers on a journey toward God's unfolding future for the church, a beloved institution in desperate need of change.   *978-1-57312-926-8 156 pages/pb* **$16.00**

Star Thrower
A Pastor's Handbook
William Powell Tuck

In *Star Thrower: A Pastor's Handbook*, William Powell Tuck draws on over fifty years of experience to share his perspective on being an effective pastor. He describes techniques for sermon preparation, pastoral care, and church administration, as well as for conducting Communion, funeral, wedding, and baptismal services. He also includes advice for working with laity and church staff, coping with church conflict, and nurturing one's own spiritual and family life.   *978-1-57312-889-6 244 pages/pb* **$15.00**

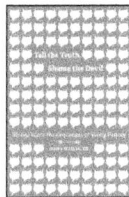

Tell the Truth, Shame the Devil
Stories about the Challenges of Young Pastors
James Elllis III, ed.

A pastor's life is uniquely difficult. *Tell the Truth, Shame the Devil*, then, is an attempt to expose some of the challenges that young clergy often face. While not exhaustive, this collection of essays is a superbly compelling and diverse introduction to how tough being a pastor under the age of thirty-five can be.   978-1-57312-839-1 198 pages/pb **$18.00**

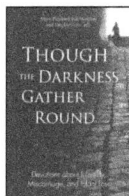

Though the Darkness Gather Round
Devotions about Infertility, Miscarriage, and Infant Loss
Mary Elizabeth Hill Hanchey and Erin McClain, eds.

Much courage is required to weather the long grief of infertility and the sudden grief of miscarriage and infant loss. This collection of devotions by men and women, ministers, chaplains, and lay leaders who can speak of such sorrow, is a much-needed resource and precious gift for families on this journey and the faith communities that walk beside them.

978-1-57312-811-7 180 pages/pb **$19.00**

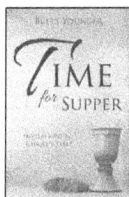

Time for Supper
Invitations to Christ's Table
Brett Younger

Some scholars suggest that every meal in literature is a communion scene. Could every meal in the Bible be a communion text? Could every passage be an invitation to God's grace? These meditations on the Lord's Supper help us listen to the myriad of ways God invites us to gratefully, reverently, and joyfully share the cup of Christ.   978-1-57312-720-2 246 pages/pb **$18.00**

A True Hope
Jedi Perils and the Way of Jesus
Joshua Hays

Star Wars offers an accessible starting point for considering substantive issues of faith, philosophy, and ethics. In *A True Hope*, Joshua Hays explores some of these challenging ideas through the sayings of the Jedi Masters, examining the ways the worldview of the Jedi is at odds with that of the Bible.   978-1-57312-770-7 186 pages/pb **$18.00**

www.ingramcontent.com/pod-product-compliance
Lightning Source LLC
Chambersburg PA
CBHW072347090426
42741CB00012B/2962